Sir Charles Oman's
War & the Middle Ages

Sir Charles Oman's War & the Middle Ages
Conflict & Politics in Europe
378-1575

ILLUSTRATED

The Art of War in the Middle Ages
378—1515

England and the Hundred Years War
1327-1485

Charles Oman

LEONAUR

Sir Charles Oman's
War & the Middle Ages
Conflict & Politics in Europe 378-1575
ILLUSTRATED
The Art of War in the Middle Ages 378—1515
and
England and the Hundred Years War 1327-1485
by Charles Oman

FIRST EDITION

First published under the titles
The Art of War in the Middle Ages A.D. 378—1515
and
England and the Hundred Years War (1327-1485 A.D.)

Leonaur is an imprint of Oakpast Ltd

Copyright in this form © 2017 Oakpast Ltd

ISBN: 978-1-78282-622-4 (hardcover)
ISBN: 978-1-78282-623-1 (softcover)

http://www.leonaur.com

Publisher's Notes

The views expressed in this book are not necessarily those of the publisher.

Contents

The Art of War in the Middle Ages 378—1515　　　7
England and the Hundred Years War 1327-1485　　165

The Art of War in the Middle Ages
378—1515

Contents

Introduction	11
The Transition from Roman to Medieval Forms in War 378–582	13
The Early Middle Ages 476–1081	26
The Byzantines and their Enemies 582–1071	42
The Supremacy of Feudal Cavalry 1066–1346	63
The Swiss 1315–1515	80
The English and their Enemies 1272–1485	117
Conclusion	152

Introduction

The Art of War has been very simply defined as 'the art which enables any commander to worst the forces opposed to him.' It is therefore conversant with an enormous variety of subjects: Strategy and Tactics are but two of the more important of its branches. Besides dealing with discipline, organisation, and armament, it is bound to investigate every means which can be adapted to increase the physical or moral efficiency of an army. The author who opened his work with a dissertation on 'the age which is preferable in a *generalissimo,*' or 'the average height which the infantry soldier should attain,' (cf. Vegetius and Maurice), was dealing with the Art of War, no less than he who confined himself to purely tactical speculations.

The complicated nature of the subject being taken into consideration; it is evident that a complete sketch of the social and political history of any period would be necessary to account fully for the state of the 'Art of War' at the time. That art has existed, in a rudimentary form, ever since the day on which two bodies of men first met in anger to settle a dispute by the arbitrament of force. At some epochs, however, military and social history have been far more closely bound up than at others.

In the present century, wars are but episodes in a people's existence: there have, however, been times when the whole national organisation was founded on the supposition of a normal state of strife. In such cases the history of the race and of its 'art of war' are one and the same. To detail the constitution of Sparta, or of Ancient Germany, is to give little more than a list of military institutions. Conversely, to speak of the characteristics of their military science involves the mention of many of their political institutions.

At no time was this interpenetration more complete than in the age which forms the central part of our period. Feudalism, in its origin and development, had a military as well as a social side, and its decline is by no means unaffected by military considerations. There is a point of view from which its history could be described as 'the rise, supremacy, and decline of heavy cavalry as the chief power in war.' To a certain extent the tracing out of this thesis will form the subject of our researches. It is here that we find the thread which links the history of the military art in the middle ages into a connected whole. Between Adrianople, the first, and Marignano, the last, of the triumphs of the mediaeval horseman, lie the chapters in the scientific history of war which we are about to investigate.

Chapter 1

The Transition from Roman to Medieval Forms in War 378–582
(From the Battle of Adrianople to the Accession of Maurice)

Between the middle of the fourth and the end of the sixth century lies a period of transition in military history, an epoch of transformations as strange and as complete as those contemporary changes which turned into a new channel the course of political history and civilisation in Europe. In war, as in all else, the institutions of the ancient world are seen to pass away, and a new order of things develops itself.

Numerous and striking as are the symptoms of that period of transition, none is more characteristic than the gradual disuse of the honoured name of '*Legion*,' the title intimately bound up with all the ages of Roman greatness. Surviving in a very limited acceptance in the time of Justinian, it had fifty years later become obsolete.

✶✶✶✶✶✶

Lord Mahon in his *Life of Belisarius,* (reprinted as *General Belisarius: Soldier of Byzantium* by Leonaur), is wrong in asserting that the legion was no longer known in Justinian's day. The term is mentioned, though rarely, in Procopius).

✶✶✶✶✶✶

It represented a form of military efficiency which had now completely vanished. That wonderful combination of strength and flexibility, so solid and yet so agile and easy to handle, had ceased to correspond to the needs of the time. The day of the sword and *pilum* had given place to that of the lance and bow. The typical Roman soldier was no longer the iron *legionary*, who, with shield fitted close to his left shoulder and sword-hilt sunk low, cut his way through the thickest hedge of pikes, and stood firm before the wildest onset of Celt or

German. (Cf. Tacitus, *Annals*, ii.) The organisation of Augustus and Trajan was swept away by Constantine, and the *legions* which for three hundred years had preserved their identity, their proud titles of honour, and their *ésprit de corps*, knew themselves no longer.

******

The old *legions* of the first century are found in full vigour at the end of the third. The coins of the British usurper Carausius commemorate as serving under him several of the *legions* which, as early as the reign of Claudius, were already stationed in Britain and Gaul.

******

Constantine, when he cut down the numbers of the military unit to a quarter of its former strength, and created many scores of new corps, (132 legions and *numeri*, besides 100 unattached *cohorts*), was acting from motives of political and not military expediency, (Gibbon, ii.) The armament and general character of the troops survived their organisation, and the infantry, the *robur peditum*, still remained the most important and numerous part of the army. At the same time, however, a tendency to strengthen the cavalry made itself felt, and the proportion of that arm to the whole number of the military establishment continued steadily to increase throughout the fourth century. Constantine himself, by depriving the *legion* of its complementary *turmae*, and uniting the horsemen into larger independent bodies, bore witness to their growing importance.

It would seem that the Empire—having finally abandoned the offensive in war, and having resolved to confine itself to the protection of its own provinces—found that there was an increasing need for troops who could transfer themselves with rapidity from one menaced point on the frontier to another. The Germans could easily distance the legion, burdened by the care of its military machines and impedimenta. Hence cavalry in larger numbers was required to intercept their raids.

But it would appear that another reason for the increase of the horsemen was even more powerful. The ascendancy of the Roman infantry over its enemies was no longer marked as in earlier ages, and it therefore required to be more strongly supported by cavalry than had been previously necessary. The Franks, Burgundians, and Allemanni of the days of Constantine were no longer the half-armed savages of the first century, who, 'without helm or mail, with weak shields of wickerwork, and armed only with the javelin,' (Tacitus, *Annals*, ii.), tried to face the embattled front of the *cohort*. They had now the iron-bound buckler, the pike, and the short stabbing sword (*scramasax*), as well as the long cutting sword (*spatha*), and the deadly *francisca* or battle-axe, which, whether thrown or wielded, would penetrate Roman armour and split the Roman shield. As weapons for hand to hand combat these so far surpassed the old *framea*, that the imperial infantry found it no light matter to defeat a German tribe.

At the same time, the morale of the Roman Army was no longer what it had once been: the corps were no longer homogeneous, and the insufficient supply of recruits was eked out by enlisting slaves and barbarians in the *legions* themselves, and not only among the auxiliary *cohorts*.

★★★★★★

When the Romans entirely abandoned the offensive an increased army became necessary, as a frontier held against raids requires to be protected on every point. Hence the conscriptions and large composition money of Constantine's epoch. He is said to have had nearly half a million of men in his forces.

★★★★★★

Though seldom wanting in courage, the troops of the fourth century had lost the self-reliance and cohesion of the old Roman infantry, and required far more careful handling on the part of the general. Few facts show this more forcibly than the proposal of the tactician Urbicius to furnish the legionaries with a large supply of portable beams and stakes, to be carried by pack-mules attached to each cohort. These were to be planted on the flanks and in the front of the legion, when there was a probability of its being attacked by hostile cavalry: behind them the Romans were to await the enemy's onset, without any attempt to assume the offensive. This proposition marks a great decay in the efficiency of the imperial foot-soldier: the troops of a previous generation would have scorned such a device, accustomed as they were to drive back with ease the assaults of the Parthian and Sarmatian *cataphracti*.

This tendency to deterioration on the part of the Roman infantry, and the consequent neglect of that arm by the generals of the time, were brought to a head by a disaster. The Battle of Adrianople was the most fearful defeat suffered by a Roman Army since Cannae; a slaughter to which it is aptly compared by the military author Ammianus Marcellinus. The Emperor Valens, all his chief officers, (Grand Masters of the infantry and cavalry, the Count of the Palace, and 45 com-

SARMATIAN CATAPHRACTI.

manders of different corps), and forty thousand men were left upon the field; indeed, the army of the East was almost annihilated, and was never reorganised upon the same lines as had previously served for it.

The military importance of Adrianople was unmistakable; it was a victory of cavalry over infantry. The imperial army had developed its attack on the position of the Goths, and the two forces were hotly engaged, when suddenly a great body of horsemen charged in upon the Roman flank. It was the main strength of the Gothic cavalry, which had been foraging at a distance; receiving news of the fight it had ridden straight for the battlefield. Two of Valens' squadrons, which covered the flank of his array, threw themselves in the way of the oncoming mass, and were ridden down and trampled underfoot.

Then the Goths swept down on the infantry of the left wing, rolled it up, and drove it in upon the centre. So tremendous was their impact that the legions and cohorts were pushed together in helpless confusion. Every attempt to stand firm failed, and in a few minutes, left, centre, and reserve were one undistinguishable mass. Imperial guards, light troops, lancers, *foederati* and infantry of the line were wedged together in a press that grew closer every moment. The Roman cavalry saw that the day was lost, and rode off without another effort. Then the abandoned infantry realised the horror of their position: equally unable to deploy or to fly, they had to stand to be cut down.

It was a sight such as had been seen once before at Cannae, and was to be seen once after at Rosbecque. Men could not raise their arms to strike a blow, so closely were they packed; spears snapped right and left, their bearers being unable to lift them to a vertical position: many soldiers were stifled in the press. Into this quivering mass the Goths rode, plying lance and sword against the helpless enemy. It was not till two-thirds of the Roman Army had fallen that the thinning of the ranks enabled a few thousand men to break out, and follow their right wing and cavalry in a headlong flight. (Cf. Ammianus Marcellinus with accounts of the Egyptian crowd at the first Battle of El Teb.)

Such was the Battle of Adrianople, the first great victory gained by that heavy cavalry which had now shown its ability to supplant the heavy infantry of Rome as the ruling power of war. During their sojourn in the *steppes* of South Russia the Goths, first of all Teutonic races, had become a nation of horsemen. Dwelling in the Ukraine, they had felt the influence of that land, ever the nurse of cavalry, from the day of the Scythian to that of the Tartar and Cossack. They had come to 'consider it more honourable to fight on horse than on foot,'

(Maurice's *Strategikon*, vi.), and every chief was followed by his warband of mounted men. Driven against their will into conflict with the empire, they found themselves face to face with the army that had so long held the world in fear. The shock came, and, probably to his own surprise, the Goth found that his stout lance and good steed would carry him through the serried ranks of the *legion*. He had become the arbiter of war, the lineal ancestor of all the knights of the middle ages, the inaugurator of that ascendancy of the horseman which was to endure for a thousand years.

Theodosius, on whom devolved the task of reorganising the troops of the Eastern empire, appears to have appreciated to its fullest extent the military meaning of the fight of Adrianople. Abandoning the old Roman theory of war, he decided that the cavalry must in future compose the most important part of the imperial army. To provide himself with a sufficient force of horsemen, he was driven to a measure destined to sever all continuity between the military organisation of the fourth and that of the fifth century. He did not, like Constantine, raise new corps, but began to enlist wholesale every Teutonic chief whom he could bribe to enter his service.

The war-bands which followed these princes were not incorporated with the national troops; they obeyed their immediate commanders alone, and were strangers to the discipline of the Roman army. Yet to them was practically entrusted the fate of the empire; since they formed the most efficient division of the imperial forces. From the time of Theodosius, the prince had to rely for the maintenance of order in the Roman world merely on the amount of loyalty which a constant stream of titles and honours could win from the commanders of the *Foederati*.

Only six years after Adrianople there were already 40,000 Gothic and other German horsemen serving under their own chiefs in the army of the East. The native troops sunk at once to an inferior position in the eyes of Roman generals, and the justice of their decision was verified a few years later when Theodosius' German mercenaries won for him the two well-contested battles which crushed the usurper Magnus Maximus and his son Victor. On both those occasions, the Roman infantry of the West, those Gallic *legions* who had always been considered the best footmen in the world, were finally ridden down by the Teutonic cavalry who followed the standard of the legitimate emperor.

★★★★★★

Soldiers of the First Crusade period

At the still fiercer fight, where the army of the usurper Eugenius almost defeated Theodosius, we find that it was the barbarian cavalry of Arbogast, not the native infantry, which had become (only seven years after Maximus' defeat) the chief force of the Western Empire.

******

A picture of the state of the Imperial Army in the Western provinces, drawn precisely at this period, has been preserved for us in the work of Vegetius, a writer whose treatise would be of far greater value had he refrained from the attempt to identify the organisation of his own day with that of the first century, by the use of the same words for entirely different things. In drawing inferences from his statements, it has also to be remembered that he frequently gives the ideal military forms of his imagination, instead of those which really existed in his day. For example, his *legion* is made to consist of 6000 men, while we know that in the end of the fourth century its establishment did not exceed 1500. His work is dedicated to one of the emperors who bore the name of Valentinian, probably to the second, as (in spite of Gibbon's arguments in favour of Valentinian III) the relations of the various arms to each other and the character of their organisation point to a date prior to the commencement of the fifth century.

A single fact mentioned by Vegetius gives us the date at which the continuity of the existence of the old Roman heavy infantry may be said to terminate. As might be expected, this epoch exactly corresponds with that of the similar change in the East, which followed the Battle of Adrianople.

> From the foundation of the city to the reign of the sainted Gratian, the *legionaries* wore helmet and *cuirass*. But when the practice of holding frequent reviews and sham-fights ceased, these arms began to seem heavy, because the soldiers seldom put them on. They therefore begged from the emperor permission to discard first their *cuirasses*, and then even their helmets, and went to face the barbarians unprotected by defensive arms. In spite of the disasters which have since ensued, the infantry have not yet resumed the use of them ... And now, how can the Roman soldier expect victory, when helmless and unarmoured, and even without a shield (for the shield cannot be used in conjunction with the bow), he goes against the enemy?—Vegetius, bk. i., ii., and iii.

Vegetius—often more of a rhetorician than a soldier—has evidently misstated the reason of this change in infantry equipment. At a time when cavalry were clothing themselves in more complete armour, it is not likely that the infantry were discarding it from mere sloth and feebleness. The real meaning of the change was that, in despair of resisting horsemen any longer by the solidity of a line of heavy infantry, the Romans had turned their attention to the use of missile weapons,—a method of resisting cavalry even more efficacious than that which they abandoned, as was to be shown a thousand years later at Cressy and Agincourt.

That Vegetius' account is also considerably exaggerated is shown by his enumeration of the *legionary* order of his own day, where the first rank was composed of men retaining shield, *pilum*, and cuirass (whom he pedantically calls *Principes*). The second rank was composed of archers, but wore the *cuirass* and carried a lance also; only the remaining half of the *legion* had entirely discarded armour, and given up all weapons but the bow.

Vegetius makes it evident that cavalry, though its importance was rapidly increasing, had not yet entirely supplanted infantry to such a large extent as in the Eastern Empire. Though no army can hope for success without them, and though they must always be at hand to protect the flanks, they are not, in his estimation, the most effective force. As an antiquary, he feels attached to the old Roman organisation, and must indeed have been somewhat behind the military experience of his day. It may, however, be remembered that the Franks and Allemanni, the chief foes against whom the Western *legions* had to contend, were—unlike the Goths—nearly all footmen.

It was not till the time of Alaric that Rome came thoroughly to know the Gothic horsemen, whose efficiency Constantinople had already comprehended and had contrived for the moment to subsidise. In the days of Honorius, however, the Goth became the terror of Italy, as he had previously been of the Balkan peninsula. His lance and steed once more asserted their supremacy: the generalship of Stilicho, the trained bowmen and pikemen of the reorganised Roman Army, the native and *foederate* squadrons whose array flanked the *legions*, were insufficient to arrest the Gothic charge. For years, the conquerors rode at their will through Italy: when they quitted it, it was by their own choice, for there were no troops left in the world who could have expelled them by force.

The day of infantry had in fact gone by in Southern Europe: they continued to exist, not as the core and strength of the army, but for various minor purposes,—to garrison towns or operate in mountainous countries. Roman and barbarian alike threw their vigour into the organisation of their cavalry. Even the duty of acting as light troops fell into the hands of the horsemen. The Roman trooper added the bow to his equipment, and in the fifth century the native force of the Empire had come to resemble that of its old enemy, the Parthian state of the first century, being composed of horsemen armed with bow and lance. Mixed with these horse-archers fought squadrons of the *Foederati*, armed with the lance alone. Such were the troops of Aetius and Ricimer, the army which faced the Huns on the plain of Chalons.

The Huns themselves were another manifestation of the strength of cavalry; formidable by their numbers, their rapidity of movement, and the constant rain of arrows which they would pour in without allowing their enemy to close. In their tactics, they were the prototypes of the hordes of Alp Arslan, of Genghiz, and Tamerlane. But mixed with the Huns in the train of Attila marched many subject German tribes, Herules and Gepidae, Scyri, Lombards, and Rugians, akin to the Goths alike in their race and their manner of fighting. Chalons then was fought by horse-archer and lancer against horse-archer and lancer, a fair conflict with equal weapons.

The Frankish allies of Aetius were by far the most important body of infantry on the field, and these were ranged, according to the traditional tactics of Rome, in the centre:—flanked on one side by the Visigothic lances, on the other by the imperial array of horse-archers and heavy cavalry intermixed. The victory was won, not by superior tactics, but by sheer hard fighting, the decisive point having been the riding down of the native Huns by Theodoric's heavier horsemen.

To trace out in detail the military meaning of all the wars of the fifth century does not fall within our province. As to the organisation of the Roman armies a few words will suffice. In the West, the *Foederati* became the sole force of the empire, so that at last one of their chiefs, breaking through the old spell of the Roman name, could make himself, in title as well as in reality, ruler of Italy.

In the East, the decline of the native troops never reached this pitch. Leo I (457-474 *a. d.*), taking warning by the fate of the Western Empire, determined on increasing the proportion of Romans to *Foederati*, and carried out his purpose, though it involved the sacrifice of the life of his benefactor, the Gothic patrician Aspar. Zeno (474-491) continued this work, and made himself noteworthy as the first

THE HUNS AT THE BATTLE OF CHALONS

emperor who utilised the military virtues of the Isaurians, or semi-Romanised mountaineers of the interior of Asia Minor. Not only did they form his imperial guard, but a considerable number of new corps were raised among them. Zeno also enlisted Armenians and other inhabitants of the Roman frontier of the East, and handed over to his successor Anastasius an army in which the barbarian element was adequately counterpoised by the native troops.

The victorious armies of Justinian were therefore composed of two distinct elements, the foreign auxiliaries serving under their own chiefs, and the regular imperial troops. The pages of Procopius give us sufficient evidence that in both these divisions the cavalry was by far the most important arm. The light horseman of the Asiatic provinces wins his especial praise. With body and limbs clothed in mail, his quiver at his right side and his sword at his left, the Roman trooper would gallop along and discharge his arrows to front or flank or rear with equal ease.

To support him marched in the second line the heavier squadrons of the subsidised Lombard, or Herule, or Gepidan princes, armed with the lance. Procopius writes:

> There are some, who regard antiquity with wonder and respect, and attach no special worth to our modern military institutions: it is, however, by means of the latter that the weightiest and most striking results have been obtained.

The men of the sixth century were, in fact, entirely satisfied with the system of cavalry tactics which they had adopted, and looked with a certain air of superiority on the infantry tactics of their Roman predecessors.

Justinian's army and its achievements were indeed worthy of all praise; its victories were its own, while its defeats were generally due to the wretched policy of the emperor, who persisted in dividing up the command among many hands,—a system which secured military obedience at the expense of military efficiency. Justinian might, however, plead in his defence that the organisation of the army had become such that it constituted a standing menace to the central power. The system of the Teutonic *comitatus*, of the 'war-band' surrounding a leader to whom the soldiers are bound by a personal tie, had become deeply ingrained in the imperial forces.

Always predominant among the *Foederati*, it had spread from them to the native corps. In the sixth century, the monarch had always to dread that the loyalty of the troops towards their immediate commanders might prevail over their higher duties. Belisarius, and even Narses, were surrounded by large bodyguards of chosen men, bound to them by oath. That of the former general at the time of his Gothic triumph amounted to 7000 veteran horsemen. The existence of such corps rendered every successful commander a possible Wallenstein, to use a name of more modern importance.

Thus, the emperor, in his desire to avert the predominance of any single officer, would join several men of discordant views in the command of an army, and usually ensure the most disastrous consequences. This organisation of the imperial force in *banda* bodies attached by personal ties to their leaders, is the characteristic military form of the sixth century. (The Teutonic word *banda* is in full acceptation in the sixth century.) Its normal prevalence is shown by the contemporary custom of speaking of each corps by the name of its commanding officer, and not by any official title. Nothing could be more opposed than this usage to old Roman precedent.

The efficiency of Justinian's army in the Vandalic, Persian, or Gothic wars, depended (as has already been implied) almost entirely on its excellent cavalry. The troops, whether Teutonic or Eastern, against which it was employed were also horsemen. Engaging them the Romans prevailed, because in each case they were able to meet their adversaries' weapons and tactics not merely with similar methods, but with a greater variety of resources. Against the Persian horse-archer was sent not only the light-cavalry equipped with arms of the same description, but the heavy *foederate* lancers, who could ride the Oriental down. Against the Gothic heavy cavalry the same lancers were supported by the mounted bowmen, to whom the Goths had nothing to oppose.

If, however, the Roman Army enjoyed all the advantages of its diverse composition, it was, on the other hand, liable to all the perils which arise from a want of homogeneity. Its various elements were kept together only by military pride, or confidence in some successful general. Hence, in the troublous times which commenced in the end of Justinian's reign and continued through those of his successors, the whole military organisation of the empire began to crumble away. A change not less sweeping than that which Theodosius had introduced was again to be taken in hand. In 582 *a.d.* the reforming Emperor Maurice came to the throne, and commenced to recast the imperial army in a new mould.

CHAPTER 2

The Early Middle Ages 476-1081

(From the Fall of the Western Empire to the Battles of Hastings and Durazzo)

THE FRANKS, ANGLO-SAXONS, SCANDINAVIANS, ETC.

In leaving the discussion of the military art of the later Romans in order to investigate that of the nations of Northern and Western Europe, we are stepping from a region of comparative light into one of doubt and obscurity. The data which in the history of the empire may occasionally seem scanty and insufficient are in the history of the Teutonic races often entirely wanting. To draw up from our fragmentary authorities an estimate of the military importance of the Eastern campaigns of Heraclius is not easy: but to discover what were the particular military causes which settled the event of the day at Vouglé or Tolbiac, at Badbury or the Heavenfield, is absolutely impossible. The state of the Art of War in the Dark Ages has to be worked out from monkish chronicles and national songs, from the casual references of Byzantine historians, from the quaint drawings of the illuminated manuscript, or the mouldering fragments found in the warrior's barrow.

It is fortunate that the general characteristics of the period render its military history comparatively simple. Of strategy, there could be little in an age when men strove to win their ends by hard fighting rather than by skilful operations or the utilising of extraneous advantages. Tactics were stereotyped by the national organisations of the various peoples. The true interest of the centuries of the early Middle Ages lies in the gradual evolution of new forms of warlike efficiency, which end in the establishment of a military class as the chief factor in war, and the decay among most peoples of the old system which made the tribe arrayed in arms the normal fighting force.

Intimately connected with this change was an alteration in arms and equipment, which transformed the outward appearance of war in a manner not less complete. This period of transition may be considered to end when, in the eleventh century, the feudal cavalier established his superiority over all the descriptions of troops which were pitted against him, from the Magyar horse-archers of the East to the Anglo-Danish axe-men of the West. The fight of Hastings, the last attempt made for three centuries by infantry to withstand cavalry, serves to mark the termination of the epoch.

The Teutonic nation of North-Western Europe did not—like the Goths and Lombards—owe their victories to the strength of their mail-clad cavalry. The Franks and Saxons of the sixth and seventh centuries were still infantry. It would appear that the moors of North Germany and Schleswig, and the heaths and marshes of Belgium, were less favourable to the growth of cavalry than the steppes of the Ukraine or the plains of the Danube valley. The Frank, as pictured to us by Sidonius Apollinaris, Procopius, and Agathias, still bore a considerable resemblance to his Sigambrian ancestors. Like them he was destitute of helmet and body-armour; his shield, however, had become a much more effective defence than the wicker framework of the first century: it was a solid oval with a large iron boss and rim.

The *framea* had now been superseded by the *angon*—'a dart neither very long nor very short, which can be used against the enemy either by grasping it as a pike or hurling it,' (Agathias). The iron of its head extended far down the shaft; at its 'neck' were two barbs, which made its extraction from a wound or a pierced shield almost impossible. The *francisca*, however, was the great weapon of the people from whom it derived its name. It was a single-bladed battle-axe, with a heavy head composed of a long blade curved on its outer face and deeply hollowed in the interior. (Though often called *bipennis* it had not necessarily two blades, that word having become a mere general name for 'axe.') It was carefully weighted, so that it could be used, like an American tomahawk, for hurling at the enemy. The skill with which the Franks discharged this weapon, just before closing with the hostile line, was extraordinary, and its effectiveness made it their favourite arm.

A sword and dagger (*scramasax*) completed the normal equipment of the warrior; the last was a broad thrusting blade, 18 inches long, the former a two-edged cutting weapon of about 2½ feet in length.

Such was the equipment of the armies which Theodebert, Buccelin, and Lothair led down into Italy in the middle of the sixth century. Procopius informs us that the first-named prince brought with him some cavalry; their numbers, however, were insignificant, a few hundreds in an army of 90,000 men. They carried the lance and a small round buckler, and served as a bodyguard round the person of the king. Their presence, though pointing to a new military departure among the Franks, only serves to show the continued predominance of infantry in their armies.

A problem interesting to the historian was worked out, when in A. D. 553 the footmen of Buccelin met the Roman Army of Narses at the Battle of Casilinum. The superiority of the tactics and armament of the imperial troops was made equally conspicuous. Formed in one deep column the Franks advanced into the centre of the semicircle in which Narses had ranged his men. The Roman infantry and the dismounted heavy cavalry of the Herule auxiliaries held them in play in front, while the horse-archers closed in on their flanks, and inflicted on them the same fate which had befallen the army of Crassus. Hardly a man of Buccelin's followers escaped from the field: the day of infantry was gone, for the Franks as much as for the rest of the world.

We are accordingly not surprised to find that from the sixth to the ninth century a steady increase in the proportion of cavalry in the Frank armies is to be found; corresponding to it is an increased employment of defensive arms. A crested helmet of classical shape becomes common among them, and shortly after a mail-shirt reaching to the hips is introduced. The Emperor Charles the Great himself contributed to the armament of his cavalry, by adopting defences for the arms and thighs: '*coxarum exteriora in eo ferreis ambiebantur bracteolis.*' (See Hewitt's *Ancient Armour*, vol. i.) This protection, however, was at first rejected by many of the Franks, who complained that it impaired their seat on horseback.

At Tours a considerable number of horsemen appear to have served in the army of Charles Martel: the general tactics of the day, however, were not those of an army mainly composed of cavalry. The Franks stood rooted to the spot, ('*terrae glacialiter adstricti*'), and fought a waiting battle, till the light-horse of the Saracens had exhausted their strength in countless unsuccessful charges: then they pushed forward and routed such of the enemy as had spirit to continue the fight.

In the time of Charles the Great we are told that all men of impor-

Charles Martel at Tours

tance, with their immediate followers, were accustomed to serve on horseback. The national forces, however, as opposed to the personal retinues of the monarch and his great officials and nobles, continued to form the infantry of the army, as can be seen from the list of the weapons which the 'Counts' are directed to provide for them. The Capitularies are explicit in declaring that the local commanders 'are to be careful that the men whom they have to lead to battle are fully equipped: that is, that they possess spear, shield, helm, mailshirt (*brunia*), a bow, two bow-strings, and twelve arrows.' (*Capitularies*, ed. Baluz, i.) The Franks had therefore become heavy infantry at the end of the eighth century: in the ninth century, they were finally to abandon their old tactics, and to entrust all important operations to their cavalry.

This transformation may be said to date from the law of Charles the Bald, providing '*ut pagenses Franci qui caballos habent, aut habere possunt, cum suis comitibus in hostem pergant.*' Whether merely ratifying an existing state of things, or instituting a new one, this order is eminently characteristic of the period, in which the defence of the country was falling into the hands of its cavalry force alone. Of the causes which led to this consummation the most important was the character of the enemies with whom the Franks had to contend in the ninth and tenth centuries. The Northman in the Western kingdom, the Magyar in the Eastern, were marauders bent on plunder alone, and owing their success to the rapidity of their movements.

The hosts of the Vikings were in the habit of seizing horses in the country which they invaded, and then rode up and down the length of the land, always distancing the slowly-moving local levies. The Hungarian horse-archers conducted forays into the heart of Germany, yet succeeded in evading pursuit. For the repression of such inroads infantry was absolutely useless; like the Romans of the fourth century, the Franks, when obliged to stand upon the defensive, had to rely upon their cavalry.

This crisis in the military history of Europe coincided with the breaking up of all central power in the shipwreck of the dynasty of Charles the Great. In the absence of any organised national resistance, the defence of the empire fell into the hands of the local counts, who now became semi-independent sovereigns. To these petty rulers the landholders of each district were now 'commending' themselves, in order to obtain protection in an age of war and anarchy. At the same time, and for the same reason, the poorer freemen were 'commending' themselves to the landholders. Thus, the feudal hierarchy was established, and a new military system appears, when the 'count' or 'duke' leads out to battle his vassals and their mounted retainers.

Politically retrogressive as was that system, it had yet its day of success: the Magyar was crushed at Merseberg and the Lechfeld, and driven back across the Leith, soon to become Christianised and grow into an orderly member of the European commonwealth. The Viking was checked in his plundering forays, expelled from his strongholds at the river-mouths, and restricted to the single possession of Normandy, where he—like the Magyar—was assimilated to the rest of feudal society. The force which had won these victories, and saved Europe from a relapse into the savagery and Paganism of the North and East, was that of the mail-clad horseman. What wonder then if his contemporaries and successors glorified him into the normal type of warriorhood, and believed that no other form of military efficiency was worth cultivating? The perpetuation of feudal chivalry for four hundred years was the reward of its triumphs in the end of the Dark Ages.

✶✶✶✶✶✶

Beyond the English Channel the course of the history of war is parallel to that which it took in the lands of the Continent, with a single exception in the form of its final development. Like the Franks, the Angles and Saxons were at the time of their conquest of Britain a nation of infantry soldiers, armed with the long ashen javelin, the broadsword, the *seax* or broad stabbing dagger, and occasionally the battle-axe. (A short weapon like the *francisca*, not the long Danish axe which afterwards became the national arm.)

Their defensive weapon was almost exclusively the shield, the 'round warboard,' with its large iron boss. Ring-mail, though known to them at a very early date, was, as all indications unite to show, extremely uncommon. The 'grey war-sark' or 'ring-locked byrnie' of Beowulf was obtainable by kings and princes alone. The helmet also, with its 'iron-wrought boar-crest,' was very restricted in its use. If the monarch and his *gesiths* wore such arms, the national levy, which formed the main fighting force of a heptarchic kingdom, was entirely without them.

Unmolested for many centuries in their island home, the English kept up the old Teutonic war customs for a longer period than other European nations. When Mercia and Wessex were at strife, the campaign was fought out by the hastily-raised hosts of the various districts, headed by their aldermen and reeves. Hence war bore the spasmodic

BATTLE OF LECHFELD

DANISH WARRIORS ON THE HUMBER.

and inconsequent character which resulted from the temporary nature of such armies. With so weak a military organisation, there was no possibility of working out schemes of steady and progressive conquest. The frays of the various kingdoms, bitter and unceasing though they might be, led to no decisive results. If in the ninth century a tendency towards unification began to show itself in England, it was caused, not by the military superiority of Wessex, but by the dying out of royal lines and the unfortunate internal condition of the other states.

While this inclination towards union was developing itself, the whole island was subjected to the stress of the same storm of foreign invasion which was shaking the Frankish empire to its foundations. The Danes came down upon England, and demonstrated, by the fearful success of their raids, that the old Teutonic military system was inadequate to the needs of the day. The Vikings were in fact superior to the forces brought against them, alike in tactics, in armament, in training, and in mobility. Personally, the Dane was the member of an old warband contending with a farmer fresh from the plough, a veteran soldier pitted against a raw militiaman.

As a professional warrior, he had provided himself with an equipment which only the chiefs among the English Army could rival, the mail *byrnie* being a normal rather than an exceptional defence, and the steel cap almost universal. The *fyrd*, on the other hand, came out against him destitute of armour, and bearing a motley array of weapons, wherein the spear and sword were mixed with the club and the stone-axe. (If these were the '*lignis imposita saxa*' of which the Norman chronicler of Hastings spoke, as being English weapons.)

If, however, the Danes had been in the habit of waiting for the local levies to come up with them, equal courage and superior numbers might have prevailed over these advantages of equipment. Plunder, however, rather than fighting, was the Viking's object: the host threw itself upon some district of the English coast, 'was there a-horsed,' (Anglo-Saxon *Chronicle*, under *a.d.* 866 and *passim*), and then rode far and wide through the land, doing all the damage in its power. The possession of the horses they had seized gave them a power of rapid movement which the *fyrd* could not hope to equal: when the local levies arrived at the spot where the invaders had been last seen, it was only to find smoke and ruins, not an enemy. When driven to bay—as, in spite of their habitual retreats, was sometimes the case—the Danes showed an instinctive tactical ability by their use of entrenchments, with which the English were unaccustomed to deal. Behind a ditch and palisade, in some commanding spot, the invaders would wait for months, till the accumulated force of the *fyrd* had melted away to its homes.

Of assaults on their positions they knew no fear: the line of axemen could generally contrive to keep down the most impetuous charge of the English levies: Reading was a more typical field than Ethandun. For one successful storm of an entrenched camp there were two bloody repulses.

Thirty years of disasters sealed the fate of the old national military organisation: something more than the *fyrd* was necessary to meet the organised war-bands of the Danes. The social results of the invasion in England had been similar to those which we have observed in the Frankish Empire. Everywhere the free *ceorls* had been 'commending' themselves to the neighbouring landowners. By accepting this 'commendation' the thegnhood had rendered itself responsible for the defence of the country.

The kingly power was in stronger hands in England than across the Channel, so that the new system did not at once develop itself into feudalism. Able to utilise, instead of bound to fear, the results of the change, Alfred and Eadward determined to use it as the basis for a new military organisation. Accordingly, all holders of five hides of land were subjected to 'Thegn-service,' and formed a permanent basis for the national army. To supplement the force thus obtained, the *fyrd* was divided into two halves, one of which was always to be available.

These arrangements had the happiest results: the tide of war turned, and England reasserted itself, till the tenth century saw the culmination of her new strength at the great Battle of Brunanburh. The *thegn*, a soldier by position like the Frankish noble, has now become the leading figure in war: arrayed in mail shirt and steel cap, and armed with sword and long pointed shield, the 'bands of chosen ones' were ready to face and hew down the Danish axemen. It is, however, worth remembering that the military problem of the day had now been much simplified for the English by the settlement of the invaders within the Danelaw.

An enemy who has towns to be burnt and homesteads to be harried can have pressure put upon him which cannot be brought to bear on a marauder whose basis of operations is the sea. It is noteworthy that Eadward utilised against the Danes that same system of fortified positions which they had employed against his predecessors; the stockades of his new *burghs* served to hold in check the *heres* of the

Battle of Brunanburh

local *jarls* of the Five Towns, while the king with his main force was busied in other quarters.

A century later than the military reforms of Alfred the feudal danger which had split up the Frankish realm began to make itself felt in England. The great ealdormen of the reign of Ethelred correspond to the counts of the time of Charles the Fat, in their tendency to pass from the position of officials into that of petty princes. Their rise is marked by the decay of the central military organisation for war; and during the new series of Danish invasions the forces of each *ealdormanry* are seen to fight and fall without any support from their neighbours. England was in all probability only saved from the fate of France by the accession of Canute. That monarch, besides reducing the provincial governors to their old position of delegates of the crown, strengthened his position by the institution of the House-*Carles*, a force sufficiently numerous to be called a small standing army rather than a mere royal guard.

These troops are not only the most characteristic token of the existence of a powerful central government, but represent the maximum of military efficiency to be found in the Anglo-Danish world. Their tactics and weapons differed entirely from those of the feudal aristocracy of the continent, against whom they were ere long to be pitted. They bore the long Danish battle-axe, a shaft five feet long fitted with a single-bladed head of enormous size. It was far too ponderous for use on horseback, and being wielded with both arms precluded the use of a shield in hand to hand combat.

★★★★★★

See in the *Roman de Rou*, ii.:—
'*Hoem ki od hache volt ferir,*
Od sez dous mainz l'estuet tenir.
Ne pot entendre a sei covrir,

S'il velt ferir de grant aïr.
Bien ferir e covrir ensemble
Ne pot l'en fair ço me semble.'

★★★★★★

The blows delivered by this weapon were tremendous: no shield or mail could resist them; they were even capable, as was shown at Hastings, of lopping off a horse's head at a single stroke. The house-*carle* in his defensive equipment did not differ from the cavalry of the lands beyond the Channel: like them he wore a mail shirt of a considerable length, reaching down to the lower thigh, and a pointed steel cap fitted with a nasal.

The tactics of the English axemen were those of the column: arranged in a compact mass they could beat off almost any attack, and hew their way through every obstacle. Their personal strength and steadiness, their confidence and *ésprit de corps*, made them the most dangerous adversaries. Their array, however, was vitiated by the two defects of slowness of movement and vulnerability by missiles. If assailed by horsemen, they were obliged to halt and remain fixed to the spot, in order to keep off the enemy by their close order. If attacked from a distance by light troops, they were also at a disadvantage, as unable to reach men who retired before them.

The Battle of Hastings, the first great mediaeval fight of which we have an account clear enough to give us an insight into the causes of its result, was the final trial of this form of military efficiency. Backed by the disorderly masses of the *fyrd*, and by the *thegns* of the home counties, the house-*carles* of King Harold stood in arms to defend the entrenchments of Senlac. Formidable as was the English array, it was opposed precisely by those arms which, in the hands of an able general, were competent to master it. The Norman knights, if unsupported by their light infantry, might have surged for ever around the impregnable palisades. The archers, if unsupported by the knights, could easily have been driven off the field by a general charge.

United, however, by the skilful tactics of William, the two divisions of the invading army won the day. The Saxon mass was subjected to exactly the same trial which befell the British squares in the Battle of Waterloo: incessant charges by a gallant cavalry were alternated with a destructive fire of missiles.

★★★★★★

The fate of the only one of Wellington's squares which attempted to deploy, in order to drive off the infantry which were annoying it, may well be compared with that of Harold's soldiery. 'The concentrated fire of this close line of skirmishers was now telling heavily upon the devoted squares of Alten's division. It was, however, impossible to deploy, as in the hollow, near La Haye Sainte, there lay in wait a body of the enemy's cavalry. At last the 5th line-battalion of the King's German Legion, forsaking its square formation, opened out, and advanced against the mass of *tirailleurs*. The French gave way as the line advanced at the charge; at the next moment, the battalion was furiously assailed by a regiment of *cuirassiers*, who, taking it in

THE BATTLE OF HASTINGS

flank, fairly rolled it up. So severe was the loss sustained, that out of the whole battalion not more than 30 men and a few officers were gradually collected in their former position.'—Siborne's *History of the Waterloo Campaign*, published in 3 shorter volumes by Leonaur, *Siborne's 1815 Campaign*, (1 before; 2 during and 3 after the principal battle.)

★★★★★★

Nothing can be more maddening than such an ordeal to the infantry soldier, rooted to the spot by the necessities of his formation. After repelling charge after charge with the greatest steadiness, the axemen could no longer bear the rain of arrows. When at last, the horsemen drew back in apparent disorder, a great part of Harold's troops stormed down into the valley after them, determined to finish the battle by an advance which should not allow the enemy time to rally. This mistake was fatal: the Norman retreat had been the result of the duke's orders, not of a wish to leave the field.

The cavalry turned, rode down the scattered mass which had pursued them, and broke into the gap in the English line which had been made by the inconsiderate charge. Desperate as was their position, the English still held out: the arrows fell thickly among them, the knights were forcing their way among the disordered ranks of the broken army, but for three hours longer the fight went on. This exhibition of courage only served to increase the number of the slain: the day was hopelessly lost, and, as evening fell, the few survivors of the English army were glad to be able to make their retreat under cover of the darkness. The tactics of the phalanx of axemen had been decisively beaten by William's combination of archers and cavalry.

Once more only—on a field far away from its native land—did the weapon of the Anglo-Danes dispute the victory with the lance and bow. Fifteen years after Harold's defeat another body of English axemen—some of them may well have fought at Senlac—were advancing against the army of a Norman prince. They were the famous Varangian guard—of the Emperor Alexius Comnenus, (such a mere synonym for Englishmen at Constantinople, that Anna Comnena considers that she defines Robert of Normandy sufficiently, when she calls him 'the brother of their king'.) That prince was engaged in an attempt to raise the siege of Dyrrhachium, then invested by Robert Guiscard.

The Norman Army was already drawn up in front of its lines, while the troops of Alexius were only slowly arriving on the field.

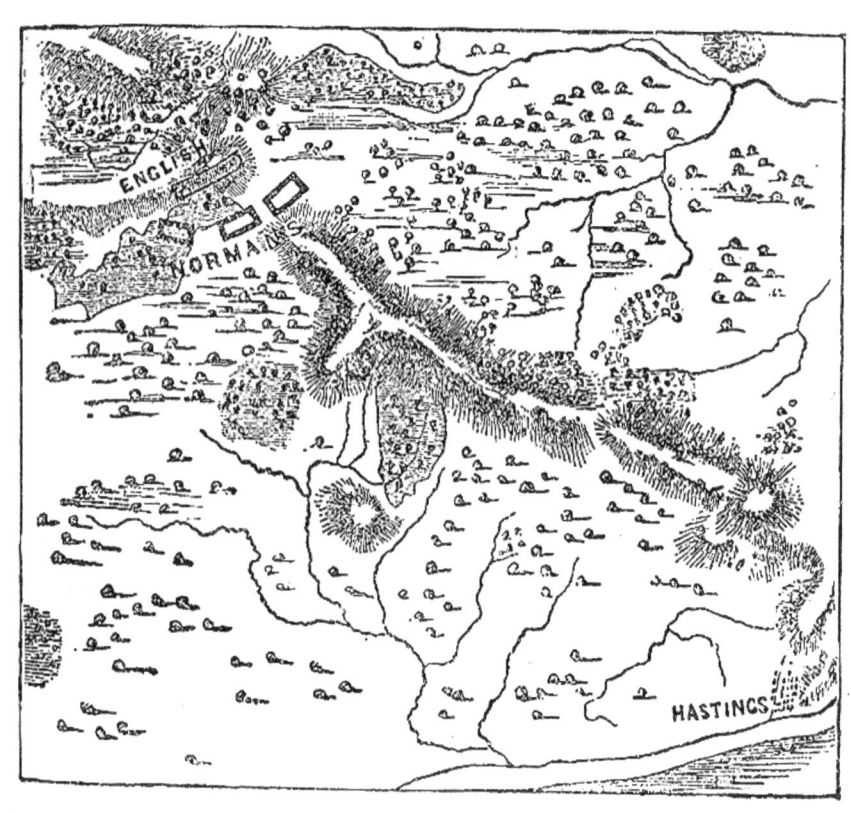

PLAN OF BATTLE OF HASTINGS.

Among the foremost of his corps were the Varangians, whom his care had provided with horses, in order that they might get to the front quickly and execute a turning movement. This they accomplished; but when they approached the enemy they were carried away by their eagerness to begin the fray. Without waiting for the main attack of the Greek Army to be developed, the axemen sent their horses to the rear, and advanced in a solid column against the Norman flank. Rushing upon the division commanded by Count Amaury of Bari, they drove it, horse and foot, into the sea.

Their success, however, had disordered their ranks, and the Norman prince was enabled, since Alexius' main body was still far distant, to turn all his forces against them. A vigorous cavalry charge cut off the greater part of the English; the remainder collected on a little mound by the sea-shore, surmounted by a deserted chapel. Here they were surrounded by the Normans, and a scene much like Senlac, but on a smaller scale, was enacted. After the horsemen and the archers had destroyed the majority of the Varangians, the remainder held out obstinately within the chapel.

Sending for fascines and timber from his camp; Robert heaped them round the building and set fire to the mass. (For these details see Anna Comnena's *Life of Alexius*.) The English sallied out to be slain one by one, or perished in the flames: not a man escaped; the whole corps suffered destruction, as a consequence of their misplaced eagerness to open the fight. Such was the fate of the last attempt made by infantry to face the feudal array of the eleventh century. No similar experiment was now to be made for more than two hundred years: the supremacy of cavalry was finally established.

CHAPTER 3

The Byzantines and their Enemies 582–1071
(From the accession of Maurice to the Battle of Manzikert)

(1) CHARACTER OF BYZANTINE STRATEGY.

Alike in composition and in organisation, the army which for 500 years held back Slav and Saracen from the frontier of the Eastern Empire, differed from the troops whose name and traditions it inherited. To the *Palatine* and *Limitary numeri* of Constantine it bore as little likeness as to the legions of Trajan. Yet in one respect at least it resembled both those forces: it was in its day the most efficient military body in the world. The men of the lower Empire have received scant justice at the hands of modern historians: their manifest faults have thrown the stronger points of their character into the shade, and Byzantinism is accepted as a synonym for effete incapacity alike in peace and war. Much might be written in general vindication of their age, but never is it easier to produce a strong defence than when their military skill and prowess are disparaged.

Gibbon, (v.) says:—

The vices of Byzantine Armies were inherent, their victories accidental.

So far is this sweeping condemnation from the truth, that it would be far more correct to call their defeats accidental, their successes normal. Bad generalship, insufficient numbers, unforeseen calamities, not the inefficiency of the troops, were the usual causes of disaster in the campaigns of the Eastern Emperors. To the excellence of the soldiery witness, direct or indirect, is borne in every one of those military treatises which give us such a vivid picture of the warfare of the age.

Unless the general is incompetent or the surrounding circumstances unusually adverse, the authors always assume that victory will follow the banner of the Empire. The troops can be trusted, like Wellington's Peninsular veterans, 'to go anywhere and do anything.'

Nicephorus Phocas says:—

The commander who has 6000 of our heavy cavalry and God's help, needs nothing more.

In a similar spirit Leo the Philosopher declares in his *Tactica* that, except the Frankish and Lombard knights, there were no horsemen in the world who could face the Byzantine *Cataphracti*, when the numbers of the combatants approached equality. Slav, Turk, or Saracen could be ridden down by a charge fairly pressed home: only with the men of the West was the result of the shock doubtful. The causes of the excellence and efficiency of the Byzantine Army are not hard to discover. In courage, they were equal to their enemies; in discipline, organisation, and armament far superior. Above all, they possessed not only the traditions of Roman strategy, but a complete system of tactics, carefully elaborated to suit the requirements of the age.

For centuries war was studied as an art in the East, while in the West it remained merely a matter of hard fighting. The young Frankish noble deemed his military education complete when he could sit his charger firmly, and handle lance and shield with skill. The Byzantine patrician, while no less exercised in arms, added theory to empiric knowledge by the study of the works of Maurice, of Leo, of Nicephorus Phocas, and of other authors whose books survive in name alone. (Nothing better attests the military spirit of the Eastern aristocracy than their duels: cf. the cases of Prusian, etc., in Finlay's *Greece*.)

The results of the opposite views taken by the two divisions of Europe are what might have been expected. The men of the West, though they regarded war as the most important occupation of life, invariably found themselves at a loss when opposed by an enemy with whose tactics they were not acquainted. The generals of the East, on the other hand, made it their boast that they knew how to face and conquer Slav or Turk, Frank or Saracen, by employing in each case the tactical means best adapted to meet their opponents' method of warfare.

The directions for the various emergencies given by the Emperor Leo impress us alike as showing the diversity of the tasks set before the Byzantine general, and the practical manner in which they were taken in hand. They serve indeed as a key to the whole system of the art of war as it was understood at Constantinople.

Leo says, (*Tactica*):—

The Frank believes that a retreat under any circumstances must be dishonourable; hence he will fight whenever you choose to offer him battle. This you must not do till you have secured all possible advantages for yourself, as his cavalry, with their long lances and large shields, charge with a tremendous impetus. You should deal with him by protracting the campaign, and if possible lead him into the hills, where his cavalry are less efficient than in the plain. After a few weeks without a great battle his troops, who are very susceptible to fatigue and weariness, will grow tired of the war, and ride home in great numbers. . . . You will find him utterly careless as to outposts and reconnaisances, so that you can easily cut off outlying parties of his men, and attack his camp at advantage.

As his forces have no bonds of discipline, but only those of kindred or oath, they fall into confusion after delivering their charge; you can therefore simulate flight, and then turn them, when you will find them in utter disarray. On the whole, however, it is easier and less costly to wear out a Frankish Army by skirmishes and protracted operations rather than to attempt to destroy it at a single blow. (The paragraphs here are a condensation of Leo's advice, and sometimes an elucidation, not a literal translation.)

The chapters of which these directions are an abstract have two distinct points of interest. They present us with a picture of a Western army of the ninth or tenth century, the exact period of the development of feudal cavalry, drawn by the critical hand of an enemy. They also show the characteristic strength and weakness of Byzantine military science. On the one hand, we note that Leo's precepts are practical and efficacious; on the other, we see that they are based upon the supposition that the imperial troops will normally act upon the defensive, a limitation which must materially lessen their efficiency. These, however, were the tactics by which the Eastern emperors succeeded in maintaining their Italian 'Themes' for 400 years, against every attack of Lombard duke or Frankish emperor.

The method which is recommended by Leo for resisting the 'Turk' (by which name he denotes the Magyars and the tribes dwelling north of the Euxine) is different in every respect from that directed against the nations of the West, The Turkish Army consisted of innumerable bands of light horsemen, who carried javelin and scimitar, but relied on their arrows for victory. Their tactics were in fact a repetition of those of Attila, a foreshadowing of those of Alp Arslan or Batu Khan. The Turks were 'given to ambushes and stratagems of every sort,' and were noted for the care with which they posted their vedettes, so that they could seldom or never be attacked by surprise.

On a fair open field, however, they could be ridden down by the Byzantine heavy cavalry, who are therefore recommended to close with them at once, and not to exchange arrows with them at a distance. Steady infantry they could not break, and indeed they were averse to attacking it, since the bows of the Byzantine foot-archers carried farther than their own shorter weapon, and they were thus liable to have their horses shot before coming within their own limit of efficacious range. Their armour protected their own bodies, but not those of their chargers; and they might thus find themselves dismounted, in which position they were absolutely helpless, the nomad of the *steppes* having never been accustomed to fight on foot. With the Turks, therefore, a pitched battle was desirable; but as they were prompt at rallying, it was always necessary to pursue them with caution, and not to allow the troops to get out of hand during the chase.

It is at once apparent from these directions how utterly the efficiency of the Byzantine infantry differed from that of the legions of an earlier day. The soldiers of the first century, armed with sword and pilum alone, were destroyed from a distance by the Parthian mounted bowmen. The adoption of the bow by infantry had now changed the aspect of affairs, and it was the horse-archer who now found himself at a disadvantage in the exchange of missiles.

Nor could he hope to retrieve the day by charging, since the *scutati* or spearmen,—one of the curious Latin survivals in Byzantine military terminology, in transliterating Latin words the Greeks paid no attention to quantity—carrying the large shield, who formed the front rank of a Byzantine *tagma*, could keep at bay horsemen armed, not with the heavy lance of the West, but merely with scimitars and short javelins. Hence the Turk avoided conflicts with the imperial infantry, and used his superior powers of locomotion to keep out of its way. It was only the cavalry which could, as a rule, come up with him.

The tactics calculated for success against the Slavs call for little notice. The Servians and the Slovenes possessed hardly any cavalry, and were chiefly formidable to the imperial troops when they kept to the mountains, where their archers and javelin-men, posted in inaccessible positions, could annoy the invader from a distance, or the spearmen could make sudden assaults on the flank of his marching columns. Such attacks could be frustrated by proper vigilance, while, if the Slavs were only surprised while engaged in their plundering expeditions into the plains, they could be ridden down and cut to pieces by the imperial cavalry.

To deal with the Saracen, on the other hand, the greatest care and skill were required.

★★★★★★

Much confusion in military history has been caused by writers attributing the archery of the Turks to the Saracens: the latter were not employers of archery-tactics, but lancers. Battles like Dorylaeum, which are given as examples of Saracen warfare, were fought really by Turks.

★★★★★★

Leo says:—

Of all barbarous nations, they are the best advised and the most prudent in their military operations.

The commander who has to meet with them will need all his tactical and strategical ability, the troops must be well disciplined and confident, if the 'barbarous and blaspheming Saracen,' (Leo), is to be driven back in rout through the *Klissuras* of Taurus.

The Arabs whom Khaled and Amrou had led in the seventh century to the conquest of Syria and Egypt, had owed their victory neither to the superiority of their arms nor to the excellence of their organisation. The fanatical courage of the fatalist had enabled them—as it has enabled their co-religionists in the present spring—to face better armed and better disciplined troops. Settled in their new homes, however, when the first outburst of their vigour had passed away, they did not disdain to learn a lesson from the nations they had defeated.

Accordingly the Byzantine Army served as a model for the forces of the *Khalifs*; 'they have copied the Romans in most of their military practices,' says Leo, both in arms and in strategy. Like the imperial generals, they placed their confidence in their mailed lancers; but the Saracen and his charger were alike at a disadvantage in the onset. Horse for horse and man for man, the Byzantines were heavier, and could ride the Orientals down when the final shock came.

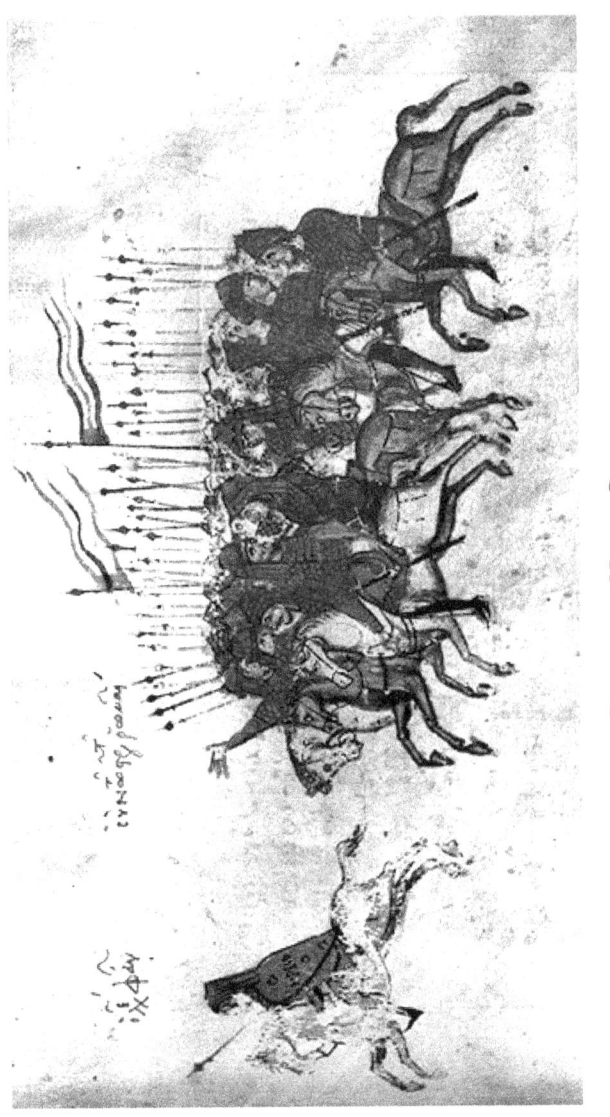

Byzantine Heavy Cavalry

Two things alone rendered the Saracens the most dangerous of foes, their numbers and their extraordinary powers of locomotion. When an inroad into Asia Minor was projected, the powers of greed and fanaticism united to draw together every unquiet spirit between Khorassan and Egypt. The wild horsemen of the East poured out in myriads from the gates of Tarsus and Adana, to harry the fertile uplands of the Anatolic Themes.

> They are no regular troops, but a mixed multitude of volunteers: the rich man serves from pride of race, the poor man from hope of plunder. Many of them go forth because they believe that God delights in war, and has promised victory to them. Those who stay at home, both men and women, aid in arming their poorer neighbours, and think that they are performing a good work thereby. Thus, there is no homogeneity in their armies, since experienced warriors and untrained plunderers march side by side.—Leo, *Tactica*: various scattered notices.

Once clear of the passes of Taurus, the great horde of Saracen horsemen cut itself loose from its communications, and rode far and wide through Phrygia and Cappadocia, burning the open towns, harrying the country side, and lading their beasts of burden with the plunder of a region which was in those days one of the richest in the world.

Now was the time for the Byzantine general to show his metal: first he had to come up with his enemies, and then to fight them. The former task was no easy matter, as the Saracen in the first days of his inroad could cover an incredible distance. It was not till he had loaded and clogged himself with plunder that he was usually to be caught.

When the news of the raid reached the general of the 'Anatolic' or 'Armeniac' theme, he had at once to collect every efficient horseman in his province, and strike at the enemy. Untrained men and weak horses were left behind, and the infantry could not hope to keep up with the rapid movements which had now to be undertaken. Accordingly, Leo would send all the disposable foot to occupy the *Klissuras* of the Taurus, where, even if the cavalry did not catch the invader, his retreat might be delayed and harassed in passes where he could not fight to advantage.

In his cavalry, however, lay the Byzantine commander's hope of success. To ascertain the enemy's position he must spare no trouble: Nicephorus Phocas writes:

SARACENS

Never turn away freeman or slave, by day or night, though you may be sleeping or eating or bathing, if he says that he has news for you.

When once the Saracen's track had been discovered, he was to be pursued without ceasing, and his force and objects discovered. If all Syria and Mesopotamia had come out for an invasion rather than a mere foray, the general must resign himself to taking the defensive, and only hang on the enemy's flanks, cutting off his stragglers and preventing any plundering by detached parties. No fighting must be taken in hand till 'all the Themes of the East have been set marching' an order which would put some 25,000 or 30,000 heavy cavalry at the disposal of the commander-in-chief, but would cost the loss of much precious time.

★★★★★★

In Leo's day, the Oriental themes had not been sub-divided, as was afterwards done by his son Constantine. There were then eight themes in Asia Minor, each of which contained a military division of the same name, and could be reckoned on for some 4000 heavy cavalry. These were 'Armeniacon, Anatolicon, Obsequium, Thracesion, Cibyrrhoeot, Bucellarion, and Paphlagonia.' Optimaton, the ninth theme, had (as Constantine tells us in his treatise on the empire), no military establishments.

★★★★★★

These Saracen 'Warden-raids' (if we may borrow an expression from the similar expeditions of our own Borderers) were of comparatively infrequent occurrence: it was seldom that the whole Byzantine force in Asia was drawn out to face the enemy in a great battle. The more typical Saracen inroad was made by the inhabitants of Cilicia and Northern Syria, with the assistance of casual adventurers from the inner Mohammedan lands.

To meet them the Byzantine commander would probably have no more than the 4000 heavy cavalry of his own Theme in hand; a force for whose handling Leo gives minute tactical directions, (see next section.) When he had come up with the raiders they would turn and offer him battle: nor was their onset to be despised. Though unequal, man for man, to their adversaries, they were usually in superior numbers, and always came on with great confidence.

They are very bold at first with expectation of victory; nor will they turn at once, even if their line is broken through by our impact.—*Tactica*.

When they suppose that their enemy's vigour is relaxing, they all charge together with a desperate effort, (*Tactica*.) If, however, this failed, a rout generally ensued.

For they think that all misfortune is sent by God, and so, if they are once beaten, they take their defeat as a sign of divine wrath, and no longer attempt to defend themselves.—*Tactica*.

Hence the Mussulman Army, when once it turned to fly, could be pursued à *l'outrance*, and the old military maxim, '*Vince sed ne nimis vincas*,' was a caution which the Byzantine officer could disregard.

The secret of success in an engagement with the Saracens lay in the cavalry tactics, which had for three centuries been in process of elaboration. By the tenth century they attained their perfection, and the experienced soldier Nicephorus Phocas vouches for their efficacy. Their distinguishing feature was that the troops were always placed in two lines and a reserve, with squadrons detached on the flanks to prevent their being turned. The enemy came on in one very deep line, and could never stand the three successive shocks as the first line, second line, and reserve were one after another flung into the *mêlée* against them.

The Byzantines had already discovered the great precept which modern military science has claimed as its own, that, 'in a cavalry combat, the side which holds back the last reserve must win.' (See Colonel Clery's *Minor Tactics*.) The exact formation used on these occasions, being carefully described by our authorities, is worth detailing, and will be found in our section treating of the organisation of the Byzantine Army.

There were several other methods of dealing with the Saracen invader. It was sometimes advisable, when his inroad was made in great force, to hang about the rear of the retreating plunderers, and only fall upon them when they were engaged in passing the *Klissuras* of the Taurus. If infantry was already on the spot to aid the pursuing cavalry, success was almost certain, when the Saracens and their train of beasts, laden with spoil, were wedged in the passes. They could then be shot down by the archers, and would not stand for a moment when they saw their horses, 'the *Pharii*, whom they esteem above all other things,' (*Tactica*), struck by arrows from a distance; for the Saracen, when not actually engaged in close combat, would do anything to save his horse from harm.

Cold and rainy weather was also distasteful to the Oriental invader: at times, when it prevailed, he did not display his ordinary firmness and daring, and could be attacked at great advantage. Much could also be done by delivering a vigorous raid into his country, and wasting Cilicia and Northern Syria, the moment his armies were reported to have passed north into Cappadocia. This destructive practice was very frequently adopted, and the sight of two enemies each ravaging the other's territory without attempting to defend his own, was only too familiar to the inhabitants of the borderlands of Christendom and Islam. Incursions by sea supplemented the forays by land. Leo says:—

> When the Saracens of Cilicia have gone off by the passes, to harry the country north of Taurus, the commander of the Cibyrrhoeot Theme should immediately go on shipboard with all available forces, and ravage their coast. If, on the other hand, they have sailed off to attempt the shore districts of Pisidia, the *Klissurarchs* of Taurus can lay waste the territories of Tarsus and Adana without danger.

Nothing can show more clearly than these directions the high average skill of the Byzantine officer. Leo himself was not a man of any great ability, and his *Tactica* are intended to codify an existing military art, rather than to construct a new one. Yet still the book is one whose equal could not have been written in Western Europe before the sixteenth century. One of its most striking points is the utter difference of its tone from that of contemporary feeling in the rest of Christendom. Of chivalry, there is not a spark in the Byzantine, though professional pride is abundantly shown. Courage is regarded as one of the requisites necessary for obtaining success, not as the sole and paramount virtue of the warrior.

Leo considers a campaign successfully concluded without a great battle as the cheapest and most satisfactory consummation in war. He has no respect for the warlike ardour which makes men eager to plunge into the fray: it is to him rather a characteristic of the brainless barbarian, and an attribute fatal to anyone who makes any pretension to generalship. He shows a strong predilection for stratagems, ambushes, and simulated retreats. For an officer who fights without having first secured all the advantages to his own side, he has the greatest contempt.

It is with a kind of intellectual pride that he gives instructions how *parlementaires* are to be sent to the enemy without any real object except that of spying out the number and efficiency of his forces. He gives, as a piece of most ordinary and moral advice, the hint that a defeated general may often find time to execute a retreat by sending an emissary to propose a surrender (which he has no intention of carrying out) to the hostile commander.

★★★★★★

Compare with this the stratagem by which the Russian Army escaped from a compromised position during the retreat before the Battle of Austerlitz. 'In agreeing to an Armistice,' wrote Kutusoff, in a very Byzantine tone, 'I had in view nothing but to gain time, and thereby obtain the means of removing to a distance from the enemy, and saving my army.' Dumas, xiv.

★★★★★★

He is not above employing the old-world trick of addressing treasonable letters to the subordinate officers of the enemy's army, and contriving that they should fall into the hands of the commander-in-chief, in order that he may be made suspicious of his lieutenants. Schemes such as these are 'Byzantine' in the worst sense of the word, but their character must not be allowed to blind us to the real and extraordinary merits of the strategical system into which they have been inserted. The 'Art of War,' as understood at Constantinople in the tenth century, was the only scheme of true scientific merit existing in the world, and was unrivalled till the sixteenth century.

(2) ARMS, ORGANISATION, AND TACTICS OF THE BYZANTINE ARMIES.

The Byzantine Army may be said to owe its peculiar form to the Emperor Maurice, a prince whose reign is one of the chief landmarks in the history of the lower empire. (The Middle Ages dimly felt this, and, as Gibbon tells us, the Italian Chroniclers name him the 'first of the Greek Emperors.') The fortunate preservation of his *Strategikon* suffices to show us that the reorganisation of the troops of the East was mainly due to him. Contemporary historians also mention his reforms, but without descending to details, and inform us that, though destined to endure, they won him much unpopularity among the soldiery.

Later writers, however, have erroneously attributed these changes to the more celebrated warrior Heraclius, the prince who bore the Roman standards further than any of his predecessors into the lands of the East. (As, for example, the Emperor Constantine Porphyrogenitus, who, in his book on the *Themata Orientis*, attributes the invention of the 'Theme' and *tagma* to Heraclius.) In reality, the army of Heraclius had already been reorganised by the worthy but unfortunate Maurice.

The most important of Maurice's alterations was the elimination of that system somewhat resembling the Teutonic *comitatus*, which had crept from among the *Foederati* into the ranks of the regular Roman Army. The loyalty of the soldier was secured rather to the emperor than to his immediate superiors, by making the appointment of all officers above the rank of centurion a care of the central government. The commander of an army or division had thus no longer in his hands the power and patronage which had given him the opportunity of becoming dangerous to the state. The men found themselves under the orders of delegates of the emperor, not of quasi-independent authorities who enlisted them as personal followers rather than as units in the military establishment of the empire.

This reform Maurice succeeded in carrying out, to the great benefit of the discipline and loyalty of his army. He next took in hand the reducing of the whole force of the empire to a single form of organisation. The rapid decrease of the revenues of the state, which had set in towards the end of Justinian's reign, and continued to make itself more and more felt, had apparently resulted in a great diminution in the number of foreign mercenaries serving in the Roman Army. To the same end contributed the fact that of the Lombards, Herules, and Gepidae, the nations who had furnished the majority of the imperial *Foederati*, one race had removed to other seats, while the others had been exterminated. At last the number of the foreign corps had sunk to such a low ebb, that there was no military danger incurred in assimilating their organisation to that of the rest of the army.

The new system introduced by Maurice was destined to last for nearly five hundred years. Its unit, alike for infantry and cavalry, was the *bandum*—a weak battalion or horse-regiment of 400 men, commanded by an officer who usually bore the vulgarised title of *comes*, but was occasionally denominated by the older name for military tribune. (*Comes* had in Constantine's days been applied to five great officers alone). Three *bands* formed a small brigade, called by the equivalent of the English word 'throng', and applied only to the masses of the barbarian army. Three '*drunges*' formed the largest military group recognised by Maurice, and the division made by their union was the '*turma*.'

Nothing can be more characteristic of the whole Byzantine military system than the curious juxtaposition of Latin, Greek, and German words in its terminology. Upon the substratum of the old Roman survivals we find first a layer of Teutonic names introduced by the '*Foederati*' of the fourth and fifth centuries, and finally numerous Greek denominations, some of them borrowed from the old Macedonian military system, others newly invented.

The whole official language of the Empire was in fact still in a state of flux; Maurice himself was hailed by his subjects as 'Pius, Felix, Augustus,' (see the evidence of coins: the title only becomes common under the Amorian dynasty), though those who used the title were, for the most part, accustomed to speak in Greek. In the *Stratêgikon* the two tongues are inextricably mixed:

> 'Before the battle,' says the emperor, 'let the counts face their bands and raise the war-cry "*Deus nobiscum*", and the troopers will shout the answering cry.'

It would appear that Maurice had intended to break down the barrier, which had been interposed in the fourth century, between the class which paid the taxes and that which recruited the national army, he writes:

> We wish that every young Roman of free condition should learn the use of the bow, and should be constantly provided with that weapon and with two javelins.

If, however, this was intended to be the first step towards the introduction of universal military service, the design was never carried any further. Three hundred years later Leo is found echoing the same words, as a pious wish rather than as a practical expedient. The rank and file, however, of the imperial forces were now raised almost entirely within the realm, and well-nigh every nation contained in its limits, except the Greeks, furnished a considerable number of soldiers. The Armenians and Isaurians in Asia, the 'Thracians' and 'Macedonians'—or more properly the semi-Romanized Slavs—in Europe, were considered the best material by the recruiting officer.

The extraordinary permanence of all Byzantine institutions is illustrated by the fact that Maurice's arrangements were found almost unchanged three hundred years after his death. The chapters of Leo's *Tactica* which deal with the armament and organisation of the troops are little more than a reedition of the similar parts of his predecessor's *Stratêgikon*. The description of the heavy and light horseman, and of the infantry soldier, are identical in the two works, except in a few points of terminology.

The heavy trooper, wore at both epochs a steel cap surmounted by a small crest, and a long mail shirt, reaching from the neck to the thighs. He was also protected by gauntlets and steel-shoes, and usually wore a light surcoat over his mail. The horses of the officers, and of the men in the front rank, were furnished with steel frontlets and poitrails. The arms of the soldier were a broad-sword, a dagger, a horseman's bow and quiver, and a long lance, fitted with a thong towards its butt, and ornamented with a little *bannerole*. The colour of *bannerole*, crest, and surcoat was that of the regimental standard, and no two *bands* in the same *turma* had standards of the same hue. Thus the line presented an uniform and orderly appearance, every band displaying its own regimental facings. Strapped to his saddle each horseman carried a long cloak, which he assumed in cold and rainy weather, or when, for purposes of concealment, he wished to avoid displaying the glitter of his armour. (*Tactica*.)

The light trooper had less complete equipment, sometimes a cuirass of mail or horn, at others only a light mail cape covering the neck and shoulders. He carried a large shield, a defence which the heavy horseman could not adopt, on account of his requiring both hands to draw his bow. For arms the light cavalry carried lance and sword.

The infantry, which was much inferior to the horsemen in importance, was, like them, divided into two descriptions, heavy and light. The *scutati*, or troops of the former class, wore a steel helmet with a crest, and a short mail shirt; they carried a large oblong shield, which, like their crests, was of the same colour as the regimental banner.

Their chief weapon was a short but heavy battle-axe (*securis*) with a blade in front and a spike behind: they were also provided with a dagger. The light infantry wore no defensive armour; they were provided with a powerful bow, which carried much further than the horseman's weapon, and was therefore very formidable to hostile horse-archers. A few corps, drawn from provinces where the bow was not well known, carried instead two or three javelins. For hand to hand fighting the *psiloi* were provided with an axe similar to that of the *scutati*, and a very small round target, which hung at their waists. (*Tactica*.)

An extensive train of non-combatants was attached to the army. Among the cavalry every four troopers had a groom; among the infantry every sixteen men were provided with an attendant, who drove a cart containing 'a hand-mill, a bill-hook, a saw, two spades, a mallet, a large wicker basket, a scythe, and two pick-axes,' (*Tactica*), besides several other utensils for whose identity the dictionary gives no clue. Thus, twenty spades and twenty pick-axes per *century* were always forthcoming for entrenching purposes; a consummation for which the modern infantry company would be glad if it could find a parallel.

******

The *century* contained 10 *decuries*, but the *decury* was 16 not 10 men: thus the *century* was 160 strong. Three *centuries* went to a *band*, which would thus be about 450 men.

******

So perfect was the organisation of the Byzantine Army that it contained not only a 'military train,' but even an ambulance-corps of bearers and surgeons. The value attached to the lives of the soldiery is shown by the fact that the *scriboni* received a *nomisma*, (gold coin, worth perhaps 12*s*. in metal value), for every wounded man whom they brought off when the troops were retiring. Special officers were told to superintend the march of this mass of non-combatants and vehicles, which is collectively styled *tuldum*, and forms not the least part among the cares of the laborious author of the *Tactica*.

Those portions of the works of Maurice and Leo which deal with tactics show a far greater difference between the methods of the sixth and the ninth centuries, than is observable in other parts of their military systems. The chapters of Leo are, as is but natural, of a more interesting character than those of his predecessor. The more important of his ordinances are well worthy our attention.

It is first observable that the old Roman system of drawing entrenchments round the army, every time that it rested for the night, had been resumed. A corps of engineers always marched with the van-guard, and, when the evening halt had been called, traced out with stakes and ropes the contour of the camp. When the main body had come up, the *tuldum* was placed in the centre of the enclosure, while the infantry *bands* drew a ditch and bank along the lines of the Mensores' ropes, each corps doing a fixed amount of the work. A thick chain of picquets was kept far out from the camp, so that a surprise, even on the darkest of nights, was almost impossible.

******

Nicephorus Phocas, says that 'Armenians must never be placed in this line of picquets, as their habitual drowsiness at night makes them untrustworthy.'

******

The main characteristic of the Byzantine system of tactics is the small size of the various units employed in the operations, a sure sign of the existence of a high degree of discipline and training. While a Western army went on its blundering way arranged in two or three enormous *battles*, each mustering many thousand men, a Byzantine Army of equal strength would be divided into many scores of fractions. Leo does not seem to contemplate the existence of any column of greater strength than that of a single *band*. The fact that order and cohesion could be found in a line composed of so many separate units, is the best testimony to the high average ability of the officers in subordinate commands. These *counts* and *moirarchs* were in the ninth and tenth centuries drawn for the most part from the ranks of the Byzantine aristocracy.

Leo says:

> Nothing prevents us from finding a sufficient supply of men of wealth, and also of courage and high birth, to officer our army. Their nobility makes them respected by the soldiers, while their wealth enables them to win the greatest popularity among their troops by the occasional and judicious gift of small creature-comforts.—*Tactica*

A true military spirit existed among the noble families of the Eastern Empire: houses like those of Skleros and Phocas, of Bryennius, Kerkuas, and Comnenus are found furnishing generation after generation of officers to the national army. The patrician left luxury and intrigue behind him when he passed through the gates of Constantinople, and became in the field a keen professional soldier.

★★★★★★

Nothing gives a better idea of the real military character of the Byzantine aristocracy than a perusal of the curious tenth century romance of *Digenes Akritas*, a member of the house of Ducas, who is *Klissurarch* of the passes of Taurus, and performs with his mighty mace all the exploits of a hero of chivalry. He really existed, and bore the name of Basil Pantherios, See *Revue des Deux Mondes*, vol. 118.

★★★★★★

Infantry plays in Leo's work a very secondary part. So much is this the case, that in many of his tactical directions he gives a sketch of the order to be observed by the cavalry alone, without mentioning the foot. This results from the fact that when the conflict was one with a rapidly moving foe like the Saracen or Turk, the infantry would at the moment of battle be in all probability many marches in the rear. It is, therefore, with the design of showing the most typical development of Byzantine tactics that we have selected for description a *turma* of nine *bands*, or 4000 men, as placed in order, before engaging with an enemy whose force consists of horsemen.

The front line consists of three *banda*, each drawn up in a line seven (or occasionally five) deep. These troops are to receive the first shock. Behind the first line is arranged a second, consisting of four half-*banda*, each drawn up ten (or occasionally eight) deep. They are placed not directly behind the front bands, but in the intervals between them, so that, if the first line is repulsed, they may fall back, not on to their comrades, but into the spaces between them. To produce, however, an impression of solidity in the second line, a single *bandon* is divided into three parts, and its men drawn up, two deep, in the spaces between the four half-*banda*.

These troops, on seeing the men of the first line beaten back and falling into the intervals of the second line, are directed to wheel to the rear, and form a support behind the centre of the array. The main reserve, however, consists of two half-*banda*, posted on the flanks of the second line, but considerably to the rear. It is in line with these that the retiring *bandon*, of which we have just spoken, would array itself. To each flank of the main body was attached a half-*bandon*, of 225 men; these were entrusted with the duty of resisting attempts to turn the flanks of the *turma*.

Still further out, and if possible under cover, were placed two other bodies of similar strength; it was their duty to endeavour to get into the enemy's rear, or at any rate to disturb his wings by unexpected assaults: these troops were called 'lyers-in-wait.' The commander's position was normally in the centre of the second line, where he would be able to obtain a better general idea of the fight, than if he at once threw himself into the *mêlée* at the head of the foremost squadrons.

This order of battle is deserving of all praise. It provides for that succession of shocks which is the key to victory in a cavalry combat; as many as five different attacks would be made on the enemy before all the impetus of the Byzantine force had been exhausted. The arrangement of the second line behind the intervals of the first, obviated the possibility of the whole force being disordered by the repulse of the first squadrons. The routed troops would have behind them a clear space in which to rally, not a close line into which they would carry their disarray. Finally, the charge of the reserve and the detached troops would be made not on the enemy's centre, which would be covered by the remains of the first and second lines, but on to his flank, his most uncovered and vulnerable point.

A further idea of the excellent organisation of the Byzantine army will be given by the fact that in minor engagements each corps was told off into two parts, one of which, the *cursores*, represented the 'skirmishing line,' the other, the *defensores*, 'the supports.' The former in the case of the infantry-*turma* would of course consist of the archers, the latter of the *Scutati*.

To give a complete sketch of Leo's *Tactics* would be tedious and unnecessary. Enough indications have now been given to show their strength and completeness. It is easy to understand, after a perusal of such directions, the permanence of the military power of the Eastern Empire. Against the undisciplined Slav and Saracen, the Imperial troops had on all normal occasions the tremendous advantages of science and discipline. It is their defeats rather than their victories which need an explanation.

We have fixed, as the termination of the period of Byzantine greatness, the Battle of Manzikert, a. d. 1071. At this fight the rashness of Romanus Diogenes led to the annihilation of the forces of the Asiatic Themes by the horse-archers of Alp-Arslan. The decay of the central power which is marked by the rise of Isaac Comnenus, the nominee of the feudal party of Asiatic nobles, may have already enfeebled the army. It was, however, the result of Manzikert which was fatal to it; as the occupation of the themes of the interior of Asia Minor by the Seljuks cut off from the empire its greatest recruiting-ground, the land of the gallant Isaurians and Armenians, who had for five hundred years formed the core of the Eastern Army.

It will be observed that we have given no long account of the famous 'Greek-fire,' the one point in Byzantine military affairs which most authors condescend to notice. If we have neglected it, it is from a conviction that, although its importance in poliorcetics and naval fighting was considerable, it was, after all, a minor engine of war, and not comparable as a cause of Byzantine success to the excellent strategical and tactical system on which we have dilated. Very much the same conclusion may be drawn from a study of the other purely mechanical devices which existed in the hands of the imperial generals.

The old skill of the Roman engineer was preserved almost in its entirety, and the armouries of Constantinople were filled with machines, whose deadly efficacy inspired the ruder peoples of the West

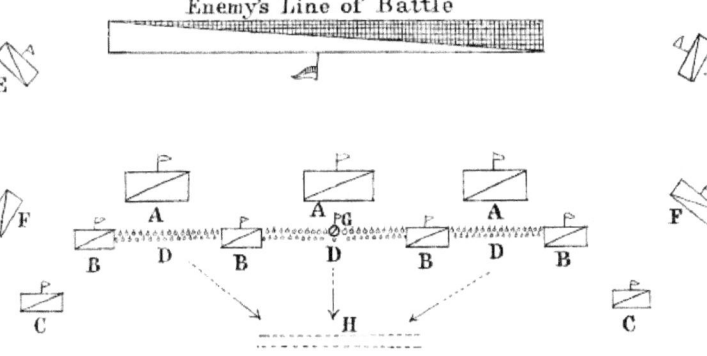

A BYZANTINE CAVALRY 'TURMA' IN ORDER OF BATTLE.

A.A.A. .... Front Line, three 'banda' of about 450 men each.
B.B.B.B. ...... Second Line, four half-'banda' of about 225 men each.
C.C. .... Reserve, two half-'banda' of same force.
D.D.D. .... One 'bandon' in double rank filling the intervals of the second line.
E.E. .... Ενεδροι, or detached bodies at the wings, who are to turn the enemy's flanks: 225 each or one bandon together.
F.F. .... Πλαγιοφύλακες, troops posted to prevent similar attempts of the enemy: 225 each, or one 'bandon' together.
G. .... The Commander and his Staff.
H. .... Place to which the troops D.D.D. would retire, when 2nd line charged.

and East with a mysterious feeling of awe. The *vinea* and *testudo*, the catapult *onager* and *balista*, were as well known in the tenth century as in the first. They were undoubtedly employed, and employed with effect, at every siege. But no amount of technical skill in the use of military machines would have sufficed to account for the ascendancy enjoyed by the Byzantines over their warlike neighbours. The sources of that superiority are to be sought in the existence of science and discipline, of strategy and tactics, of a professional and yet national army, of an upper class at once educated and military.

When the aristocracy became mere courtiers, when foreign mercenaries superseded the Isaurian bowman and the Anatolic cavalier, when the traditions of old Roman organisation gave place to mere centralisation, then no amount of the inherited mechanical skill of past ages could save the Byzantine Empire from its fall. The rude vigour of the Western knight accomplished the task which Chosroes and Crumn, Moslemah and Sviatoslaf, had found too hard for them. But it was not the empire of Heraclius or John Zimisces, of Leo the Isaurian, or Leo the Armenian, that was subdued by the piratical Crusaders, it was only the diminished and disorganised realm of the miserable Alexius Angelus.

CHAPTER 4

The Supremacy of Feudal Cavalry 1066-1346

(From the Battle of Hastings to the Battles of Morgarten and Cressy)

Between the last struggles of the infantry of the Anglo-Dane, and the rise of the pikemen and bowmen of the fourteenth century lies the period of the supremacy of the mail-clad feudal horseman. The epoch is, as far as strategy and tactics are concerned, one of almost complete stagnation: only in the single branch of Poliorcetics does the art of war make any appreciable progress.

The feudal organisation of society made every person of gentle blood a fighting man, but it cannot be said that it made him a soldier. If he could sit his charger steadily, and handle lance and sword with skill, the horseman of the twelfth or thirteenth century imagined himself to be a model of military efficiency. That discipline or tactical skill may be as important to an army as mere courage, he had no conception. Assembled with difficulty, insubordinate, unable to manoeuvre, ready to melt away from its standard the moment that its short period of service was over,—a feudal force presented an assemblage of unsoldierlike qualities such as has seldom been known to coexist.

Primarily intended to defend its own borders from the Magyar, the Northman, or the Saracen, the foes who in the tenth century had been a real danger to Christendom, the institution was utterly unadapted to take the offensive. When a number of tenants-in-chief had come together, each blindly jealous of his fellows and recognising no superior but the king, it would require a leader of uncommon skill to persuade them to institute that hierarchy of command, which must be established in every army that is to be something more than an undisciplined mob. Monarchs might try to obviate the danger by the creation of offices such as those of the Constable and Marshal, but these expedients were mere palliatives.

The radical vice of insubordination continued to exist. It was always possible that at some critical moment a battle might be precipitated, a formation broken, a plan disconcerted, by the rashness of some petty baron or banneret, who could listen to nothing but the promptings of his own heady valour. When the hierarchy of command was based on social status rather than on professional experience, the noble who led the largest contingent or held the highest rank, felt himself entitled to assume the direction of the battle. The veteran who brought only a few lances to the array could seldom aspire to influencing the movements of his superiors.

When mere courage takes the place of skill and experience, tactics and strategy alike disappear. Arrogance and stupidity combine to give a certain definite colour to the proceedings of the average feudal host. The century and the land may differ, but the incidents of battle are the same: Mansoura is like Aljubarotta, Nicopolis is like Courtrai. When the enemy came in sight, nothing could restrain the Western knights: the shield was shifted into position, the lance dropped into rest, the spur touched the charger, and the mail-clad line thundered on, regardless of what might be before it.

As often as not its career ended in being dashed against a stone wall or tumbled into a canal, in painful flounderings in a bog, or futile surgings around a palisade. The enemy who possessed even a rudimentary system of tactics could hardly fail to be successful against such armies. The fight of Mansoura may be taken as a fair specimen of the military customs of the thirteenth century. When the French vanguard saw a fair field before them and the lances of the *infidel* gleaming among the palm-groves, they could not restrain their eagerness. With the Count of Artois at their head, they started off in a headlong charge, in spite of St. Louis' strict prohibition of an engagement.

The Mamelukes retreated, allowed their pursuers to entangle themselves in the streets of a town, and then turned fiercely on them from all sides at once. In a short time, the whole *battle* of the Count of Artois was dispersed and cut to pieces. Meanwhile the main-body, hearing of the danger of their companions, had ridden off hastily to their aid. However, as each commander took his own route and made what speed he could, the French Army arrived upon the field in dozens of small scattered bodies. These were attacked in detail, and in many cases routed by the Mamelukes. No general battle was fought, but a number of detached and incoherent cavalry combats had all the results of a great defeat. A skirmish and a street fight could overthrow the chivalry of the West, even when it went forth in great strength, and was inspired by all the enthusiasm of a Crusade.

The array of a feudal force was stereotyped to a single pattern. As it was impossible to combine the movements of many small bodies, when the troops were neither disciplined nor accustomed to act together, it was usual to form the whole of the cavalry into three great masses, or *battles*, as they were called, and launch them at the enemy. The refinement of keeping a reserve in hand was practised by a few commanders, but these were men distinctly in advance of their age. Indeed, it would often have been hard to persuade a feudal chief to take a position out of the front line, and to incur the risk of losing his share in the hard fighting. When two *battles* met, a fearful *mêlée* ensued, and would often be continued for hours.

Sometimes, as if by agreement, the two parties wheeled to the rear, to give their horses breath, and then rushed at each other again, to renew the conflict till one side grew overmatched and left the field. An engagement like Brenville or Bouvines or Benevento was nothing more than a huge scuffle and scramble of horses and men over a convenient heath or hillside. The most ordinary precautions, such as directing a reserve on a critical point, or detaching a corps to take the enemy in flank, or selecting a good position in which to receive battle, were considered instances of surpassing military skill.

Charles of Anjou, for instance, has received the name of a great commander, because at Tagliacozzo he retained a body of knights under cover, and launched it against Conradin's rear, when the Ghibellines had dispersed in pursuit of the routed Angevin main-*battle*. Simon de Montfort earned high repute; but if at Lewes he kept and utilised a reserve, we must not forget that at Evesham he allowed himself to be surprised and forced to fight with his back to a river, in a position from which no retreat was possible. The commendation of the age was, in short, the meed of striking feats of arms rather than of real generalship. If much attention were to be paid to the chroniclers, we should believe that commanders of merit were numerous; but, if we examine the actions of these much-belauded individuals rather than the opinions of their contemporaries, our belief in their ability almost invariably receives a rude shock. (Eustace de Ribeaumont, for instance, who gave the madly impractical advice which lost the Battle of Poictiers, was, we are told, an officer of high ability.)

If the minor operations of war were badly understood, strategy—the higher branch of the military art—was absolutely non-existent. An invading army moved into hostile territory, not in order to strike at some great strategical point, but merely to burn and harry the land. As no organised commissariat existed, the resources of even the richest districts were soon exhausted, and the invader moved off in search of subsistence, rather than for any higher aim.

It is only towards the end of the period with which we are dealing that any traces of systematic arrangements for the provisioning of an army are found. Even these were for the most part the results of sheer necessity: in attacking a poor and uncultivated territory, like Wales or Scotland, the English kings found that they could not live on the country, and were compelled to take measures to keep their troops from starvation. But a French or German Army, when it entered Flanders or Lombardy, or an English force in France, trusted, as all facts unite to demonstrate, for its maintenance to its power of plundering the invaded district.

✶✶✶✶✶✶

The Black Prince's campaign in South France, for example, before the Battle of Poictiers, was merely an enormous and destructive raid. He besieged no important town, and did not attempt to establish any posts to command the country through which he passed.

✶✶✶✶✶✶

Great battles were, on the whole, infrequent: a fact which appears strange, when the long-continued wars of the period are taken into consideration. Whole years of hostilities produced only a few partial skirmishes: compared with modern campaigns, the general engagements were incredibly few. Frederick the Great or Napoleon I. fought more battles in one year than a mediaeval commander in ten. The fact would appear to be that the opposing armies, being guided by no very definite aims, and invariably neglecting to keep touch of each other by means of outposts and vedettes, might often miss each other altogether. When they met, it was usually from the existence of some topographical necessity, of an old Roman road, or a ford or bridge on which all routes converged.

Nothing could show the primitive state of the military art better than the fact that generals solemnly sent and accepted challenges to meet in battle at a given place and on a given day. Without such precautions, there was apparently a danger lest the armies should lose sight of each other, and stray away in different directions. When maps were non-existent, and geographical knowledge both scanty and inaccurate, this was no inconceivable event. Even when two forces were actually in presence, it sometimes required more skill than the commanders owned to bring on a battle. Bela of Hungary and Ottokar of Bohemia were in arms in 1252, and both were equally bent on fighting; but when they sighted each other it was only to find that the River March was between them.

To pass a stream in face of an enemy was a task far beyond the ability of a thirteenth-century general, (the difficulty experienced by Edward III and Henry V in crossing the Somme is equally remarkable)—as St. Louis had found, two years earlier, on the banks of the Achmoum Canal. Accordingly, it was reckoned nothing strange when the Bohemian courteously invited his adversary either to cross the March unhindered, and fight in due form on the west bank, or to give him the same opportunity and grant a free passage to the Hungarian side. Bela chose the former alternative, forded the river without molestation, and fought on the other side the disastrous Battle of Cressenbrunn.

Infantry was in the twelfth and thirteenth centuries absolutely insignificant: foot-soldiers accompanied the army for no better purpose than to perform the menial duties of the camp, or to assist in the numerous sieges of the period. Occasionally they were employed as light troops, to open the battle by their ineffective demonstrations. There was, however, no really important part for them to play. Indeed, their lords were sometimes affronted if they presumed to delay too long the opening of the cavalry charges, and ended the skirmishing by riding into and over their wretched followers.

At Bouvines the Count of Boulogne could find no better use for his infantry than to form them into a great circle, inside which he and his horsemen took shelter when their chargers were fatigued and needed a short rest. If great bodies of foot occasionally appeared upon the field, they came because it was the duty of every able-bodied man to join the *arrière-ban* when summoned, not because the addition of 20,000 or 100,000 half-armed peasants and burghers was calculated to increase the real strength of the levy. The chief cause of their military worthlessness may be said to have been the miscellaneous nature of their armament.

Troops like the Scotch Lowlanders, with their long spears, or the Saracen auxiliaries of Frederick II, with their cross-bows, deserved and obtained some respect on account of the uniformity of their equipment. But with ordinary infantry the case was different; exposed, without discipline and with a miscellaneous assortment of dissimilar weapons, to a cavalry charge, they could not combine to withstand it, but were ridden down and crushed.

A few infantry successes which appear towards the end of the period were altogether exceptional in character. The infantry of the 'Great Company,' in the East beat the Duke of Athens, by inducing him to charge with all his men-at-arms into a swamp. In a similar way, the victory of Courtrai was secured, not by the mallets and iron-shod staves of the Flemings, but by the canal, into which the headlong onset of the French cavalry thrust rank after rank of their companions.

The attempt to introduce some degree of efficiency into a feudal force drove monarchs to various expedients. Frederick Barbarossa strove to enforce discipline by a strict code of 'Camp Laws;' an undertaking in which he won no great success, if we may judge of their observance by certain recorded incidents. In 1158, for example, Egbert von Buten, a young Austrian noble, left his post and started off with a thousand men to endeavour to seize one of the gates of Milan, a presumptuous violation of orders in which he lost his life. This was only in accordance with the spirit of the times, and by no means exceptional. If the stern and imposing personality of the great emperor could not win obedience, the task was hopeless for weaker rulers.

Most monarchs were driven into the use of another description of troops, inferior in morale to the feudal force, but more amenable to discipline. The mercenary comes to the fore in the second half of the twelfth century. A stranger to all the nobler incentives to valour, an enemy to his God and his neighbour, the most deservedly hated man in Europe, he was yet the instrument which kings, even those of the better sort, were obliged to seek out and cherish. When wars ceased to be mere frontier raids, and were carried on for long periods at a great distance from the homes of most of the baronage, it became impossible to rely on the services of the feudal levy. But how to provide the large sums necessary for the payment of mercenaries was not always obvious.

Notable among the expedients employed was that of Henry II of England, who substituted for the personal service of each knight the system of *scutage*. By this the majority of the tenants of the crown compounded for their personal service by paying two *marks* for each knight's fee. Thus, the king was enabled to pass the seas at the head of

Combat in the 12th Century

a force of mercenaries who were, for most military purposes, infinitely preferable to the feudal array. (*Capitales barones suos cum paucis secum duxit, solidarios vero milites innumeros.*—Rob. de Monte, 1159.)

However objectionable the hired foreigner might be, on the score of his greed and ferocity, he could, at least, be trusted to stand by his colours as long as he was regularly paid. Every ruler found him a necessity in time of war, but to the unconstitutional and oppressive ruler his existence was especially profitable: it was solely by the lavish use of mercenaries that the warlike nobility could be held in check. Despotism could only begin when the monarch became able to surround himself with a strong force of men whose desires and feelings were alien to those of the nation. The tyrant in modern Europe, as in ancient Greece, found his natural support in foreign hired soldiery. King John, when he drew to himself his 'Routiers,' 'Brabançons,' and 'Satellites,' was unconsciously imitating Pisistratus and Polycrates.

The military efficiency of the mercenary of the thirteenth century was, however, only a development of that of the ordinary feudal cavalier. Like the latter, he was a heavily-armed horseman; his rise did not bring with it any radical change in the methods of war. Though he was a more practised warrior, he still worked on the old system—or want of system—which characterised the cavalry tactics of the time.

The final stage in the history of mercenary troops was reached when the bands which had served through a long war instead of dispersing at its conclusion, held together, and moved across the continent in search of a state which might be willing to buy their services. But the age of the 'Great Company' and the Italian *Condottieri* lies rather in the fourteenth than the thirteenth century, and its discussion must be deferred to another chapter.

In the whole military history of the period the most striking feature is undoubtedly the importance of fortified places, and the ascendancy assumed by the defensive in poliorcetics.

If battles were few, sieges were numerous and abnormally lengthy. The castle was as integral a part of feudal organisation as the mailed knight, and just as the noble continued to heap defence after defence on to the persons of himself and his charger, so he continued to surround his dwelling with more and more fortifications. The simple Norman castle of the eleventh century, with its great keep and plain rectangular enclosure, developed into elaborate systems of concentric works, like those of Caerphilly and Carnarvon. The walls of the town rivalled those of the citadel, and every country bristled with forts and

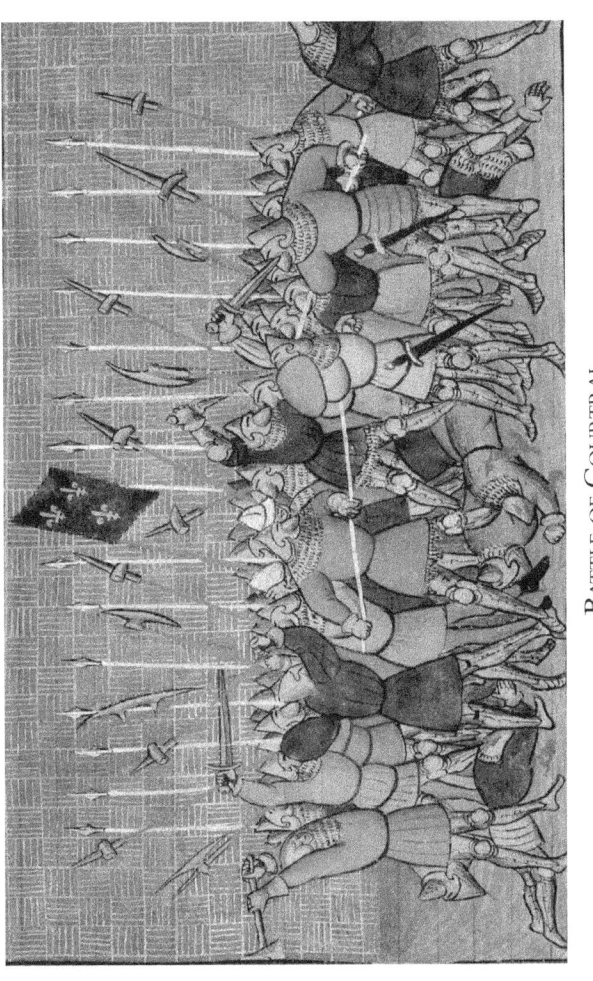

Battle of Courtrai

places of strength, large and small.

The one particular in which real military capacity is displayed in the period is the choice of commanding sites for fortresses. A single stronghold was often so well placed that it served as the key to an entire district. The best claim to the possession of a general's eye which can be made in behalf of Richard I. rests on the fact that he chose the position for Château Gaillard, the great castle which sufficed to protect the whole of Eastern Normandy as long as it was adequately held.

The strength of a mediaeval fortress lay in the extraordinary solidity of its construction. Against walls fifteen to thirty feet thick, the feeble siege-artillery of the day, *perriéres*, catapults, *trebuchets*, and so forth, beat without perceptible effect. A Norman keep, solid and tall, with no wood-work to be set on fire, and no openings near the ground to be battered in, had an almost endless capacity for passive resistance. Even a weak garrison could hold out as long as its provisions lasted. Mining was perhaps the device which had most hope of success against such a stronghold; but if the castle was provided with a deep moat, or was built directly on a rock, mining was of no avail. (The classical instances of the successful employment of the mine in England are the captures of Rochester Castle in 1215, and Bedford Castle in 1224, both works of enormous labour.)

There remained the laborious expedient of demolishing the lower parts of the walls by approaches made under cover of a pent-house, or *cat*, as it was called. If the moat could be filled, and the cat brought close to the foot of the fortifications, this method might be of some use against a fortress of the simple Norman type. Before bastions were invented, there was no means by which the missiles of the besieged could adequately command the ground immediately below the ramparts. If the defenders showed themselves over the walls—as would be necessary in order to reach men perpendicularly below them—they were at once exposed to the archers and cross-bowmen who, under cover of mantlets, protected the working of the besieger's pioneers. Hence something might be done by the method of demolishing the lower parts of the walls: but the process was always slow, laborious, and exceedingly costly in the matter of human lives. Unless pressed for time a good commander would almost invariably prefer to starve out a garrison.

The success—however partial and hardly won—of this form of attack, led to several developments on the part of the defence. The moat was sometimes strengthened with palisading: occasionally small

A Norman keep

detached forts were constructed just outside the walls on any favourable spot. But the most generally used expedients were the brattice (*bretêche*) and the construction of large towers, projecting from the wall and flanking the long sketches of 'curtain' which had been found the weak point in the Norman system of fortification.

The brattice was a wooden gallery fitted with apertures in its floor, and running along the top of the wall, from which it projected several feet. It was supported by beams built out from the rampart, and commanded, by means of its apertures, the ground immediately at the foot of the walls. Thus, the besieger could no longer get out of the range of the missiles of the besieged, and continued exposed to them, however close he drew to the fortifications. The objection to the brattice was that, being wooden, it could be set on fire by inflammatory substances projected by the catapults of the besieger. It was therefore superseded ere long by the use of machicolation, where a projecting stone gallery replaced the woodwork.

Far more important was the utilisation of the flanking action of towers, (revival of the old Roman system of fortification), the other great improvement made by the defence. This rendered it possible to direct a converging fire from the sides on the point selected for attack by the besieger. The towers also served to cut off a captured stretch of wall from any communication with the rest of the fortifications. By closing the iron-bound doors in the two on each side of the breach, the enemy was left isolated on the piece of wall he had won, and could not push to right or left without storming a tower. This development of the defensive again reduced the offensive to impotence.

Starvation was the only weapon likely to reduce a well-defended place, and fortresses were therefore blockaded rather than attacked. The besieger, having built a line of circumvallation and an entrenched camp, sat down to wait for hunger to do its work. (As, for example, did Edward III before Calais. He fortified all approaches passable for a relieving army, and waited quietly in his lines.) It will be observed that by fortifying his position he gave himself the advantage of the defensive in repelling attacks of relieving armies. His other expedients, such as endeavours to fire the internal buildings of the invested place, to cut off its water supply, or to carry it by nocturnal escalade, were seldom of much avail.

The number and strength of the fortified places of Western Europe explain the apparent futility of many campaigns of the period. A land could not be conquered with rapidity when every district was

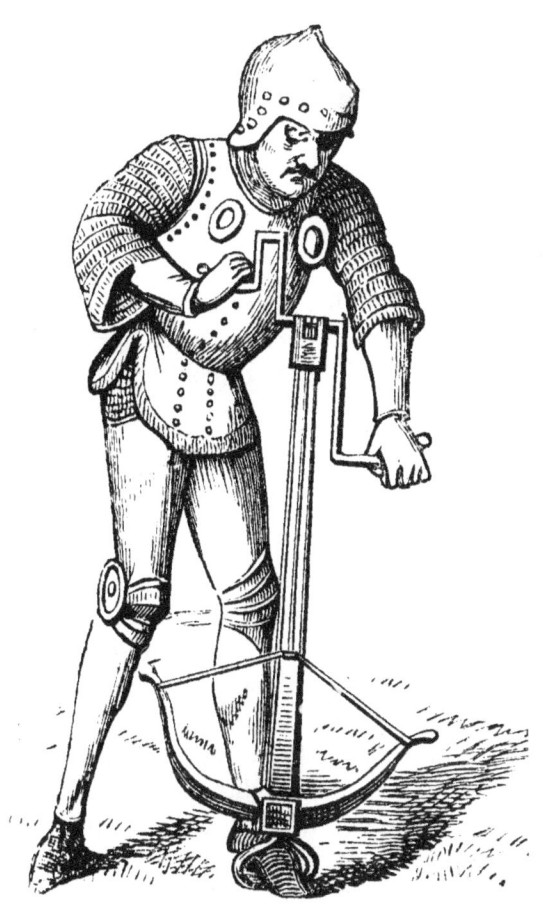
CROSSBOWMAN

guarded by three or four castles and walled towns, which would each need several months' siege before they could be reduced. Campaigns tended to become either plundering raids, which left the strongholds alone, or to be occupied in the prolonged blockade of a single fortified place. The invention of gunpowder was the first advantage thrown on the side of the attack for three centuries. Even cannon, however, were at the period of their invention, and for long years afterward, of very little practical importance. The taking of Constantinople by Mahomet II is perhaps the first event of European importance in which the power of artillery played the leading part.

Before proceeding to discuss the rise of the new forms of military efficiency which brought about the end of the supremacy of feudal cavalry, it may be well to cast a glance at those curious military episodes, the Crusades. Considering their extraordinary and abnormal nature, more results might have been expected to follow them than can in fact be traced. When opposed by a system of tactics to which they were unaccustomed the Western nobles were invariably disconcerted.

At fights, such as Dorylaeum they were only preserved from disaster by their indomitable energy: tactically beaten they extricated themselves by sheer hard fighting. On fairly-disputed fields, such as that of Antioch, they asserted the same superiority over Oriental horsemen which the Byzantine had previously enjoyed. But after a short experience of Western tactics the Turks and Saracens foreswore the battle-field. They normally acted in great bodies of light cavalry, moving rapidly from point to point, and cutting off convoys or attacking detached parties. The Crusaders were seldom indulged in the twelfth century with those pitched battles for which they craved. The Mahometan leaders would only fight when they had placed all the advantages on their own side; normally they declined the contest.

In the East, just as in Europe, the war was one of sieges: armies numbered by the hundred thousand were arrested before the walls of a second-class fortress such as Acre, and in despair at reducing it by their operations, had to resort to the lengthy process of starving out the garrison. On the other hand nothing but the ascendancy enjoyed by the defensive could have protracted the existence of the 'Kingdom of Jerusalem,' when it had sunk to a chain of isolated fortresses, dotting the shore of the Levant from Alexandretta to Acre and Jaffa.

If we can point to any modifications introduced into European warfare by the Eastern experience of the Crusaders, they are not of

Knights Templar before Jerusalem

any great importance. Greek fire, if its composition was really ascertained, would seem to have had very little use in the West: the horse-bowman, copied from the cavalry of the Turkish and Mameluke *sultans*, did not prove a great military success: the adoption of the curved sabre, the 'Morris-pike,' the horseman's mace, (borrowed either from the Byzantine or the Saracen: it is quite distinct from the rude club occasionally found in the West at an earlier date, as, for example, in the hands of Bishop Odo at Hastings), and a few other weapons, is hardly worth mentioning. On the whole, the military results of the Crusades were curiously small. As lessons, they were wholly disregarded by the European world. When, after the interval of a hundred and fifty years, a Western army once more faced an Oriental foe, it committed at Nicopolis exactly the same blunder which led to the loss of the day at Mansoura.

SIEGE OF ACRE, 1291

CHAPTER 5

The Swiss 1315-1515
(From the Battle of Morgarten to the Battle of Marignano)

(1) THEIR CHARACTER, ARMS, AND ORGANISATION.

In the fourteenth century infantry, after a thousand years of depression and neglect, at last regained its due share of military importance. Almost simultaneously there appeared two peoples asserting a mastery in European politics by the efficiency of their foot-soldiery. Their manners of fighting were as different as their national character and geographical position, but although they never met either in peace or war, they were practically allied for the destruction of feudal chivalry. The knight, who had for so long ridden roughshod over the populations of Europe, was now to recognise his masters in the art of war. The free yeomanry of England and the free herdsmen of the Alps were about to enter on their career of conquest.

When war is reduced to its simplest elements, we find that there are only two ways in which an enemy can be met and defeated. Either the shock or the missile must be employed against him. In the one case the victor achieves success by throwing himself on his opponent, and worsting him in a hand-to-hand struggle by his numbers, his weight, the superiority of his arms, or the greater strength and skill with which he wields them.

In the second case he wins the day by keeping up such a constant and deadly rain of missiles, that his enemy is destroyed or driven back before he can come to close quarters. Each of these methods can be combined with the use of very different arms and tactics, and is susceptible of innumerable variations. In the course of history, they have alternately asserted their preponderance: in the early middle ages shock-tactics were entirely in the ascendant, while in our own day the use of the missile has driven the rival system out of the field, nor does it appear possible that this final verdict can ever be reversed.

The English archer and the Swiss pikeman represented these two great forms of military efficiency in their simplest and most elementary shapes. The one relied on his power to defeat his enemy's attack by rapid and accurate shooting. The other was capable of driving before him far superior numbers by the irresistible impact and steady pressure of his solid column with its serried hedge of spear-points. When tried against the mail-clad cavalry which had previously held the ascendancy in Europe, each of these methods was found adequate to secure the victory for those who employed it.

Hence the whole military system of the middle ages received a profound modification. To the unquestioned predominance of a single form, that of the charge delivered by cavalry, succeeded a rapid alternation of successful and unsuccessful experiments in the correlation and combination of cavalry and infantry, of shock-tactics and missile-tactics. Further complicated by the results of the introduction of firearms, this struggle has been prolonged down to the present day. It is only in the last few years that the military world has learnt that the attempt to utilise the shock of the infantry column or the charging squadron must be abandoned in face of the extraordinary development of modern firearms.

The Swiss of the fourteenth and fifteenth centuries have been compared with much aptness to the Romans of the early Republic. In the Swiss, as in the Roman, character we find the most intense patriotism combined with an utter want of moral sense and a certain meanness and pettiness of conception, which prevent us from calling either nation truly great. In both the steadiest courage and the fervour of the noblest self-sacrifice were allied to an appalling ferocity and a cynical contempt and pitiless disregard for the rights of others. Among each people the warlike pride generated by successful wars of independence led ere long to wars of conquest and plunder.

As neighbours, both were rendered insufferable by their haughtiness and proneness to take offence on the slightest provocation.

※※※※※※

For example, the case cited in Von Elgger's *Kriegswesen der Schweizerischen Eidgenossen*, where a patrician of Constance having refused to accept a Bernese *plappert* (small coin) in payment of a wager, and having scornfully called the bear represented on it a cow, the Confederates took the matter up as a national insult, and ravaged the territory of Constance without any declaration of war.

✶✶✶✶✶✶

As enemies, both were distinguished for their deliberate and cold-blooded cruelty. The resolution to give no quarter, which appears almost pardonable in patriots desperately defending their native soil, becomes brutal when retained in wars of aggression, but reaches the climax of fiendish inhumanity when the slayer is a mere mercenary, fighting for a cause in which he has no national interest. Repulsive as was the bloodthirstiness of the Roman, it was far from equalling in moral guilt the needless ferocity displayed by the hired Swiss soldiery on many a battlefield of the sixteenth century. (At Novara, for instance, they put to death after the battle several hundred German prisoners.)

In no point, do we find a greater resemblance between the histories of the two peoples, than in the causes of their success in war. Rome and Switzerland alike are examples of the fact that a good military organisation and a sound system of national tactics are the surest basis for a sustained career of conquest. Provided with these a vigorous state needs no unbroken series of great commanders. A succession of respectable mediocrities suffices to guide the great engine of war, which works almost automatically, and seldom fails to cleave its way to success.

The elected consuls of Rome, the elected or nominated 'captains' of the Confederates, could never have led their troops to victory, had it not been for the systems which the experience of their predecessors had brought to perfection. The combination of pliability and solid strength in the legion, the powers of rapid movement and irresistible impact which met in the Swiss column, were competent to win a field without the exertion of any extraordinary ability by the generals who set them in motion.

The battle-array which the Confederates invariably employed, was one whose prototype had been seen in the Macedonian *phalanx*. It was always in masses of enormous depth that they presented themselves on the battlefield. Their great national weapon in the days of their highest reputation was the pike, an ashen shaft eighteen feet long, fitted with a head of steel which added another foot to its length. It was grasped with two hands widely extended, and poised at the level of the shoulder with the point slightly sunk, so as to deliver a downward thrust. (Montluc's *Commentaries*.)

Before the line projected not only the pikes of the front rank, but

SWISS PIKEMEN

those of the second, third, and fourth, an impenetrable hedge of bristling points. The men in the interior of the column held their weapons upright, till called upon to step forward in order to replace those who had fallen in the foremost ranks. Thus, the pikes, rising twelve feet above the heads of the men who bore them, gave to the charging mass the appearance of a moving wood. Above it floated numberless flags, the pennons of districts, towns, and guilds, the banners of the cantons, sometimes the great standard of 'the Ancient League of High Germany,' the white cross on the red ground.

★★★★★★

At Morat the contingent of Bern alone brought with them (besides the great standard of the canton) the flags of twenty-four towns and districts (Thun, Aarau, Lenzburg, Interlaken, Burgdorf, the Haslithal, the Emmenthal, etc. etc.) and of eight craft-guilds and six other associations.

★★★★★★

The pike, however, was not the only weapon of the Swiss. In the earlier days of their independence, when the Confederacy consisted of three or four cantons, the halberd was their favourite arm, and even in the sixteenth century a considerable proportion of the army continued to employ it. Eight feet in length—with a heavy head which ended in a sharp point and bore on its front a blade like that of a hatchet, on its back a strong hook—the halberd was the most murderous, if also the most ponderous, of weapons. Swung by the strong arms of the Alpine herdsmen it would cleave helmet, shield, or coat-of-mail, like pasteboard. The sight of the ghastly wounds which it inflicted might well appal the stoutest foeman: he who had once felt its edge required no second stroke. It was the halberd which laid Leopold of Hapsburg dead across his fallen banner at Sempach, and struck down Charles of Burgundy—all his face one gash from temple to teeth—in the frozen ditch by Nancy. (The halberd only differed from the English 'brown-bill' in having a spike.)

The halberdiers had their recognised station in the Confederates' battle-array. They were drawn up in the centre of the column, around the chief banner, which was placed under their care. If the enemy succeeded in checking the onset of the pikemen, it was their duty to pass between the front ranks, which opened out to give them egress, and throw themselves into the fray. They were joined in their charge by the bearers of two-handed swords, 'Morning-Stars,' and 'Lucern Hammers,' all weapons of the most fearful efficiency in a hand-to-hand combat.

✶✶✶✶✶✶

The 'Morning-Star' was a club five feet long, set thickly at its end with iron spikes. It had disappeared by the middle of the 15th century. The 'Lucern Hammer' was like a halberd, but had three curved prongs instead of the hatchet-blade: it inflicted a horrible jagged wound.

✶✶✶✶✶✶

It was seldom that a hostile force, whether infantry or cavalry, sustained this final attack, when the infuriated Swiss dashed in among them, slashing right and left, sweeping off the legs of horses, and cleaving armour and flesh with the same tremendous blow.

In repelling cavalry charges, however, the halberd was found, owing to its shortness, a far less useful weapon than the pike. The disastrous fight near Bellinzona in 1422, where the Swiss, having a large proportion of halberdiers in their front rank, were broken by the Milanese gendarmes, was the final cause of its relegation to the second epoch of the battle. From the first shock of the opposing forces it was banished, being reserved for the *mêlée* which afterwards ensued.

Next to its solidity the most formidable quality of the Swiss infantry was its rapidity of movement.

No troops were ever more expeditious on a march, or in forming themselves for battle, because they were not overloaded with armour.—Machiavelli, *Art of War*, republished by Leonaur in a double volume *The Prince and the Art of War*.

When emergencies arrived a Confederate army could be raised with extraordinary speed; a people who regarded military glory as the one thing which made life worth living, flocked to arms without needing a second summons. The outlying contingents marched day and night in order to reach the mustering place in good time. There was no need to waste days in the weary work of organisation, when every man stood among his kinsmen and neighbours, beneath the pennon of his native town or valley.

The troops of the democratic cantons elected their officers, those of the larger states received leaders appointed by their councils, and then without further delay the army marched to meet the enemy. Thus, an invader, however unexpected his attack, might in the course of three or four days find twenty thousand men on his hands. They would often be within a few miles of him, before he had heard that a

Swiss force was in the field.

In face of such an army it was impossible for the slowly-moving troops of the fourteenth or fifteenth centuries to execute manoeuvres. An attempt to alter the line of battle,—as Charles the Rash discovered to his dismay at Granson,—was sure to lead to disaster. When once the Confederates were in motion, their enemy had to resign himself to fighting in whatever order he found himself at the moment. They always made it their rule to begin the fight, and never to allow themselves to be attacked. The composition of their various columns was settled early on the battle morning, and the men moved off to the field already drawn up in their fighting-array. There was no pause needed to draw the army out in line of battle; each phalanx marched on the enemy at a steady but swift pace, which covered the ground in an incredibly short time.

The solid masses glided forward in perfect order and in deep silence, until the war-cry burst out in one simultaneous roar and the column dashed itself against the hostile front. The rapidity of the Swiss advance had in it something portentous: the great wood of pikes and halberds came rolling over the brow of some neighbouring hill; a moment later it was pursuing its even way towards the front, and then—almost before the opponent had time to realise his position—it was upon him, with its four rows of spear-points projecting in front and the impetus of file upon file surging up from the rear.

This power of swift movement was—as Machiavelli observed—the result of the Confederates' determination not to burden themselves with heavy armour. Their abstention from its use was originally due to their poverty alone, but was confirmed by the discovery that a heavy panoply would clog and hamper the efficiency of their national tactics. The normal equipment of the pikeman or halberdier was therefore light, consisting of a steel-cap and breastplate alone. Even these were not in universal employment; many of the soldiery trusted the defence of their persons to their weapons, and wore only felt hats and leather jerkins.

******

Machiavelli even says that the pikemen in his day did not wear the steel-cap, which was entirely confined to the halberdiers. But this can be shown from other sources to be an exaggeration.

******

The use of back-plates, arm-pieces, and greaves was by no means common; indeed, the men wearing them were often not sufficient in number to form a single rank at the head of the column, the post in which they were always placed. The leaders alone were required to present themselves in full armour; they were therefore obliged to ride while on the march, in order to keep up with their lightly-armed followers. When they arrived in sight of the enemy they dismounted and led their men to the charge on foot. A few of the patricians and men of knightly family from Bern were found in the fifteenth century serving as cavalry, but their numbers were absolutely insignificant, a few scores at the most. (See Kirk's *Charles the Bold,* book iv.)

Although the strength and pride of the Confederates lay in their pikemen and halberdiers, the light troops were by no means neglected. On occasion, they were known to form as much as a fourth of the army, and they never sank below a tenth of the whole number.

******

At Morat, according to Commines, they were nearly a third, 10,000 out of 35,000. At Arbedo they were a seventh: among the Confederates who joined Charles VIII in his march to Naples only a tenth of the force.

******

They were originally armed with the crossbow—the weapon of the fabulous Tell—but even before the great Burgundian war the use of the clumsy firearms of the day was general among them. It was their duty to precede the main body, and to endeavour to draw on themselves the attention of the enemy's artillery and light troops, so that the columns behind them might advance as far as possible without being molested. Thus, the true use of a line of skirmishers was already appreciated among the Swiss in the fifteenth century. When the pikemen had come up with them, they retired into the intervals between the various masses, and took no part in the great charge, for which their weapons were not adapted.

It is at once evident that in the simplicity of its component elements lay one of the chief sources of the strength of a Confederate army. Its commanders were not troubled by any of those problems as to the correlation and subordination of the various arms, which led to so many unhappy experiments among the generals of other nations. Cavalry and artillery were practically non-existent; nor were the operations hampered by the necessity of finding some employment for those masses of troops of inferior quality who so often increased the numbers, but not the efficiency, of a mediaeval army. A Swiss force—

however hastily gathered—was always homogeneous and coherent; there was no residuum of untried or disloyal soldiery for whose conduct special precautions would have to be taken. The larger proportion of the men among a nation devoted to war had seen a considerable amount of service; while if local jealousies were ever remembered in the field, they only served to spur the rival contingents on to a healthy emulation in valour. However much the cantons might wrangle among themselves, they were always found united against a foreign attack. (*E. g.* the Forest Cantons were bitterly opposed to the Bernese policy of engaging in war with Charles the Bold; but their troops did no worse service than the rest at Granson or Morat.)

(2) TACTICS AND STRATEGY.

The character and organisation of the Confederate army were exceedingly unfavourable to the rise of great generals. The soldier rested his hope of success rather on an entire confidence in the fighting power of himself and his comrades, than on the skill of his commander. Troops who have proved in a hundred fields their ability to bear up against the most overwhelming odds, are comparatively indifferent as to the personality of their leader. If he is competent they work out his plan with success, if not, they cheerfully set themselves to repair his faults by sheer hard fighting. Another consideration was even more important among the Swiss; there was a universal prejudice felt against placing the troops of one canton under the orders of the citizen of another.

So strong was this feeling that an extraordinary result ensued: the appointment of a commander-in-chief remained, throughout the brilliant period of Swiss history, an exception rather than a rule. Neither in the time of Sempach, in the old war of Zurich, in the great struggle with Burgundy, nor in the Swabian campaign against Maximilian of Austria, was any single general entrusted with supreme authority.

★★★★★★

Rudolf von Erlach's position as commander-in-chief at Laupen was quite exceptional. If we hear in the cases mentioned above of Swiss commanders, we must remember that they were co-ordinate authorities, among whom one man might exert more influence than another, but only by his personal ascendancy, not by legal right. It is a mistake to say that Rene of Lorraine formally commanded at Morat or Nancy.

★★★★★★

The conduct of affairs was in the hands of a 'council of war;' but it was a council which, contrary to the old proverb about such bodies, was always ready and willing to fight. It was composed of the 'captains' of each cantonal contingent, and settled the questions which came under discussion by a simple majority of voices. Before a battle it entrusted the command of van, rear, main-body, and light troops to different officers, but the holders of such posts enjoyed a mere delegated authority, which expired with the cessation of the emergency.

The existence of this curious subdivision of power, to which the nearest parallel would be found in early Byzantine days, would suffice by itself to explain the lack of all strategical skill and unity of purpose which was observable in Swiss warfare. The compromise which forms the mean between several rival schemes usually combines their faults, not their merits. But in addition to this, we may suspect that to find any one Swiss officer capable of working out a coherent plan of campaign would have been difficult. The 'Captain' was an old soldier who had won distinction on bygone battlefields, but except in his experience nowise different to the men under his orders. Of elaborating the more difficult strategical combinations a Swiss 'Council of War' was not much more capable than an average party of veteran sergeant-majors would be in our own day.

With tactics, however, the case was different. The best means of adapting the attack in column to the accidents of locality or the quality and armament of the opposing troops were studied in the school of experience. A real tactical system was developed, whose efficiency was proved again and again in the battles of the fifteenth century. For dealing with the mediaeval men-at-arms and infantry against whom it had been designed, the Swiss method was unrivalled: it was only when a new age introduced different conditions into war that it gradually became obsolete.

The normal order of battle employed by the Confederates, however small or large their army might be, was an advance in an *échelon* of three divisions. (Machiavelli has a very clear account of this form of advance, see *Art of War*.) The first corps (*vorhut*), that which had formed the van while the force was on the march, made for a given point in the enemy's line. The second corps (*gewaltshaufen*), instead of coming up in line with the first, advanced parallel to it, but at a short distance to its right or left rear. The third corps (*nachhut*) advanced still further back, and often halted until the effect of the first attack was seen, in order that it might be able to act, if necessary, as a reserve.

This disposition left a clear space behind each column, so that if it was repulsed it could retire without throwing into disorder the rest of the army.

Other nations (*e. g.* the French at Agincourt), who were in the habit of placing one corps directly in front of another, had often to pay the penalty for their tactical crime, by seeing the defeat of their first line entail the rout of the whole army, each division being rolled back in confusion on that immediately in its rear. The Swiss order of attack had another strong point in rendering it almost impossible for the enemy's troops to wheel inwards and attack the most advanced column: if they did so they at once exposed their own flank to the second column, which was just coming up and commencing its charge.

The advance in *échelon* of columns was not the only form employed by the Confederates. At Laupen the centre or *gewaltshaufen* moved forward and opened the fight before the wings were engaged. At the combat of Frastenz in 1499, on the other hand, the wings commenced the onset, while the centre was refused, and only came up to complete the overthrow.

Even the traditional array in three masses was sometimes discarded for a different formation. At Sempach the men of the Forest Cantons were drawn up in a single 'wedge' (*Keil*). This order was not, as might be expected from its name, triangular, but merely a column of more than ordinary depth in proportion to its frontage. Its object was to break a hostile line of unusual firmness by a concentrated shock delivered against its centre. In 1468, during the fighting which preceded the siege of Waldshut, the whole Confederate army moved out to meet the Austrian cavalry in a great hollow square, in the midst of which were placed the banners with their escort of halberdiers.

When such a body was attacked, the men faced outwards to receive the onset of the horsemen; this they called 'forming the hedgehog,' (Elgger's *Kriegswesen der Schweizerische.*) So steady were they that, with very inferior numbers, they could face the most energetic charge: in the Swabian war of 1498, six hundred men of Zurich, caught in the open plain by a thousand imperial men-at-arms, 'formed a hedgehog, and drove off the enemy with ease and much jesting,' (Elgger), Machiavelli, (*Art of War*), speaks of another Swiss order of battle, which he calls 'the Cross:' 'between the arms of which they place their musketeers, to shelter them from the first shock of the hostile column.' His description, however, is anything but explicit, and we can find no trace of any formation of the kind in any recorded engagement.

(3) Development of Swiss Military Supremacy.

The first victory of the Confederates was won, not by the tactics which afterwards rendered them famous, but by a judicious choice of a battlefield. Morgarten was a fearful example of the normal uselessness of feudal cavalry in a mountainous country. On a frosty November day, when the roads were like ice underfoot, Leopold of Austria thrust his long narrow column into the defiles leading to the valley of Schwytz. In front rode the knights, who had of course claimed the honour of opening the contest, while the 6000 infantry blocked the way behind. In the narrow pass of Morgarten, where the road passes between a precipitous slope on the right and the waters of the Egeri lake on the left, the 1500 Confederates awaited the Austrians.

Full of the carelessness which accompanies overweening arrogance, the duke had neglected the most ordinary precaution of exploring his road, and only discovered the vicinity of the enemy when a shower of boulders and tree-trunks came rolling down the slope on his right flank, where a party of Swiss were posted in a position entirely inaccessible to horsemen. A moment later the head of the helpless column was charged by the main body of the mountaineers. Before the Austrians had realised that the battle had commenced, the halberds and 'morning-stars' of the Confederates were working havoc in their van.

The front ranks of the knights, wedged so tightly together by the impact of the enemy that they could not lay their lances in rest, much less spur their horses to the charge, fought and died. The centre and rear were compelled to halt and stand motionless, unable to push forward on account of the narrowness of the pass, or to retreat on account of the infantry, who choked the road behind. For a short time, they endured the deadly shower of rocks and logs, which continued to bound down the slope, tear through the crowded ranks, and hurl man and horse into the lake below. Then, by a simultaneous impulse, the greater part of the mass turned their reins and made for the rear.

In the press hundreds were pushed over the edge of the road, to drown in the deep water on the left. The main body burst into the column of their own infantry, and, trampling down their unfortunate followers, fled with such speed as was possible on the slippery path. The Swiss, having now exterminated the few knights in the van who had remained to fight, came down on the rear of the panic-stricken crowd, and cut down horseman and footman alike without meeting any resistance. John of Winterthur, a contemporary chronicler, says:

BATTLE OF AGINCOURT

It was not a battle, but a mere butchery of duke Leopold's men; for the mountain folk slew them like sheep in the shambles: no one gave any quarter, but they cut down all, without distinction, till there were none left to kill. So great was the fierceness of the Confederates that scores of the Austrian footmen, when they saw the bravest knights falling helplessly, threw themselves in panic into the lake, preferring to sink in its depths rather than to fall under the fearful weapons of their enemies.—Quoted at length in Elgger.

In short, the Swiss won their freedom, because, with instinctive tactical skill, they gave the feudal cavalry no opportunity for attacking them at advantage.

They were lords of the field, because it was they, and not their foe, who settled where the fighting should take place.'

On the steep and slippery road, where they could not win impetus for their charge, and where the narrowness of the defile prevented them from making use of their superior numbers, the Austrians were helpless. The crushing character of the defeat, however, was due to Leopold's inexcusable carelessness, in leaving the way unexplored and suffering himself to be surprised in the fatal trap of the pass.

Morgarten exhibits the Swiss military system in a rudimentary condition. Though won, like all Confederate victories, by the charge of a column, it was the work of the halberd, not of the pike. The latter weapon was not yet in general use among the mountaineers of the three cantons: it was, in fact, never adopted by them to so great an extent as was the case among the Swiss of the lower Alpine lands and Aar valley, the Bernese and people of Zurich and Lucern. The halberd, murderous though it might be, was not an arm whose possession would give an unqualified ascendancy to its wielders: it was the position, not the weapons nor the tactics, of the Swiss which won Morgarten. But their second great success bears a far higher military importance.

At Laupen, for the first time almost since the days of the Romans, infantry, entirely unsupported by horsemen, ranged on a fair field in the plains, withstood an army complete in all arms and superior in numbers. (At Bannockburn, the Scots had made good use of their cavalry, which, though not strong, gave them an advantage wanting to the Swiss at Laupen.)

It was twenty-four years after duke Leopold's defeat that the Con-

THE BATTLE AT MORGARTEN.

federates and their newly-allied fellows of Bern met the forces of the Burgundian nobility of the valleys of the Aar and Rhone, mustered by all the feudal chiefs between Elsass and Lake Leman. Count Gerard of Vallangin, the commander of the baronial army, evidently intended to settle the day by turning one wing of the enemy, and crushing it. With this object, he drew up the whole of his cavalry on the right of his array, his centre and left being entirely composed of infantry. The Swiss formed the three columns which were henceforth to be their normal order of battle. They were under a single commander, Rudolf of Erlach, to whom the credit of having first employed the formation apparently belongs.

The Bernese, who were mainly armed with the pike, formed the centre column, the wings were drawn back. That on the left was composed of the men of the three old cantons, who were still employing the halberd as their chief weapon, while the right was made up of other allies of Bern. In this order, they moved on to the attack, the centre considerably in advance. The infantry of the barons proved to be no match for the Confederates: with a steady impulse, the Bernese pushed it back, trampled down the front ranks, and drove the rest off the field.

A moment later the Burgundian left suffered the same fate at the hands of the Swiss right column. Then, without wasting time in pursuit, the two victorious masses turned to aid the men of the Forest Cantons. Surrounded by a raging flood of horsemen on all sides, the left column was hard pressed. The halberd, though inflicting the most ghastly wounds, could not prevent the cavalry from occasionally closing in. Like a rock, however, the mountaineers withstood the incessant charges, and succeeded in holding their own for the all-important period during which the hostile infantry was being driven off the field. Then the two successful columns came down on the left and rear of the Baronial horsemen, and steadily met their charge. Apparently, the enemy was already exhausted by his attempt to overcome the men of the Forest Cantons, for, after one vain attempt to ride down the Bernese pikemen, he turned and rode off the field, not without considerable loss, as many of his rear-guard were intercepted and driven into the River Sense.

Laupen was neither so bloody nor so dramatic a field as Morgarten; but it is one of three great battles which mark the beginning of a new period in the history of war. Bannockburn had already sounded the same note in the distant West, but for the Continent Laupen was the first revelation as to the power of good infantry. The experiment which had been tried a few years before at Cassel and Mons-en-Puelle with such ill success, was renewed with a very different result. The Swiss had accomplished the feat which the Flemings had undertaken with inadequate means and experience. Seven years later a yet more striking lesson was to be administered to feudal chivalry, when the archer faced the knight at Cressy. The mail-clad horseman was found unable to break the *phalanx* of pikes, unable to approach the line from which the deadly arrow reached him, but still the old superstition which gave the most honourable name in war to the mounted man, was strong enough to perpetuate for another century the cavalry whose day had really gone by. A system which was so intimately bound up with mediaeval life and ideas could not be destroyed by one, or by twenty disasters.

Sempach, the third great victory won by the Confederates, shares with the less famous fight of Arbedo a peculiar interest. Both were attempts to break the Swiss column by the adoption of a similar method of attack to that which rendered it so formidable. Leopold the Proud, remembering no doubt the powerlessness of the horsemen which had been shown at Laupen, made his knights dismount, as Edward of England had done with such splendid results thirty years earlier. Perhaps he may have borne in mind a similar order given by his ancestor the Emperor Albert, when he fought the Bavarians at Hasenbühl in 1298.

At any rate the duke awaited the enemy's attack with his 4000 mailed men-at-arms formed in one massive column,—their lances levelled in front,—ready to meet the Swiss with tactics similar to their own and with the advantage which the superior protection of armour gave in a contest otherwise equal. (Similarly at the Battle of the Standard the English knights dismounted to meet the furious rush of the Galwegians.) Leopold had also posted in reserve a considerable body of foot and horse, who were to fall on the flanks and rear of the Confederates, when they were fully engaged in front.

Arrayed in a single deep column (*Keil*), the Swiss came rushing down from the hills with their usual impetuosity, the horns of Uri and Unterwalden braying in their midst and the banners of the four Forest Cantons waving above them.

★★★★★★

The numbers which the Swiss Chroniclers allow to have been present at Sempach are evidently minimised. The whole force of four cantons was there, yet we are told of only 1500 men!

Burgundians

Yet the *three* cantons seventy-one years before put the same number in the field, and the populous state of Lucern had now joined them.

★★★★★★

The first shock between the two masses was tremendous, but when it was ended the Confederates found themselves thrust back. Their whole front rank had gone down, and the Austrian column was unshaken. In a moment, they rallied; Uri replaced Lucern as the head of the *phalanx*, and again they dashed at the mail-clad line before them. But the second charge was no more successful than the first: Schwytz had to succeed Uri, and again Unterwalden took the place of Schwytz, and yet nothing more was effected. The Austrians stood victorious, while in front of them a long bank of Swiss corpses lay heaped.

At the same moment the duke's reserve began to move, with the intention of encircling the Confederate flank. The critical moment had come; without some desperate effort, the day was lost: but while the Swiss were raging along the line of bristling points, vainly hacking at the spears which pierced them, the necessary impulse was at last given.

To detail once more Winkelried's heroic death is unnecessary: everyone knows how the Austrian column was broken, how in the close combat which followed the lance and long horseman's sword proved no match for the halberd, the battle-axe and the cutlass, how the duke and his knights, weighed down by their heavy armour, neither could nor would flee, and fell to a man around their banner.

Historians tell us all this, but what they forget to impress upon us is that, in spite of his failure, duke Leopold was nearer to success than any other commander, one exception alone being made, who faced the Swiss down to the day of Marignano. His idea of meeting the shock of the Swiss phalanx with a heavier shock of his own was feasible. His mistakes in detail ruined a plan which in itself was good. The first fault was that he halted to receive the enemy's charge, and did not advance to meet it. Thus, he lost most of the advantage which the superior weight of his men would have given in the clashing of the columns. He was equally misguided in making no attempt to press on the Confederates when their first three charges had failed, and so allowing them time to rally.

Moreover, he made no adequate use of his mounted squadron in reserve, his light troops, and the artillery, which we know that he had with him.

******

The Confederates were forming their column in Sempach Wood, when Leopold's artillery opened on them—

With their long lances levelled before the fight they stood,
And set their cannon firing at those within the wood;
Then to the good Confederates the battle was not sweet,
When all around the mighty boughs dropped crashing at their feet.

(Rough translation of Halbshuter's contemporary *Sempacherlied*.)

******

If these had been employed on the Swiss flanks at the proper moment, they would have decided the day. But Leopold only used his artillery to open the combat, and kept his crossbowmen and slingers in the rear, probably out of that feudal superstition which demanded that the knight should have the most important part in the battle. Neglecting these precautions, he lost the day, but only after some of the hardest fighting which the Swiss ever experienced.

What a better general could do by the employment of Leopold's tactical experiment was shown thirty-seven years later on the field of Arbedo. On that occasion Carmagnola the Milanese general,—who then met the Confederates for the first time,—opened the engagement with a cavalry charge. Observing its entire failure, the experienced *condottiere* at once resorted to another form of attack. He dismounted the whole of his 6000 men-at-arms, and launched them in a single column against the Swiss *phalanx*. The enemy, a body of 4000 men from Uri, Unterwalden, Zug, and Lucern, were mainly halberdiers, the pikemen and crossbowmen forming only a third of their force. The two masses met, and engaged in a fair duel between lance and sword on the one hand and pike and halberd on the other.

The impetus of the larger force bore down that of the smaller, and, in spite of the desperate fighting of their enemies, the Milanese began to gain ground. So hardly were the Confederates now pressed that the Schultheiss of Lucern even thought of surrender, and planted his halberd in the ground in token of submission. Carmagnola, however, heated with the fight, cried out that men who gave no quarter should receive none, and continued his advance. He was on the very point of victory, when a new Swiss force suddenly appeared in his rear.

******

Sismondi, who writes entirely from Swiss sources as to this fight, gives a very different impression from Machiavelli. The later cites Arbedo as the best known check received by the Swiss, and puts their loss down at several thousands (*Art of War*). Müller evidently tries to minimise the check; but we may judge from our knowledge of Swiss character how great must have been the pressure required to make a Confederate officer think of surrender. Forty-four members of the Cantonal councils of Lucern fell in the fight: 'The contingent of Lucern had crossed the lake of the four Cantons in ten large barges, when setting out on this expedition: it returned in two!' These facts, acknowledged by the Swiss themselves, seem to show that the figure of 400 men for their loss is placed absurdly low.

★★★★★★

Believing them to be the contingents of Zurich, Schwytz, Glarus, and Appenzell, which he knew to be at no great distance, Carmagnola drew off his men and began to reform. But in reality the new-comers were only a band of 600 foragers; they made no attack; while the Swiss main-body took advantage of the relaxation of the pressure to retire in good order. They had lost 400 men according to their own acknowledgment, many more if Italian accounts are to be received. Carmagnola's loss, though numerically larger, bore no such proportion to his whole force, and had indeed been mainly incurred in the unsuccessful cavalry charge which opened the action.

From the results of Sempach and Arbedo it seems natural to draw the conclusion that a judicious employment of dismounted men-at-arms might have led to success, if properly combined with the use of other arms. The experiment, however, was never repeated by the enemies of the Swiss: indeed almost the only consequence which we can attribute to it is a decree of the Council of Lucern, that 'since things had not gone altogether well with the Confederates' a larger proportion of the army was in future to be furnished with the pike, a weapon which, unlike the halberd, could contend on superior terms with the lance. (From a Lucern *Raths-Protocoll* of 1422, '*Da es den Eidgenossen nicht so wohl ergangen seie*,' etc.)

Putting aside the two battles which we have last examined, we may say that for the first 150 years of their career the Swiss were so fortunate as never to meet either with a master of the art of war, or with any new form of tactical efficiency which could rival their own phalanx. It was still with the mailed horsemen or the motley and undisciplined infantry-array of the middle ages that they had to deal. Their tactics had been framed for successful conflict with such forces, and continued to preserve an ascendancy over them. The free lances of Enguerrand de Coucy, the *burghers* and nobles of Swabia, the knights who followed Frederick or Leopold or Sigismund of Hapsburg, were none of them exponents of a new system, and served each in their turn to demonstrate yet more clearly the superiority of the Confederates in military skill.

Even the most dangerous attack ever aimed against Switzerland, the invasion by the 'Armagnac' mercenaries of the Dauphin Louis in 1444, was destined to result in the increase of the warlike reputation of its soldiery. The Battle of St. Jacob, mad and unnecessary though it was, might serve as an example to deter the boldest enemy from meddling with men who preferred annihilation to retreat. Possessed by the single idea that their *phalanx* could bear down any obstacle, the Confederates deliberately crossed the Birs in face of an army of fifteen times their strength. They attacked it, broke its centre, and were then surrounded by its overwhelming numbers. Compelled to 'form the hedgehog' in order to resist the tremendous cavalry charges directed against them, they remained rooted to the spot for the remainder of the day.

The *Dauphin* launched squadron after squadron at them, but each in its turn was hurled back in disorder. In the intervals between these onsets the French light troops poured in their missiles, but though the clump of pikes and halberds grew smaller it still remained impenetrable. Not until the evening was the fighting ended, and then 6000 Armagnacs lay dead around the heap of Swiss corpses in the centre. Louis saw that a few such victories would destroy his whole army, and turned back into Alsace, leaving Switzerland unmolested.

From that day, the Confederates were able to reckon their reputation for obstinate and invincible courage, as one of the chief causes which gave them political importance. The generals and armies who afterwards faced them, went into battle without full confidence in themselves. It was no light matter to engage with an enemy who would not retire before any superiority in numbers, who was always ready for the fight, who would neither give nor take quarter. The enemies of the Swiss found these considerations the reverse of inspiriting before a combat: it may almost be said that they came into the field expecting a defeat, and therefore earned one.

This fact is especially noticeable in the great Burgundian war. If Charles the Rash himself was unawed by the warlike renown of his enemies, the same cannot be said of his troops. (Yet even the duke said, that 'Against the Swiss it will never do to march unprepared.' Panagirola, quoted by Kirk, vol. iii.)

A large portion of his motley army could not be trusted in any dangerous crisis: the German, Italian, and Savoyard mercenaries knew too well the horrors of Swiss warfare, and shrank instinctively from the shock of the phalanx of pikes. The duke might range his men in order of battle, but he could not be sure that they would fight. The old proverb that '*God was on the side of the Confederates*' was ever ringing in their ears, and so they were half beaten before a blow was struck. Charles had endeavoured to secure the efficiency of his army, by enlisting from each warlike nation of Europe the class of troops for which it was celebrated.

The archers of England, the arquebusiers of Germany, the light cavalry of Italy, the pikemen of Flanders, marched side by side with the feudal chivalry of his Burgundian vassals. But the duke had forgotten that, in assembling so many nationalities under his banner, he had thrown away the cohesion which is all-important in battle. Without mutual confidence or certainty that each comrade would do his best for the common cause, the soldiery would not stand firm. Granson was lost merely because the nerve of the infantry failed them at the decisive moment, although they had not yet been engaged.

In that fight the unskilful generalship of the Swiss had placed the tactical advantages on the side of Charles: he had both outflanked them and attacked one division of their army before the others came up. He had, however, to learn that an army superior in morale and homogeneity, and thoroughly knowing its weapon, may be victorious in spite of all disadvantages. Owing to their eagerness for battle the Confederate vanguard (*vorhut*), composed of the troops of Bern, Freiburg, and Schwytz, had far outstripped the remainder of the force. Coming swiftly over the hill side in one of their usual deep columns, they found the whole Burgundian army spread out before them in battle array on the plain of Granson.

As they reached the foot of the hill they at once saw that the duke's cavalry was preparing to attack them. Old experience had made them callous to such sights: facing outwards the column awaited the onset. The first charge was made by the cavalry of Charles' left wing: it failed, although the gallant lord of Chateauguyon, who led it, forced his horse among the pikes and died at the foot of the Standard of Schwytz. Next the duke himself led on the lances of his guard, a force who had long been esteemed the best troops in Europe: they did all

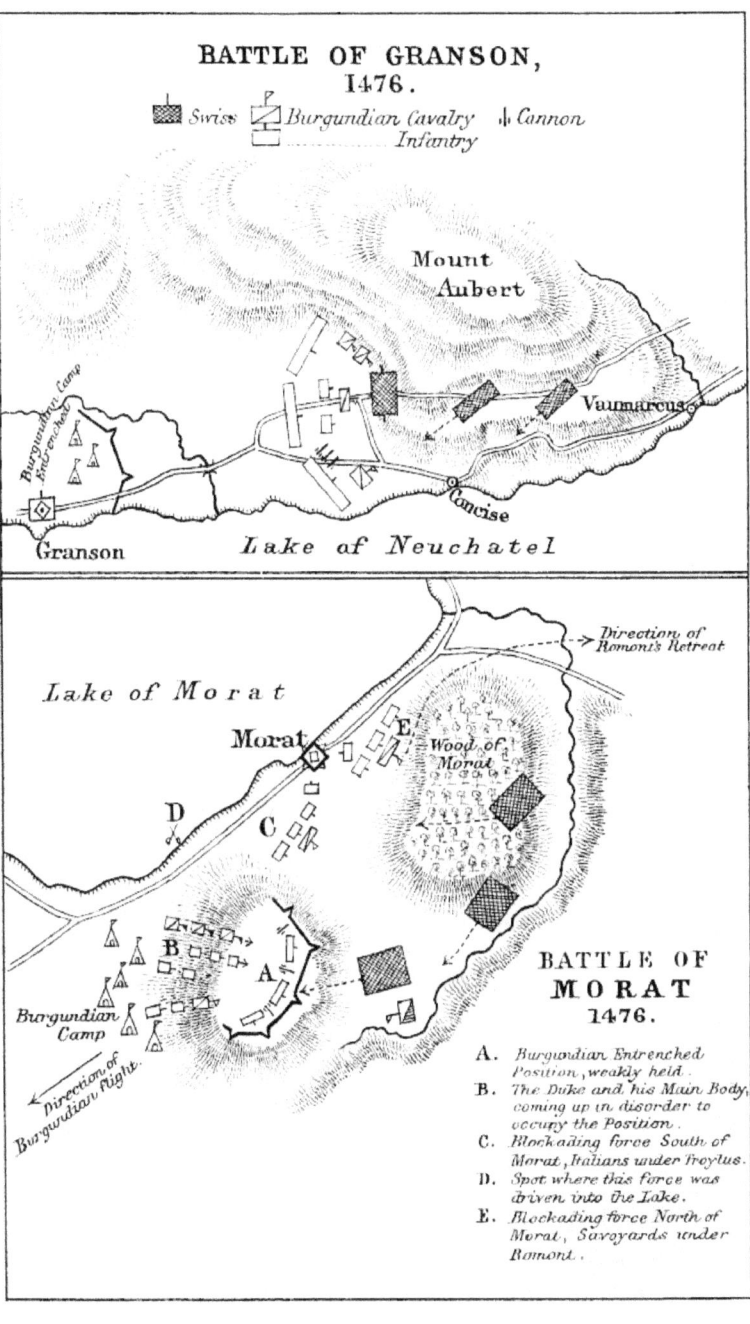

that brave men could, but were dashed back in confusion from the steady line of spear-points.

The Swiss now began to move forward into the plain, eager to try the effect of the impact of their *phalanx* on the Burgundian line. To meet this advance Charles determined to draw back his centre, and when the enemy advanced against it, to wheel both his wings round upon their flank. The manoeuvre appeared feasible, as the remainder of the Confederate Army was not yet in sight. Orders were accordingly sent to the infantry and guns who were immediately facing the approaching column, directing them to retire; while at the same time the reserve was sent to strengthen the left wing, the body with which the duke intended to deliver his most crushing stroke.

The Burgundian Army was in fact engaged in repeating the movement which had given Hannibal victory at Cannae: their fortune, however, was very different. At the moment when the centre had begun to draw back, and when the wings were not yet engaged, the heads of the two Swiss columns, which had not before appeared, came over the brow of Mont Aubert; moving rapidly towards the battlefield with the usual majestic steadiness of their formation. This of course would have frustrated Charles' scheme for surrounding the first *phalanx*; the *échelon* of divisions, which was the normal Swiss array, being now established. The aspect of the fight, however, was changed even more suddenly than might have been expected. Connecting the retreat of their centre with the advance of the Swiss, the whole of the infantry of the Burgundian wings broke and fled, long before the Confederate masses had come into contact with them.

It was a sheer panic, caused by the fact that the duke's army had no cohesion or confidence in itself; the various corps in the moment of danger could not rely on each others' steadiness, and seeing what they imagined to be the rout of their centre, had no further thought of endeavouring to turn the fortune of the day. It may be said that no general could have foreseen such a disgraceful flight; but at the same time the duke may be censured for attempting a delicate manoeuvre with an army destitute of homogeneity, and in face of an enterprising opponent. 'Strategical movements to the rear' have always a tendency to degenerate into undisguised retreats, unless the men are perfectly in hand, and should therefore be avoided as much as possible. Granson was for the Swiss only one more example of the powerlessness of the best cavalry against their columns: of infantry fighting there was none at all.

ARQUEBUSIER

In the second great defeat, which he suffered at the hands of the Confederates the duke was guilty of far more flagrant faults in his generalship. His army was divided into three parts, which in the event of a flank attack could bring each other no succour. The position which he had chosen and fortified for the covering of his siege-operations, only protected them against an assault from the south-east. Still more strange was it that the Burgundian light troops were held back so close to the main-body, that the duke had no accurate knowledge of the movements of his enemies till they appeared in front of his lines.

It was thus possible for the Confederate Army to march, under cover of the Wood of Morat, right across the front of the two corps which virtually composed the centre and left of Charles' array. As it was well known that the enemy were in the immediate vicinity, it is hard to conceive how the duke could be content to wait in battle-order for six hours, without sending out troops to obtain information. It is nevertheless certain that when the Swiss did not show themselves, he sent back his main-body to camp, and left the carefully entrenched position in the charge of a few thousand men. Hardly had this fault been committed, when the Confederate vanguard appeared on the outskirts of the Wood of Morat, and marched straight on the palisade.

The utterly inadequate garrison made a bold endeavour to hold their ground, but in a few minutes, were driven down the reverse slope of the hill, into the arms of the troops who were coming up in hot haste from the camp to their succour. The Swiss following hard in their rear pushed the disordered mass before them, and crushed in detail each supporting corps as it straggled up to attack them. The greater part of the Burgundian infantry turned and fled,—with far more excuse than at Granson. Many of the cavalry corps endeavoured to change the fortune of the day by desperate but isolated charges, in which they met the usual fate of those who endeavoured to break a Swiss *phalanx*.

The fighting, however, was soon at an end, and mere slaughter took its place. While the van and main-body of the Confederates followed the flying crowd, who made off in the direction of Avenches, the rear came down on the Italian infantry, who had formed the besieging force south of the town of Morat. These unfortunates, whose retreat was cut off by the direction which the flight of the main-body had taken, were trodden under foot or pushed into the lake by the impact of the Swiss column, and entirely annihilated, scarcely a single man escaping out of a force of six thousand. The Savoyard corps, under Romont, who had composed the duke's extreme left, and were posted to the north of Morat, escaped by a hazardous march which took them round the rear of the Confederates.

Though Charles had done his best to prepare a victory for his enemies by the faultiness of his dispositions, the management of the Swiss army at Morat was the cause of the completeness of his overthrow. A successful attack on the Burgundian right would cut off the retreat of the two isolated corps which composed the duke's centre and left; the Confederate leaders therefore determined to assault this point, although to reach it they had to march straight across their opponent's front.

★★★★★★

'If we attack Romont,' said Ulrich Kätzy at the Swiss council of war, 'while we are beating him the duke will have time and opportunity to escape; let us go round the hills against the mainbody, and when that is routed, we shall have the rest without a stroke.' This showed real tactical skill.

★★★★★★

Favoured by his astonishing oversight in leaving their march unobserved, they were able to surprise him, and destroy his army in detail, before it could manage to form even a rudimentary line of battle.

At Nancy, the Swiss commanders again displayed considerable skill in their dispositions: the main battle and the small rear column held back and attracted the attention of the Burgundian army, while the van executed a turning movement through the woods, which brought it out on the enemy's flank, and made his position perfectly untenable. The duke's troops assailed in front and on their right at the same moment, and having to deal with very superior numbers, were not merely defeated but dispersed or destroyed. Charles himself refusing to fly, and fighting desperately to cover the retreat of his scattered forces, was surrounded, and cleft through helmet and skull by the tremendous blow of a Swiss halberd.

The generalship displayed at Nancy and Morat was, however, exceptional among the Confederates. After those battles, just as before, we find that their victories continued to be won by a headlong and desperate onset, rather than by the display of any great strategical ability. In the Swabian war of 1499 the credit of their successes falls to the troops rather than to their leaders. The stormings of the fortified camps of Hard and Malsheide were wonderful examples of the power of unshrinking courage; but on each occasion the Swiss officers seem to have considered that they were discharging their whole duty, when they led their men straight against the enemy's entrenchments.

At Frastenz the day was won by a desperate charge up the face of a cliff which the Tyrolese had left unguarded, as being inaccessible. Even at Dornach—the last battle fought on Swiss soil against an invader till the eighteenth century—the fortune of the fight turned on the superiority of the Confederate to the Swabian pikemen man for man, and on the fact that the lances of Gueldres could not break the flank column by their most determined onset. Of manoeuvring there appears to have been little, of strategical planning none at all; it was considered sufficient to launch the *phalanx* against the enemy, and trust to its power of bearing down every obstacle that came in its way.

(4) CAUSES OF THE DECLINE OF SWISS ASCENDENCY.

Their disregard for the higher and more delicate problems of military science, was destined to enfeeble the power and destroy the reputation of the Confederates. At a time when the great struggle in Italy was serving as a school for the soldiery of other European nations, they alone refused to learn. Broad theories, drawn from the newly-discovered works of the ancients, were being co-ordinated with the modern experience of professional officers, and were developing into an art of war far superior to anything known in mediaeval times. Scientific engineers and artillerists had begun to modify the conditions of warfare, and feudal tradition was everywhere discarded. New forms of military efficiency, such as the sword-and-buckler men of Spain, the Stradiot light cavalry, the German 'black bands' of musketeers, were coming to the front. The improvement of the firearms placed in the hands of infantry was only less important than the superior mobility which was given to field artillery.

The Swiss, however, paid no attention to these changes; the world around them might alter, but they would hold fast to the tactics of their ancestors. At first, indeed, their arms were still crowned with success: they were seen in Italy, as in more northern lands, to:

> .....march with ten or fifteen thousand pikemen against any number of horse, and to win a general opinion of their excellence from the many remarkable services they performed.— Machiavelli, *Art of War*.

They enjoyed for a time supreme importance, and left their mark on the military history of every nation of central and southern Europe. But it was impossible that a single stereotyped tactical method, applied by men destitute of any broad and scientific knowledge of the art of war, should continue to assert an undisputed ascendancy. The victories of the Swiss set every officer of capacity and versatile talent searching for an efficient way of dealing with the onset of the phalanx. Such a search was rendered comparatively easy by the fact that the old feudal cavalry and the worthless mediaeval infantry were being rapidly replaced by disciplined troops, men capable of keeping cool and collected even before the desperate rush of the Confederate pikemen.

The standing army of Charles of Burgundy had been rendered inefficient by its want of homogeneity and cohesion, as well as by the bad generalship of its leader. The standing armies which fought in Italy thirty years later were very different bodies. Although still raised from among various nations, they were united by the bonds of old comradeship, of ésprit *de corps*, of professional pride, or of confidence in some favourite general. The Swiss had therefore to face troops of a far higher military value than they had ever before encountered.

The first experiment tried against the Confederates was that of the Emperor Maximilian, who raised in Germany corps of pikemen and halberdiers, trained to act in a manner exactly similar to that of their enemies. The 'Landsknechts' soon won for themselves a reputation only second to that of the Swiss, whom they boldly met in many a bloody field. The conflicts between them were rendered obstinate by military as well as national rivalry: The Confederates being indignant that any troops should dare to face them with their own peculiar tactics, while the Germans were determined to show that they were not inferior in courage to their Alpine kinsmen.

The shock of the contending columns was therefore tremendous. The two bristling lines of pikes crossed, and the leading files were thrust upon each other's weapons by the irresistible pressure from behind. Often the whole front rank of each *phalanx* went down in the first onset, but their comrades stepped forward over their bodies to continue the fight.

★★★★★★

Frundsberg, the old captain of *landsknechts*, gives a cool and business-like account of these shocks, '*Wo unter den langen Wehren etliche Glieder zu grund gehen, werden die Personen, so dahinter stehen, etwas zaghaft*,' etc.

★★★★★★

When the masses had been for some time 'pushing against each other,' their order became confused and their pikes interlocked: then was the time for the halberdiers to act. (The two-handed sword had almost entirely, and the 'morning-star' and 'Lucern hammer' quite, disappeared from use by the end of the fifteenth century.) The columns opened out to let them pass, or they rushed round from the rear, and threw themselves into the *mêlée*. This was the most deadly epoch of the strife: the combatants mowed each other down with fearful rapidity. Their ponderous weapons allowed of little fencing and parrying, and inflicted wounds which were almost invariably mortal. Everyone who missed his blow, or stumbled over a fallen comrade, or turned to fly, was a doomed man. Quarter was neither expected nor given.

Of course, these fearful hand-to-hand combats could not be of great duration; one party had ere long to give ground, and suffer the most fearful losses in its retreat. It was in a struggle of this kind that the Landsknechts lost a full half of their strength, when the Swiss bore them down at Novara. Even, however, when they were victorious, the Confederates found that their military ascendancy was growing less: they could no longer sweep the enemy from the field by a single unchecked onset, but were confronted by troops who were ready to turn their own weapons against them, and who required the hardest pressure before they would give ground. In spite of their defeats the *Landsknechts* kept the field, and finally took their revenge when the Swiss recoiled in disorder from the fatal trenches of Bicocca.

There was, however, an enemy even more formidable than the German, who was to appear upon the scene at a slightly later date. The Spanish infantry of Gonsalvo de Cordova displayed once more to the military world the strength of the tactics of old Rome. They were armed, like the men of the ancient legion, with the short thrusting sword and buckler, and wore the steel cap, breast- and back-plates and greaves. Thus, they were far stronger in their defensive armour than the Swiss whom they were about to encounter. When the pikeman and the swordsman first met in 1502, under the walls of Barletta, the old problem of Pydna and Cynoscephalae was once more worked out.

A *phalanx* as solid and efficient as that of Philip the Macedonian was met by troops whose tactics were those of the *legionaries* of Æmilius Paullus. Then, as in an earlier age, the wielders of the shorter weapon prevailed.

> When they came to engage, the Swiss at first pressed so hard on
> their enemy with the pike, that they opened out their ranks; but

the Spaniards, under the cover of their bucklers, nimbly rushed in upon them with their swords, and laid about them so furiously, that they made a great slaughter of the Swiss, and gained a complete victory.—Machiavelli, *Art of War*.

The vanquished, in fact, suffered at the hands of the Spaniard the treatment which they themselves had inflicted on the Austrians at Sempach. The bearer of the longer weapon becomes helpless when his opponent has closed with him, whether the arms concerned be lance and halberd or pike and sword. The moment a breach had been made in a Macedonian or Swiss *phalanx* the great length of their spears became their ruin. There was nothing to do but to drop them, and in the combat which then ensued troops using the sword alone, and without defensive armour, were at a hopeless disadvantage in attacking men furnished with the buckler as well as the sword, and protected by a more complete panoply.

Whatever may be the result of a duel between sword and spear alone, it is certain that when a light shield is added to the swordsman's equipment, he at once obtains the ascendancy. The buckler serves to turn aside the spear-point, and then the thrusting weapon is free to do its work.

✶✶✶✶✶✶

It is a curious fact that Chaka, one of Cetywayo's predecessors as king of the Zulus, set himself to solve this problem. He took a hundred men and armed them with the shield and the 'short *assegai*,' a thrusting weapon resembling a sword rather than a spear in its use. He then set them to fight another hundred furnished with the shield and the 'long *assegai*,' the slender javelin which had previously been the weapon of his tribe. The wielders of the shorter weapon won with ease, and the king thereupon ordered its adoption throughout the Zulu Army. It was this change which originally gave the Zulus their superiority over their neighbours.

✶✶✶✶✶✶

It was, therefore, natural that when Spanish and Swiss infantry met, the former should in almost every case obtain success. The powerlessness of the pike, however, was most strikingly displayed at a battle in which the fortune of the day had not been favourable to Spain. At the fight of Ravenna Gaston de Foix had succeeded in driving Don Ramon de Cardona from his entrenchments, and was endeavouring to secure the fruits of victory by a vigorous pursuit. To intercept the retreat of the Spanish infantry, who were retiring in good order, Gaston sent forward the pikemen of Jacob Empser, then serving as auxiliaries beneath the French banner. These troops accordingly fell on the retreating column and attempted to arrest its march.

The Spaniards, however, turned at once and fell furiously on the Germans, 'rushing at the pikes, or throwing themselves on the ground and slipping below the points, so that they darted in among the legs of the pikemen,'—a manoeuvre which reminds us of the conduct of the Soudanese Arabs at El Teb. In this way, they succeeded in closing with their opponents, and 'made such good use of their swords that not a German would have escaped, had not the French horse come up to their rescue.' (*Machiavelli*.)

This fight was typical of many more, in which during the first quarter of the sixteenth century the sword and buckler were proved to be able to master the pike. It may, therefore, be asked why, in the face of these facts, the Swiss weapon remained in use, while the Spanish infantry finally discarded their peculiar tactics. To this question the answer is found in the consideration that the sword was not suited for repulsing a cavalry charge, while the pike continued to be used for that purpose down to the invention of the bayonet in the end of the seventeenth century.

Machiavelli was, from his studies in Roman antiquity, the most devoted admirer of the Spanish system, which seemed to bring back the days of the ancient legion. Yet even he conceded that the pike, a weapon which he is on every occasion ready to disparage, must be retained by a considerable portion of those ideal armies for whose guidance he drew up his *Art of War*. He could think of no other arm which could resist a charge of cavalry steadily pressed home, and was therefore obliged to combine pikemen with his *velites* and 'bucklermen.'

The rapid development of the arts of the engineer and artillerist aimed another heavy blow at the Swiss supremacy. The many-sided energy of the Renaissance period not unfrequently made the professional soldier a scholar, and set him to adapt the science of the ancients to the requirements of modern warfare. The most cursory study of Vegetius Hyginus or Vitruvius, all of them authors much esteemed at the time, would suffice to show the strength of the Roman fortified camp. Accordingly, the art of Castramentation revived, and corps of pioneers were attached to every army. It became common to en-trench not merely permanent positions, but camps which were to be held for a few days only. Advantage was taken of favourable sites, and lines of greater or less strength with emplacements for artillery were constructed for the protection of the army which felt itself inferior in the field.

Many of the greatest battles of the Italian wars were fought in and around such positions; Ravenna, Bicocca, and Pavia are obvious examples. Still more frequently a general threw himself with all his forces into a fortified town and covered it with outworks and redoubts till it resembled an entrenched camp rather than a mere fortress. Such a phase in war was most disadvantageous to the Swiss: even the most desperate courage cannot carry men over stone walls or through flooded ditches, if they neglect the art which teaches them how to approach such obstacles.

The Confederates in their earlier days had never displayed much skill in attacking places of strength; and now, when the enemy's position was as frequently behind defences as in the open plain, they refused to adapt their tactics to the altered circumstances. Occasionally, as for example at the storming of the outworks of Genoa in 1507, they were still able to sweep the enemy before them by the mere vehemence of their onset. But more frequently disaster followed the headlong rush delivered against lines held by an adequate number of steady troops. Of this the most striking instance was seen in 1522, when the Swiss columns attempted to dislodge the enemy from the fortified park of Bicocca.

Under a severe fire from the Spanish hackbutmen they crossed several hedges and flooded trenches, which covered the main position of the imperialists. But when they came to the last ditch and bank, along which were ranged the landsknechts of Frundsberg; they found an obstacle which they could not pass. Leaping into the deep excavation the front ranks endeavoured to scramble up its further slope; but every man who made the attempt fell beneath the pike-thrusts of the Germans, who, standing on a higher level in their serried ranks, kept back the incessant rushes with the greatest steadiness. Three thousand corpses were left in the ditch before the Swiss would desist from their hopeless undertaking; it was an attack which, for misplaced daring, rivals the British assault on Ticonderoga in 1758.

The improved artillery of the early sixteenth century worked even more havoc with the Confederates. Of all formations, the *phalanx* is the easiest at which to aim, and the one which suffers most loss from each cannon ball which strikes it. A single shot ploughing through its serried ranks might disable twenty men, yet the Swiss persisted in rushing straight for the front of batteries and storming them in spite of their murderous fire.

Such conduct might conceivably have been justifiable in the fifteenth century, when the clumsy guns of the day could seldom deliver more than a single discharge between the moment at which the enemy came within range and that at which he reached their muzzles. Scientific artillerists, however, such as Pietro Navarro and Alphonso D'Este, made cannon a real power in battles by increasing its mobility and the rapidity of its fire. None the less the Confederates continued to employ the front attack, which had become four or five times more dangerous in the space of forty years.

A fearful lesson as to the recklessness of such tactics was given them at Marignano, where, in spite of the gallantry of the French *gendarmerie*, it was the artillery which really won the day. The system which Francis' advisers there employed was to deliver charge after charge of cavalry on the flanks of the Swiss columns, while the artillery played upon them from the front. The onsets of the cavalry, though they never succeeded in breaking the phalanx, forced it to halt and 'form the hedgehog.' The men at arms came on in bodies of about five hundred strong, one taking up the fight when the first had been beaten off. The king wrote to his mother:

> In this way more than thirty fine charges were delivered, and no one will in future be able to say that cavalry are of no more use than hares in armour.

Of course, these attacks would by themselves have been fruitless; it was the fact that they checked the advance of the Swiss, and obliged them to stand halted under artillery fire that settled the result of the battle. (Sismondi's *Italian History*, vol. ix.) At last the columns had suffered so severely that they gave up the attempt to advance, and retired in good order, unbroken but diminished by a half in their size.

Last but not least important among the causes of the decline of the military ascendancy of the Confederates, was the continual deterioration of their discipline. While among other nations the commanders were becoming more and more masters of the art of war, among the Swiss they were growing more and more the slaves of their own soldiery. The division of their authority had always been detrimental to the development of strategical skill, but it now began to make even

16th Century Germans and Swiss

tactical arrangements impossible. The army looked upon itself as a democracy entitled to direct the proceedings of its ministry, rather than a body under military discipline. Filled with a blind confidence in the invincibility of their onset, they calmly neglected the orders which appeared to them superfluous.

On several occasions, they delivered an attack on the front of a position which it had been intended to turn; on others, they began the conflict, although they had been directed to wait for the arrival of other divisions before giving battle. If things were not going well they threw away even the semblance of obedience to their leaders. Before Bicocca the cry was raised, 'Where are the officers, the pensioners, the double-pay men? Let them come out and earn their money fairly for once: they shall all fight in the front rank today.'

What was even more astonishing than the arrogance of the demand, was the fact that it was obeyed. The commanders and captains stepped forward and formed the head of the leading column; hardly one of them survived the fight, and Winkelried of Unterwalden, the leader of the van-guard, was the first to fall under the lances of Frundsberg's *landsknechts*. What was to be expected from an army in which the men gave the orders and the officers executed them? Brute strength and heedless courage were the only qualities now employed by the Swiss, while against them were pitted the scientific generals of the new school of war. The result was what might have been expected: the pike tactics, which had been the admiration of Europe, were superseded, because they had become stereotyped, and the Swiss lost their proud position as the most formidable infantry in the world.

CHAPTER 6

The English and their Enemies 1272-1485

(From the accession of Edward I to the end of the Wars of the Roses)

The use of the long-bow is as much the key to the successes of the English armies in the fourteenth and fifteenth centuries, as that of the pike is to the successes of the Swiss. Dissimilar as were the characters of the two weapons, and the national tactics to which their use led, they were both employed for the same end of terminating the ascendancy in war of the mailed horseman of the feudal *régime*. It is certainly not the least curious part of the military history of the period, that the commanders who made such good use of their archery, had no conception of the tendencies of their action. Edward the Black Prince and his father regarded themselves as the flower of chivalry, and would have been horrified had they realised that their own tactics were going far to make chivalrous warfare impossible.

Such, however, was the case: that unscientific kind of combat which resembled a huge tilting match could not continue, if one side persisted in bringing into the field auxiliaries who could prevent their opponents from approaching near enough to break a lance. The needs of the moment, however, prevented the English commanders being troubled by such thoughts; they made the best use of the material at their disposal, and if they thus found themselves able to beat the enemy, they were satisfied.

It is not till the last quarter of the thirteenth century that we find the long-bow taking up its position as the national weapon of England. In the armies of our Norman and Angevin kings archers were indeed to be found, but they formed neither the most numerous nor the most effective part of the array. On this side of the Channel, just

LONG-BOWMEN

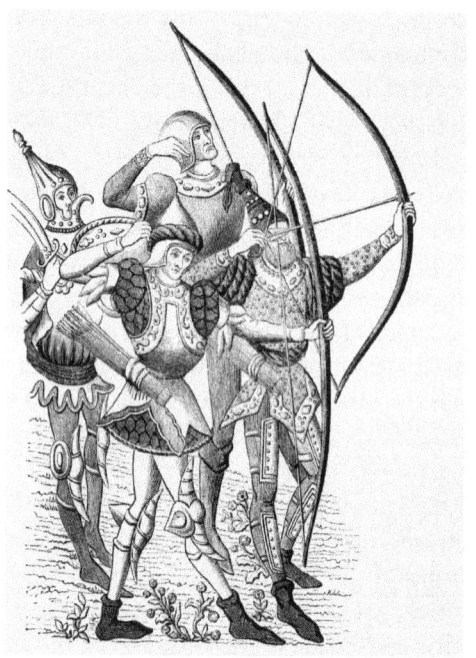

as beyond it, the supremacy of the mailed horseman was still unquestioned. It is indeed noteworthy that the theory which attributes to the Normans the introduction of the long-bow is difficult to substantiate. If we are to trust the Bayeux Tapestry—whose accuracy is in other matters thoroughly borne out by all contemporary evidence—the weapon of William's archers was in no way different to that already known in England, and used by a few of the English in the fight of Senlac. (*E.g.* by the diminutive archer who crouches under a *thegn's* shield, like Teucer protected by Ajax.)

It is the short bow, drawn to the breast and not to the ear. The bowmen who are occasionally mentioned during the succeeding century, as, for example, those present at the Battle of the Standard, do not appear to form any very important part of the national force. Nothing can be more conclusive as to the insignificance of the weapon than the fact that it is not mentioned at all in the 'Assize of Arms' of 1181. In the reign of Henry II, therefore, we may fairly conclude that the bow did not form the proper weapon of any class of English society.

A similar deduction is suggested by Richard Coeur de Lion's predilection for the arbalest: it is impossible that he should have introduced that weapon as a new and superior arm, if he had been acquainted with the splendid long-bow of the fourteenth century. It is evident that the bow must always preserve an advantage in rapidity of fire over the arbalest; the latter must therefore have been considered by Richard to surpass in range and penetrating power. But nothing is better established than the fact that the trained archer of the Hundred Years' War was able to beat the cross-bowmen on both these points. It is, therefore, rational to conclude that the weapon superseded by the arbalest was merely the old short-bow, which had been in constant use since Saxon times.

However, this may be, the cross-bowmen continued to occupy the first place among light troops during the reigns of Richard and John. The former monarch devised for them a system of tactics, in which the pavise was made to play a prominent part. The latter entertained great numbers both of horse- and foot-arbalesters among those mercenary bands who were such a scourge to England. It would appear that the barons, in their contest with John, suffered greatly from having no adequate provision of infantry armed with missiles to oppose the cross-bowmen of Fawkes de Breauté and his fellows. Even in the reign of Henry III, the epoch in which the long-bow begins to come into use, the arbalest was still reckoned the more effective arm. At the

BATTLE OF NEVILLE'S CROSS

BATTLE OF FLODDEN

Battle of Taillebourg, in 1242, a corps of 700 men armed with it were considered to be the flower of the English infantry.

To trace the true origin of the long-bow is not easy: there are reasons for believing that it may have been borrowed from the South Welsh, who were certainly provided with it as early as *a. d.* 1150.

✶✶✶✶✶✶

Giraldus Cambrensis, Itin. Cambriae, c. 3, speaks of the Welsh bowmen as being able to send an arrow through an oak door four fingers thick. The people of Gwent (Monmouth and Glamorgan) were reckoned the best archers. Those of North Wales were always spearmen, not archers.

✶✶✶✶✶✶

Against this derivation, however, may be pleaded the fact that in the first half of the thirteenth century it appears to have been in greater vogue in the northern than in the western counties of England. As a national weapon, it is first accepted in the Assize of Arms of 1252, wherein all holders of 40*s.* in land or nine *marks* in chattels are desired to provide themselves with sword, dagger, bow and arrows. (Stubbs' *Select Charters.*) Contemporary documents often speak of the obligation of various manors to provide the king with one or more archers 'when he makes an expedition against the Welsh.' It is curious to observe that even as late as 1281 the preference for the cross-bow seems to have been kept up, the wages of its bearer being considerably more than those of the archer.

✶✶✶✶✶✶

In the *Pay Roll* of the garrison of Rhuddlan castle, 1281, we find 'paid to Geoffrey le Chamberlin for the wages of twelve cross-bowmen, and thirteen archers, for twenty-four days, £7 8*s.*, each cross-bowman receiving by the day 4*d.*, and each archer 2*d.*'

✶✶✶✶✶✶

To Edward I the long-bow owes its original rise into favour: that monarch, like his grandson and great-grandson, was an able soldier, and capable of devising new expedients in war. His long experience in Welsh campaigns led him to introduce a scientific use of archery, much like that which William the Conqueror had employed at Hastings. We are informed that it was first put in practice in a combat fought against Prince Llewellin at Orewin Bridge, and afterwards copied by the Earl of Warwick in another engagement during the year 1295.

CHARGE OF THE SCOTS AT HALIDON HILL

BATTLE OF HOMILDON

The Welsh, on the earl's approach, set themselves fronting his force with exceeding long spears, which, being suddenly turned toward the earl and his company, with their ends placed in the earth and their points upward, broke the force of the English cavalry. But the earl well provided against them, by placing archers between his men-at-arms, so that by these missive weapons those who held the lances were put to rout.—Nic. Trivet, *Annales*.

The Battle of Falkirk, however (1298), is the first engagement of real importance in which the bowmen, properly supplemented by cavalry, played the leading part. Its circumstances, indeed, bore such striking witness to the power of the arrow, that it could not fail to serve as a lesson to English commanders. The Scots of the Lowlands, who formed the army of Wallace, consisted mainly of spearmen; armed, like the Swiss, with a pike of many feet in length. They had in their ranks a small body of horse, a few hundred in number, and a certain proportion of archers, mainly drawn from the Ettrick and Selkirk district. Wallace, having selected an excellent position behind a marsh, formed his spearmen in four great masses (or *schiltrons*, as the Scotch called them) of circular form, ready to face outward in any direction.

The light troops formed a line in the intervals of these columns, while the cavalry were placed in reserve. Edward came on with his horsemen in three divisions, and his archers disposed between them. The foremost English *battle*, that of the Earl Marshal, rode into the morass, was stopped by it, and suffered severely from the Scotch missile weapons. The second division, commanded by the Bishop of Durham, observing this check, rode round the flank of the marsh, in order to turn Wallace's position. The small body of Scotch cavalry endeavoured to stay their advance, but were driven completely off the field by superior numbers.

★★★★★★

It is surely unnecessary to call in the aid of treachery—as historians have so frequently done—in order to account for the rout of a force numbered by hundreds, by one numbered by thousands.

★★★★★★

Then the bishop's horsemen charged the hostile line from the rear. The squadrons opposed to the light troops succeeded in riding them down, as Wallace's archers were only armed with the short-bow, and

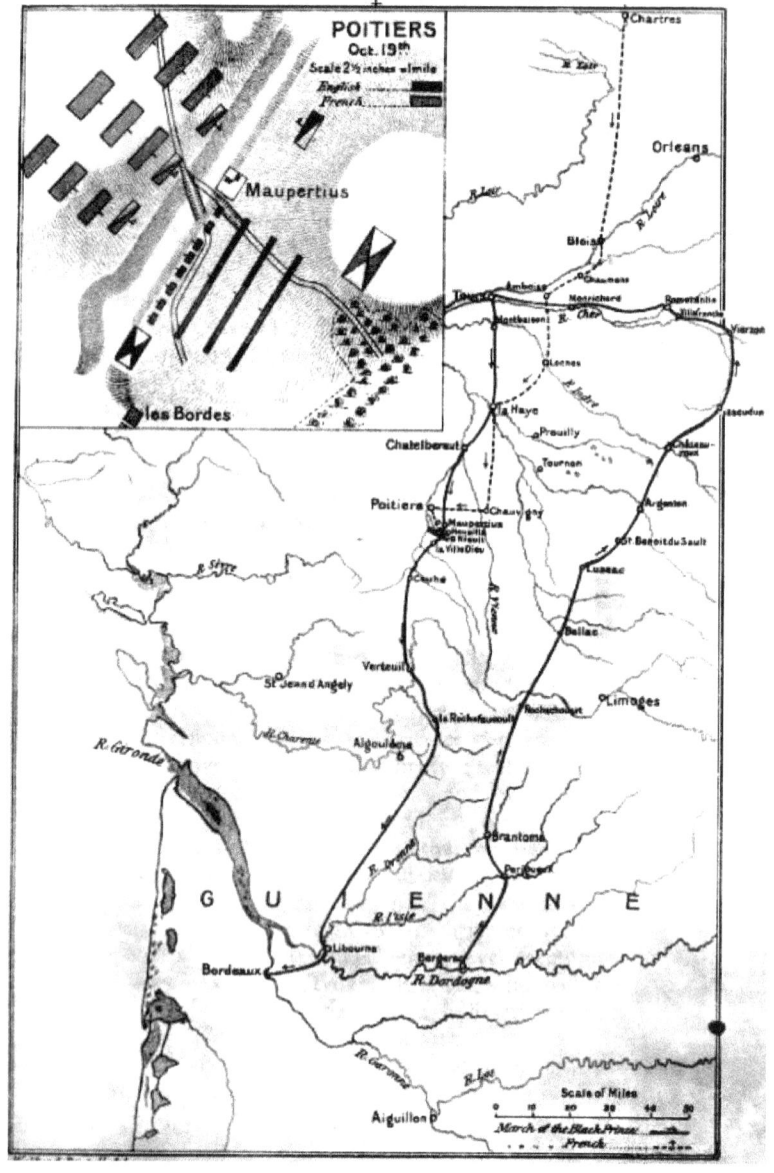

were not particularly skilled in its use. Those of the English, however, who faced the masses of pikemen received a sanguinary check, and were thrown back in disorder. The Bishop had therefore to await the arrival of the king, who was leading the infantry and the remainder of the cavalry round the end of the marsh. When this had been done, Edward brought up his bowmen close to the Scotch masses, who were unable to reply (as their own light troops had been driven away) or to charge, on account of the nearness of the English men-at-arms.

Concentrating the rain of arrows on particular points in the columns, the king fairly riddled the Scotch ranks, and then sent in his cavalry with a sudden impetus. The plan succeeded, the shaken parts of the masses were pierced, and the knights, having once got within the pikes, made a fearful slaughter of the enemy. The moral of the fight was evident: cavalry could not beat the Scotch tactics, but archers supplemented by horsemen could easily accomplish the required task. Accordingly, for the next two centuries, the characteristics of the fight of Falkirk were continually repeated whenever the English and Scotch met. Halidon Hill, Neville's Cross, Homildon, Flodden, were all variations on the same theme.

The steady but slowly-moving masses of the Lowland infantry fell a sacrifice to their own persistent bravery, when they staggered on in a vain endeavour to reach the line of archers, flanked by men-at-arms, whom the English commander opposed to them. The bowman might boast with truth that he 'carried twelve Scots' lives at his girdle;' he had but to launch his shaft into the easy target of the great surging mass of pikemen, and it was sure to do execution.

Bannockburn, indeed, forms a notable exception to the general rule. Its result, however, was due not to an attempt to discard the tactics of Falkirk, but to an unskilful application of them. The forces of Robert Bruce, much like those of Wallace in composition, consisted of 40,000 pikemen, a certain proportion of light troops, and less than 1000 cavalry. They were drawn up in a very compact position, flanked by marshy ground to the right, and to the left by a quantity of small pits destined to arrest the charge of the English cavalry. Edward II refrained from any attempt to turn Bruce's army, and by endeavouring to make 100,000 men cover no more space in frontage than 40,000, cramped his array, and made manoeuvres impossible.

His most fatal mistake, however, was to place all his archers in the front line, without any protecting body of horsemen. The arrows were already falling among the Scotch columns before the English cavalry

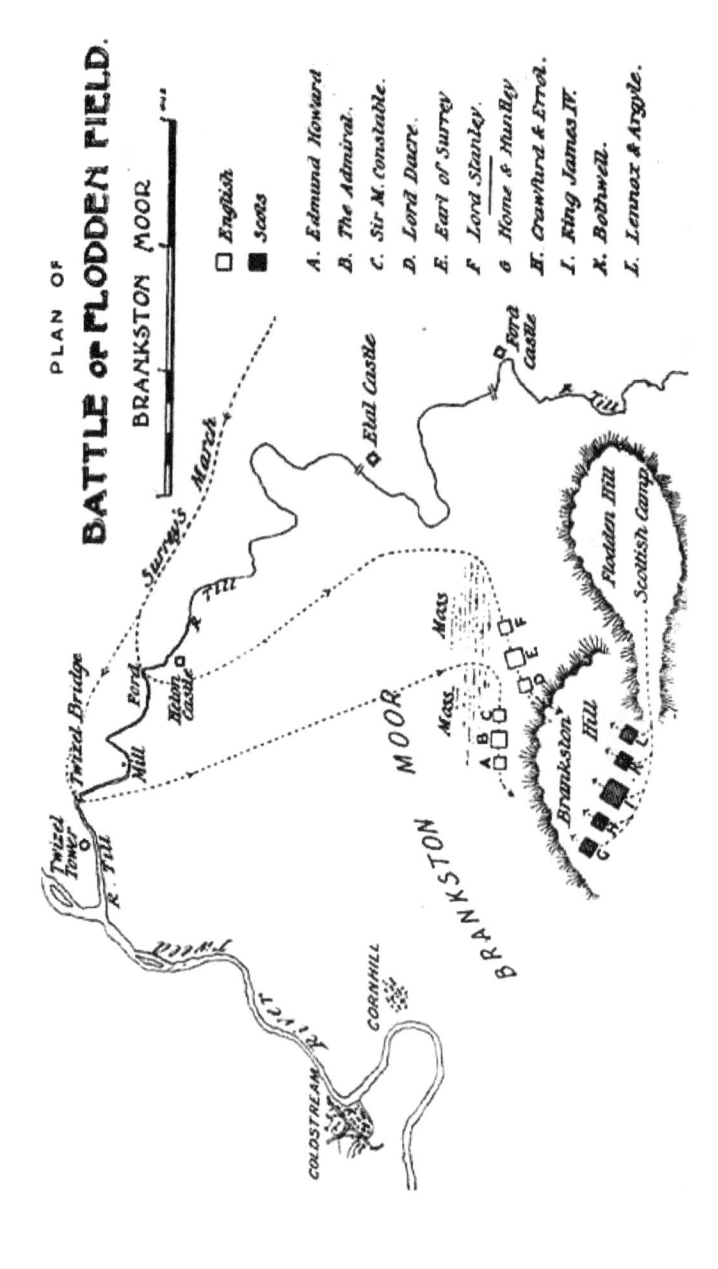

had fully arrived upon the field. Bruce at once saw his opportunity: his small body of men-at-arms was promptly put in motion against the bowmen. A front attack on them would of course have been futile, but a flank charge was rendered possible by the absence of the English squadrons, which ought to have covered the wings. Riding rapidly round the edge of the morass, the Scotch horse fell on the uncovered line, rolled it up from end to end, and wrought fearful damage by their unexpected onset.

The archers were so maltreated that they took no further effective part in the battle. Enraged at the sudden rout of his first line, Edward flung his great masses of cavalry on the comparatively narrow front of the Scotch army. The steady columns received them, and drove them back again and again with ease. At last every man-at-arms had been thrown into the *mêlée*, and the splendid force of English horsemen had become a mere mob, surging helplessly in front of the enemy's line, and executing partial and ineffective charges on a cramped terrain. Finally, their spirit for fighting was exhausted, and when a body of camp-followers appeared on the hill behind Bruce's position, a rumour spread around that reinforcements were arriving for the Scots.

The English were already hopeless of success, and now turned their reins to retreat. When the Scotch masses moved on in pursuit, a panic seized the broken army, and the whole force dispersed in disorder. Many galloped into the pits on the left; these were dismounted and slain or captured. A few stayed behind to fight, and met a similar fate. The majority made at once for the English border, and considered themselves fortunate if they reached Berwick or Carlisle without being intercepted and slaughtered by the peasantry. The moral of the day had been that the archery must be adequately supported on its flanks by troops capable of arresting a cavalry charge. The lesson was not thrown away, and at Creçy and Maupertuis the requisite assistance was given, with the happiest of results.

The next series of campaigns in which the English bowman was to take part, were directed against an enemy different in every respect from the sturdy spearman of the Lowlands. In France those absurd perversions of the art of war which covered themselves under the name of Chivalry were more omnipotent than in any other country of Europe. The strength of the armies of Philip and John of Valois was composed of a fiery and undisciplined aristocracy, which imagined itself to be the most efficient military force in the world, but was in reality little removed from an armed mob.

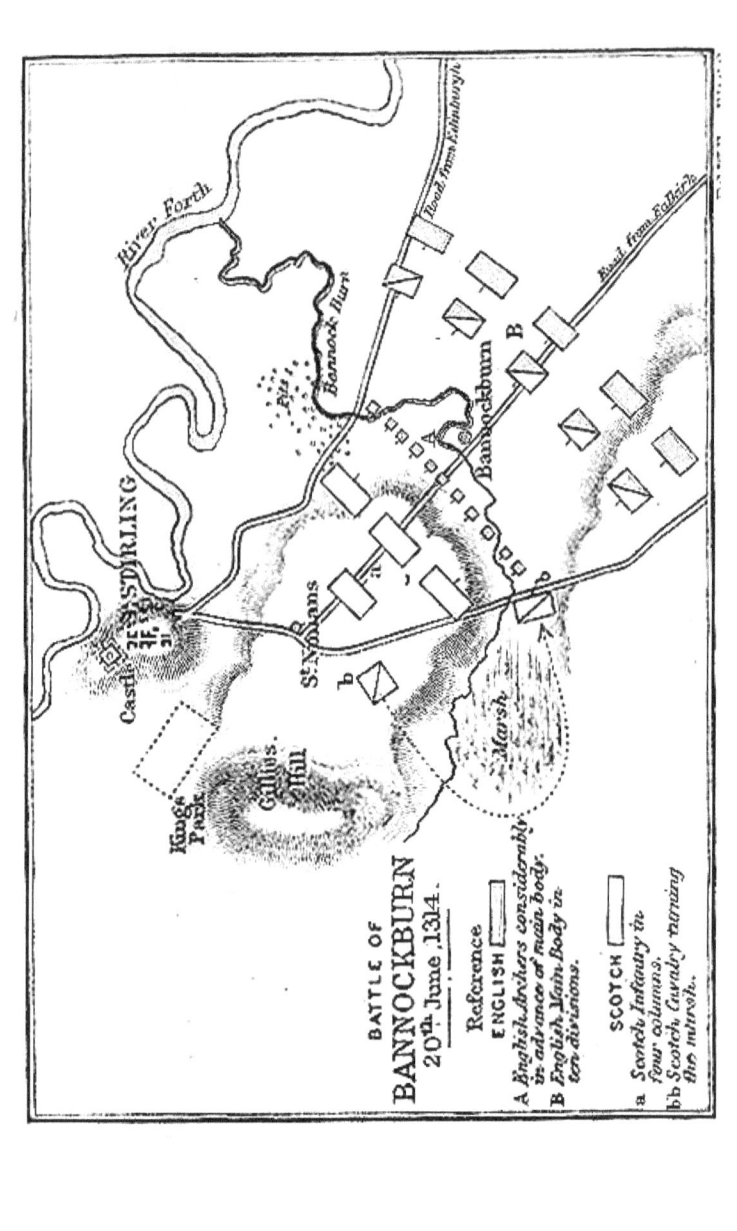

A system which reproduced on the battlefield the distinctions of feudal society, was considered by the French noble to represent the ideal form of warlike organisation. He firmly believed that, since he was infinitely superior to any peasant in the social scale, he must consequently excel him to the same extent in military value. He was, therefore, prone not only to despise all descriptions of infantry, but to regard their appearance on the field against him as a species of insult to his class-pride. The self-confidence of the French nobility—shaken for the moment by the result of Courtray—had re-asserted itself after the bloody days of Mons-en-Puelle and Cassel. The fate which had on those occasions befallen the gallant but ill-trained *burghers* of Flanders, was believed to be only typical of that which awaited any foot-soldier who dared to match himself against the chivalry of the most warlike aristocracy in Christendom. Pride goes before a fall, and the French noble was now to meet infantry of a quality such as he had never supposed to exist.

Against these presumptuous cavaliers, their mercenaries, and the wretched band of half-armed villains whom they dragged with them to the battlefield, the English archer was now matched. He was by this time almost a professional soldier, being usually not a pressed man, but a volunteer, raised by one of those barons or knights with whom the king contracted for a supply of soldiers. Led to enlist by sheer love of fighting, desire for adventures, or national pride, he possessed a great moral ascendancy over the spiritless hordes who followed the French nobility to the wars.

Historians, however, have laid too much stress on this superiority, real as it was. No amount of mere readiness to fight would have accounted for the English victories of the fourteenth century. Self-confidence and pugnacity were not wanting in the Fleming at Rosbecque or the Scot at Falkirk, yet they did not secure success. It was the excellent armament and tactics of our yeomanry, even more than their courage, which made them masters of the field at Crecy or Poictiers.

The long-bow had as yet been employed only in offensive warfare, and against an enemy inferior in cavalry to the English army. When, however, Edward III led his invading force into France, the conditions of war were entirely changed. The French were invariably superior in the numbers of their horsemen, and the tactics of the archer had to be adapted to the defensive. He was soon to find that the charging squadron presented as good a mark for his shaft as the stationary column of infantry.

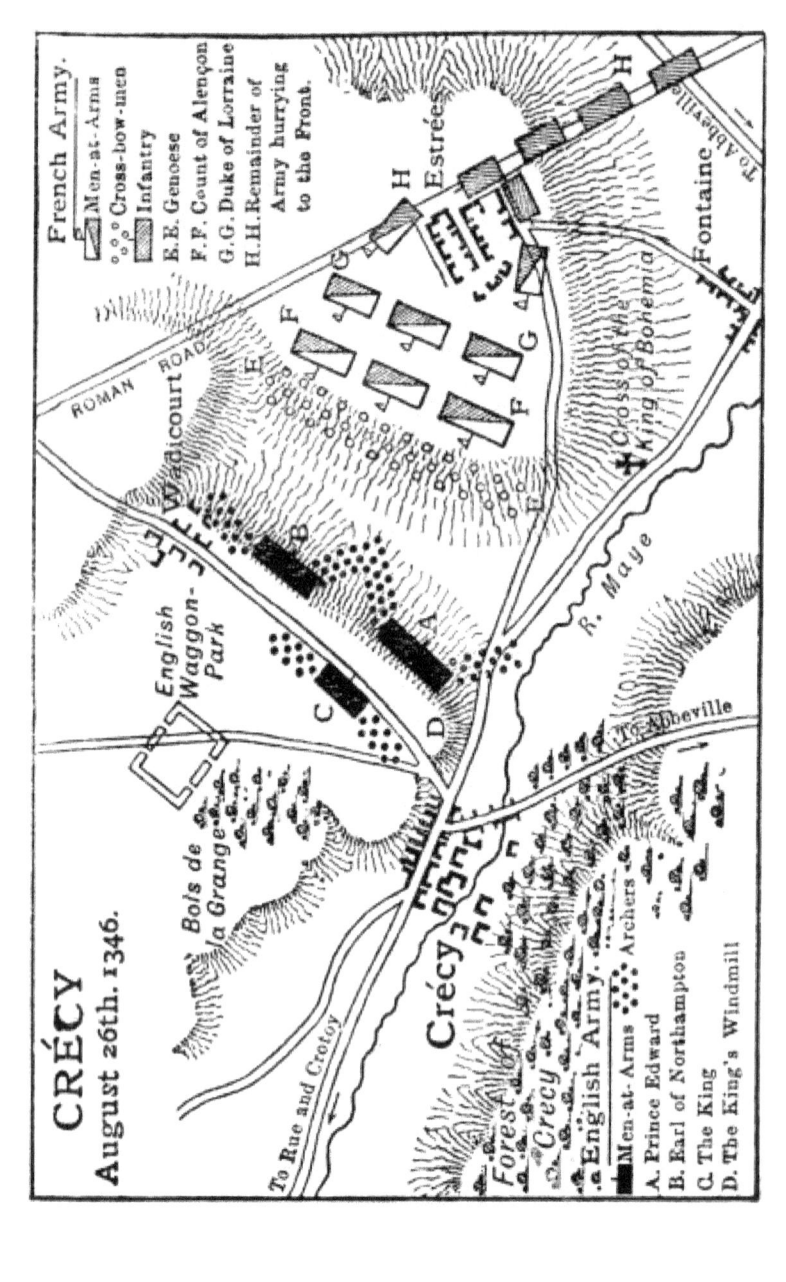

Nothing indeed could be more discomposing to a body of cavalry than a flight of arrows: not only did it lay low a certain proportion of the riders, but it caused such disorder by setting the wounded horses plunging and rearing among their fellows, that it was most effective in checking the impetus of the onset. As the distance grew shorter and the range more easy, the wounds to horse and man became more numerous: the disorder increased, the pace continued to slacken, and at last a limit was reached, beyond which the squadron could not pass. To force a line of long-bowmen by a mere front attack was a task almost as hopeless for cavalry as the breaking of a modern square. This, however, was a fact which the continental world had yet to learn in the year 1346.

The scientific method of receiving a charge of horsemen by archers flanked with supporting troops was first practised by Edward III at Creçy. When he determined to fight, he chose an excellent position on the gentle slope of a hill, whose flanks were protected by woods and a little brook, which also ran along the front of the line. Following the immemorial usage of the middle ages, the army was drawn up in three *battles*, of which the foremost was commanded by the Prince of Wales, the second by the Earl of Northampton, and the third by the king himself.

In the front *battle*, on which the greater part of the fighting was to fall, 2000 archers were flanked by two bodies of 800 dismounted men-at-arms, who stood in solid *phalanx* with their lances before them, to receive cavalry charges directed against the wings of the archers. The second line was formed in similar order, while between the two were ranged 1000 Welsh and Cornish light infantry armed with javelins and long knives. The reserve of 2000 archers and 700 mounted men occupied the summit of the hill.

Nothing could be more characteristic of the indiscipline of the French Army than the fact that it forced on the battle a day sooner than its leader had intended. On observing the English position, Philip and his marshals had determined to defer the conflict till the next morning, as the troops had been marching since daybreak. When, however, the order to halt reached the vanguard, the nobles at the head of the column believed that they were to be deprived of the honour of opening the fight, as they could see that some of the troops in the rear were still advancing.

They therefore pushed on, and, as the main-body persisted in following them, the whole army arrived so close to the English position

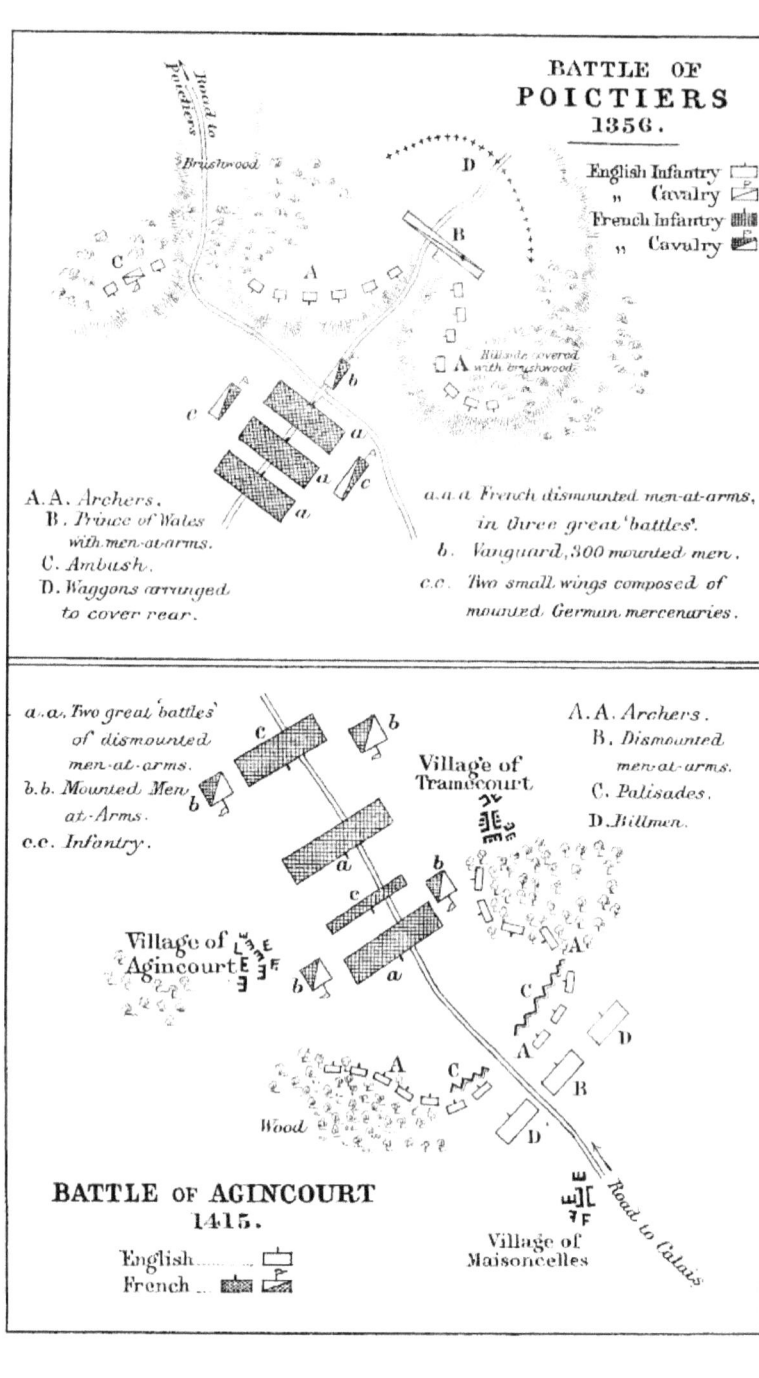

that a battle became unavoidable. The circumstances of that day have often been described: it is unnecessary to detail the mishap of the unfortunate Genoese crossbowmen, who were shot down in scores while going through the cumbrous process of winding up their arbalests. The fruitless charges of the cavalry against the front of the line of archers led to endless slaughter, till the ground was heaped with the bodies of men and horses, and further attempts to advance became impossible.

Only on the flanks was the charge pressed home; but when the counts of Flanders and Alençon came on the compact masses of dismounted cavalry who covered the wings of the archery, their progress was at an end. They fell before the line of lances which they were unable to break, and fared no better than their comrades in the centre. At evening the French fell back in disorder, and their whole army dispersed. The English had won the day without stirring a foot from their position: the enemy had come to them to be killed. Considerably more than a third of his numbers lay dead in front of the English line, and of these far the greater number had fallen by the arrows of the bowmen.

Creçy had proved that the archer, when adequately supported on his flanks, could beat off the most-determined charges of cavalry. The moral, however, which was drawn from it by the French was one of a different kind. Unwilling, in the bitterness of their class-pride, to ascribe the victory to the arms of mere peasants, they came to the conclusion that it was due to the stability of the *phalanx* of dismounted knights.

Bearing this in mind. King John, at the Battle of Poictiers, resolved to imitate the successful expedient of King Edward. He commanded the whole of his cavalry, with the exception of two corps, to shorten their spears, take off their spurs, and send their horses to the rear. He had failed to observe that the circumstances of attack and defence are absolutely different. Troops who intend to root themselves to a given spot of ground adopt tactics the very opposite of those required for an assault on a strong position. The device which was well chosen for the protection of Edward's flanks at Creçy, was ludicrous when adopted as a means for storming the hill of Maupertuis.

Vigorous impact and not stability was the quality at which the king should have aimed. Nothing, indeed, could have been more fatal than John's conduct throughout the day. The battle itself was most unnecessary, since the Black Prince could have been starved into sur-

CHARGE OF FRENCH KNIGHTS AT CREÇY

render in less than a week. If, however, fighting was to take place, it was absolutely insane to form the whole French Army into a gigantic wedge—where corps after corps was massed behind the first and narrowest line—and to dash it against the strongest point of the English front. This, however, was the plan which the king determined to adopt. The only access to the plateau of Maupertuis lay up a lane, along whose banks the English archers were posted in hundreds.

Through this opening John thrust his vanguard, a chosen body of 300 horsemen, while the rest of his forces, three great masses of dismounted cavalry, followed close behind. It is needless to say that the archers shot down the greater part of the advanced corps, and sent the survivors reeling back against the first *battle* in their rear. This at once fell into disorder, which was largely increased when the archers proceeded to concentrate their attention on its ranks. Before a blow had been struck at close quarters, the French were growing demoralised under the shower of arrows.

Seeing his opportunity, the prince at once came down from the plateau, and fell on the front of the shaken column with all his men-at-arms. At the same moment, a small ambuscade of 600 men, which he had placed in a wood to the left, appeared on the French flank. This was too much for King John's men: without waiting for further attacks about two-thirds of them left the field. A corps of Germans in the second 'battle' and the troops immediately around the monarch's person were the only portions of the army which made a creditable resistance. The English, however, were able to surround these bodies at their leisure, and ply bow and lance alternately against them till they broke up. Then John, his son Philip, and such of his nobles as had remained with him, were forced to surrender.

This was a splendid tactical triumph for the prince, who secured the victory by the excellence of the position he had chosen, and the judicious use made of his archery. John's new device for attacking an English army had failed, with far greater ignominy than had attended the rout of his predecessor's feudal chivalry at Creçy. So greatly did the result of the day of Poictiers affect the French mind, that no further attempt was made to meet the invader in a pitched battle during the continuance of the war. Confounded at the blow which had been delivered against their old military system, the *noblesse*. of France foreswore the open field, and sullenly shut themselves up in their castles, resolved to confine their operations to petty sieges and incursions.

The English might march through the length and breadth of the

Black Prince at Poictiers

land—as did the Earl of Lancaster in 1373—but they could no longer draw their opponents out to fight. Entrenched behind walls which the invader had no leisure to attack, the French allowed him to waste his strength in toilsome marches through a deserted country. Opposed as was this form of war to all the precepts of chivalry—which bid the good knight to accept every challenge—they were on the whole well suited to the exigencies of the time. The tactics of Charles V and Du Guesclin won back all that those of King John had lost. The English found that the war was no longer a means of displaying great feats of arms, but a monotonous and inglorious occupation, which involved a constant drain of blood and money, and no longer maintained itself from the resources of the enemy.

Common sense, and not aphorisms drawn from the customs of the tournament, guided the campaigns of Du Guesclin. He took the field, not in the spirit of adventure, but in the spirit of business. His end being to edge and worry the English out of France, he did not care whether that consummation was accomplished by showy exploits or by unobtrusive hard work. He would fight if necessary, but was just as ready to reach his goal by craft as by hard blows. Night surprises, ambuscades, and stratagems of every description were his choice, in preference to open attacks.

Provided with a continual supply of men by his 'free companies,' he was never obliged to hazard an engagement for fear that his forces might melt away without having done any service. This relieved him from that necessity to hurry operations, which had been fatal to so many generals commanding the temporary hosts of feudalism. The English were better fitted for winning great battles than for carrying on a series of harassing campaigns. Tactics, not strategy, was their forte, and a succession of petty sieges and inglorious retreats put an end to their ill-judged attempt to hold by force a foreign dominion beyond the Channel.

Du Guesclin, however, had only cleared the way for the re-appearance of the French *noblesse* on the field. Shut up in their castles while the free companies were re-conquering the country, they had apparently 'forgotten nothing and remembered nothing.' (The characteristic of their descendants in the second decade of the present century.) With the fear of the English no longer before their eyes, they at once reverted to their old chivalrous superstitions. The last years of the century were similar to the first: if Cassel reproduced itself at Rosbecque, a nemesis awaited the revived tactics of feudalism, and Nicopolis was a more disastrous edition of Courtray. Thirty years of anarchy, during the reign of an imbecile king, fostered the reactionary and unscientific tendency of the wars of the time, and made France a fit prey to a new series of English invasions.

If subsequent campaigns had not proved that Henry V was a master of strategical combinations, we should be inclined to pronounce his march to Agincourt a rash and unjustifiable undertaking. It is, however, probable that he had taken the measure of his enemies and gauged their imbecility, before he sacrificed his communications and threw himself into Picardy. The rapidity of his movements between the 6th and 24th of October, (320 miles in eighteen days; a rate surpassing any *continuous* marching recorded of late years), shows that he had that appreciation of the value of time which was so rare among mediaeval commanders, while the perfect organisation of his columns on the march proved that his genius could condescend to details.

Near St. Pol the French barred Henry's further progress with a great feudal army of sixty thousand combatants, of whom full fifteen thousand were mounted men of gentle blood. Like the two Edwards at Creçy and Maupertuis, the king resolved to fight a defensive battle, in spite of the scantiness of his force. He had with him not more than fourteen thousand men, of whom two-thirds were archers. The position chosen by Henry was as excellent in its way as could be desired; it had a frontage of not more than twelve hundred yards, and was covered by woods on either flank.

The land over which the enemy would have to advance consisted of ploughed fields, thoroughly sodden by a week of rain. The king's archers were sufficient in number not only to furnish a double line along the front of the army, but to occupy the woods to right and left. Those in the plain strengthened their position by planting in front of themselves the stakes which they habitually carried. In rear of the archers were disposed the rest of the force, the infantry with bills and pikes at the wings, the small force of men-at-arms in the centre.

The Constable of France committed as many faults in drawing up his array, as could have been expected from an average feudal nobleman. He could not resist the temptation of following the example set him by King John at Poictiers, and therefore dismounted three-fourths of his cavalry. These he drew up in two deep *battles*, flanked by small squadrons of mounted men. Behind the first line, where it could be of no possible use, was stationed a corps of 4000 cross-bowmen. The reserve was formed by a great mass of 20,000 infantry, who were relegated to the rear lest they should dispute the honour of the day with their masters. At eleven o'clock the French began to move towards the English position: presently they passed the village of Agincourt, and found themselves between the woods, and in the ploughed land.

Struggling on for a few hundred yards, they began to sink in the deep clay of the fields: horsemen and dismounted knight alike found their pace growing slower and slower. By this time the English archery was commencing to play upon them, first from the front, then from the troops concealed in the woods also. Pulling themselves together as best they could, the French lurched heavily on, sinking to the ankle or even to the knee in the sodden soil. Not one in ten of the horsemen ever reached the line of stakes, and of the infantry not a man struggled on so far. Stuck fast in the mud they stood as a target for the bowmen, at a distance of from fifty to a hundred yards from the English front.

After remaining for a short time in this unenviable position, they broke and turned to the rear. Then the whole English Army, archers and men-at-arms alike, left their position and charged down on the mass, as it staggered slowly back towards the second *battle*. Perfectly helpless and up to their knees in mire, the exhausted knights were cast down, or constrained to surrender to the lighter troops who poured among them, 'beating upon the armour as though they were hammering upon anvils.'

The few who contrived to escape, and the body of arbalesters who had formed the rear of the first line, ran in upon the second *battle*, which was now well engaged in the miry fields, just beyond Agincourt village, and threw it into disorder. Close in their rear the English followed, came down upon the second mass, and inflicted upon it the fate which had befallen the first. The infantry-reserve very wisely resolved not to meddle with their masters' business, and quietly withdrew from the field.

Few commanders could have committed a more glaring series of blunders than did the constable: but the chief fault of his design lay in attempting to attack an English Army, established in a good position, at all. The power of the bow was such that not even if the fields had been dry, could the French Army have succeeded in forcing the English line. The true course here, as at Poictiers, would have been to have starved the king, who was living merely on the resources of the neighbourhood, out of his position. If, however, an attack was projected, it should have been accompanied by a turning movement round the woods, and preceded by the use of all the arbalesters and archers of the army, a force which we know to have consisted of 15,000 men.

Such a day as Agincourt might have been expected to break the French *noblesse* of its love for an obsolete system of tactics. So intimately, however, was the feudal array bound up with the feudal scheme of society, that it yet remained the ideal order of battle. Three bloody defeats, Crevant, Verneuil, and the 'Day of the Herrings,' were the consequences of a fanatical adherence to the old method of fighting. On each of those occasions the French columns, sometimes composed of horsemen, sometimes of dismounted knights, made a desperate attempt to break an English line of archers by a front attack, and on each occasion, they were driven back in utter rout.

It was not till the conduct of the war fell into the hands of professional soldiers like Xaintrailles, La Hire, and Dunois, that these insane tactics were discarded. Their abandonment, however, was only the first step towards success for the French. The position of the country was infinitely worse than it had been in the days of Du Guesclin, since the greater part of the districts north of the Loire were not only occupied by the English, but had resigned themselves to their fate, and showed no desire to join the national party. A petty warfare such as had won back the lands of Acquitaine from the Black Prince, would have been totally inadequate to rescue France in 1428.

It is on this ground that we must base the importance of the influence of the Maid of Orleans. Her successes represent, not a new tactical system, but the awakening of a popular enthusiasm which was to make the further stay of the English in France impossible. The smaller country could not hold down the larger, unless the population of the latter were supine; when they ceased to be so, the undertaking—in spite of all military superiority—became impossible.

While ascribing the expulsion of the English from France to political rather than strategical reasons, we must not forget that the professional officers of the fifteenth century had at last discovered a method of minimizing the ascendancy of the English soldiery. When they found the invaders drawn up in a good defensive position, they invariably refrained from attacking them. There was no object in making the troops a target to be riddled with arrows, when success was almost impossible. Accordingly, the French victories of the second quarter of the century will be found to have resulted in most cases from attacking an English Army at a moment when it was on the march or in some other position which rendered it impossible for an order of battle to be rapidly formed.

Patay is a fair example of a conflict of this description; the battle was lost because Talbot when attacked was not immediately ready. Expecting to see the whole French Army arrive on the field and draw itself up in battle array, he paid no attention to the mere vanguard which was before him, and commenced falling back on the village of Patay, where he intended to form his line. La Hire, however, without waiting for the main-body to come up, attacked the retreating columns, and forced his way among them 'before the archers had time to fix their stakes.' (Viollet-le-Duc's *Tactique des Armées Françaises au Moyen Age*.) The superiority of the bow to the lance depended on the ability of the bearer of the missile weapon to keep his enemy at a distance. If once, by any accident, the cavalry got among their opponents, a mere melee ensued, and numbers and weight carried the day.

Such was the case on this occasion: La Hire having succeeded in closing, the battle resolved itself into a hand-to-hand struggle, and when the main-body of the French came up, the English were overpowered by numerical superiority. Such were the usual tactical causes of English defeats in the fifteenth century. The fall of the empire which Henry V had established in France was therefore due, from the military point of view, to the inadequacy of a purely defensive system to meet all the vicissitudes of a series of campaigns.

The commanders who had received the tradition of Agincourt and Poictiers disliked assuming the offensive. Accustomed to win success by receiving the enemy's attack on a carefully chosen ground, and after deliberate preparations, they frequently failed when opposed to officers who refrained on principle from assailing a position, but were continually appearing when least expected. In the open field or on the march, in camp or the town, the English were always liable to a sudden onslaught. They were too good soldiers to be demoralised, but lost the old confidence which had distinguished them in the days when the French still persisted in keeping up their ancient feudal tactics.

A fortunate chance has preserved for us, in the pages of Blondel's *Reductio Normanniae* a full account of the disastrous field of Formigny, the last battle but one fought by the English in their attempt to hold down their dominion beyond the Channel. The narrative is most instructive, as explaining the changes of fortune during the later years of the Great War. The fight itself—though destined to decide the fate of all Normandy—was an engagement on a very small scale. Some five thousand English, half of them archers, the remainder billmen for the most part, with a few hundred men-at-arms, had been collected for a desperate attempt to open the way to Caen.

In that town, the Duke of Somerset, commander of all the English armies in France, was threatened by an overwhelming host led by King Charles, in person. To draw together a force capable of taking the field all the Norman fortresses had been stripped of their garrisons, and such reinforcements as could be procured, some 2000 men at most, had been brought across from England. The relieving army succeeded in taking Valognes and forcing the dangerous fords of the Douve and Vire, but hard by the village of Formigny it was confronted by a French corps under the Count of Clermont, one of several divisions which had been sent out to arrest the march of the English.

Clermont's troops did not greatly exceed their enemies in number: they appear, as far as conflicting accounts allow us to judge, to have consisted of six hundred *lances garnis* (i. e. 3000 cavalry) and three thousand infantry. The obligation to take the offensive rested with the English, who were bound to force their way to Caen. Nevertheless, Sir Thomas Kyriel and Sir Matthew Gough, the two veterans who commanded the relieving army, refused to assume the initiative. The old prejudice in favour of fighting defensive battles was so strong that, forgetting the object of their expedition, they fell back and looked for a position in which to receive the attack of Clermont's troops.

Finding a brook lined with orchards and plantations, which was well calculated to cover their rear, they halted in front of it, and drew up their men in a convex line, the centre projecting, the wings drawn back so as to touch the stream. Three bodies of archers—each seven hundred strong—formed the main-*battle*; on the flanks of this force were stationed two *battles* of billmen, not in a line with the centre but drawn back from it, while these corps were themselves flanked by the small force of cavalry, which was formed close in front of the orchards and the brook. Clermont did not attack immediately, so that the archers had ample time to fix their stakes, according to their invariable custom, and the whole force was beginning to cover itself with a trench when the enemy at last began to move. (*Gladio ad usum fossarum verso, et ungue verrente tellurem concavant: et ante se campum equis inadibilem mira hostium astucia efficiebat.*—Blondel, iv.)

Through long experience the French had grown too wary to attack an English line of archers from the front: after feeling the position, they tried several partial assaults on the flanks, which were repulsed. Skirmishing had been going on for three hours without any decisive result, when Giraud 'master of the royal ordnance' brought up two culverins, and placed them in a spot from which they enfiladed the English line. Galled by the fire of these pieces, part of the archers rushed out from behind their stakes, and with the aid of one of the wings of billmen charged the French, seized the culverins, and routed the troops which protected them. If the whole of Kyriel's force had advanced at this moment the battle would have been won. (*Et si Anglici, incaepto conflictu praestantes, Gallos retrogresses insequi ausi fuissent,* etc.—Blondel, iv.)

But the English commander adhered rigidly to his defensive tactics, and while he waited motionless, the fate of the battle was changed. The troops who had charged were attacked by one of the flank *battles* of French men-at-arms, who had dismounted and advanced to win back the lost cannon: a desperate fight took place, while the English strove to drag the pieces towards their lines, and the enemy to recapture them. At last the French prevailed, and pushing the retreating body before them reached the English position. The archers were unable to use their arrows, so closely were friend and foe intermixed in the crowd of combatants which slowly rolled back towards them.

Thus, the two armies met all along the line in a hand-to-hand combat, and a sanguinary *mêlée* began. The fate of the battle was still doubtful when a new French force arrived in the field. The Counts of Richemont and Laval, coming up from St. Lo, appeared on the rear of the English position with 1200 men-at-arms. All Kyriel's troops were engaged, and he was unable to meet this new attack. His men recoiled to the brook at their backs, and were at once broken into several isolated corps.

Gough cut his way through the French, and reached Bayeux with the cavalry. But Kyriel and the infantry were surrounded, and the whole main-*battle* was annihilated. A few hundred archers escaped, and their commander, with some scores more, was taken prisoner, but the French gave little quarter, and their heralds counted next day three thousand seven hundred and seventy-four English corpses lying on the field.

★★★★★★

Fusis enim Anglorum bellis robusti quingenti sagittarii in hortum sentibus conseptum prosiliunt . . . ac inexorabili Gallorum ferocitate, ut quisque genu flexo arcum traderet, (in sign of surrender) *omnes (nec unus evasit) gladio confodiuntur.*—Blondel, iv.

★★★★★★

Seldom has an army suffered such a complete disaster: of Kyriel's small force not less than four-fifths was destroyed. What number of the French fell we are unable to ascertain: their annalists speak of the death of twelve knights, none of them men of note, but make no further mention of their losses. an English chronicler sarcastically observes:

> They declare what number they slew, but they write not how many of themselves were slain and destroyed. This was well-nigh the first foughten field they gat on the English, wherefore I blame them not; though they of a little make much, and set forth all, and hide nothing that may sound to their glory.—Grafton, *Henry VI*, year xxvii.

The moral of Formigny was evident: an unintelligent application of the defensive tactics of Edward III and Henry V could only lead to disaster, when the French had improved in military skill, and were no longer accustomed to make gross blunders at every engagement. Unless some new method of dealing with the superior numbers and cautious manoeuvres of the disciplined '*compagnies d'ordonnance*' of Charles VII could be devised, the English were foredoomed by their numerical inferiority to defeat. It was probably a perception of this fact which induced the great Talbot to discard his old tactics, and employ at his last fight a method of attack totally unlike that practised in the rest of the Hundred Years' War.

The accounts of the Battle of Chatillon recall the warfare of the Swiss rather than of the English armies. That engagement was a desperate attempt of a column of dismounted men-at-arms and billmen, flanked by archers, to storm an entrenched camp protected by artillery. The English—like the Swiss at Bicocca—found the task too hard for them, and only increased the disaster by their gallant persistence in attempting to accomplish the impossible.

The expulsion of the English from their continental possessions had no permanent effect in discrediting the power of the bow. The weapon still retained its supremacy as a missile over the clumsy arbalest with its complicated array of wheels and levers. It was hardly less superior to the newly-invented hand-guns and arquebuses, which did not attain to any great degree of efficiency before the end of the century.

The testimony of all Europe was given in favour of the long-bow. Charles of Burgundy considered a corps of three thousand English bowmen the flower of his infantry. Charles of France, thirty years earlier, had made the 'archer' the basis of his new militia, in a vain attempt to naturalise the weapon of his enemies beyond the Channel. James of Scotland, after a similar endeavour, had resigned himself to ill success, and turned the archery of his subjects to ridicule.

There are few periods which appear more likely to present to the enquirer a series of interesting military problems, than the years of the great struggle, in which the national weapons and national tactics of the English were turned against each other. The Wars of the Roses were, however, unfortunate in their historians. The dearth of exact information concerning the various engagements is remarkable, when we consider the ample materials which are to be found for the history of the preceding periods.

The meagre annals of William of Worcester, Warkworth, Fabyan, of the continuer of the *Croyland Chronicle*, and the author of the 'arrival of king Edward IV,' with the ignorant generalities of Whethamstede, are insufficiently supplemented by the later works of Grafton and Hall. When all has been collated, we still fail to grasp the details of most of the battles. Not in one single instance can we reconstruct the exact array of a Yorkist or a Lancastrian army. Enough, however, survives to make us regret the scantiness of the sources of our information.

That some considerable amount of tactical and strategical skill was employed by many of the English commanders is evident, when we analyse the general characteristics of their campaigns. The engagements show no stereotyped similarity of incident, such as would have resulted from a general adherence f to a single form of attack or defence. Each combat had its own individuality, resulting from the particular tactics employed in it. The fierce street-fight which is known as the first Battle of St. Albans, has nothing in common with the irregular skirmishing of Hedgeley Moor. The stormings of the fortified positions of Northampton and Tewkesbury bear no resemblance to the pitched Battles of Towton and Barnet. The superiority of tactics which won Bloreheath contrasts with the superiority of armament which won Edgecot Field.

Prominent among the features of the war stands out the generalship of King Edward IV. Already a skilful commander in his nineteenth year, it was he who at Northampton turned the Lancastrian position, by forcing the 'streight places' which covered the flank of the 'line of high banks and deep trenches' behind which the army of King Henry was sheltered. (Hall.)

A year later he saved a cause which seemed desperate, by his rapid march from Hereford to London; a march executed in the inclement month of February and over the miry roads of the South-Midland counties. The decision of mind which led him to attempt at all hazards to throw himself into the capital, won him his crown and turned the balance at the decisive crisis of the war. If, when settled on the throne, he imperilled his position by carelessness and presumption, he was himself again at the first blast of the trumpet. His vigorous struggle in the spring of 1470, when all around him were showing themselves traitors, was a wonderful example of the success of prompt action.

******

The whole country being disaffected and ready—as the events of the autumn proved—to revolt in favour of Warwick or Henry VI, the suppression of the Lincolnshire rebellion and the expulsion of the King-maker were remarkable achievements.

******

Nor was his genius less marked in his last great military success, the campaign of Barnet and Tewkesbury.

To have marched from York to London, threading his way among the hosts of his foes without disaster, was a skilful achievement, even if the treachery of some of the hostile commanders be taken into consideration. At Barnet, he showed that tactics no less than strategy lay within the compass of his powers, by turning the casual circumstance of the fog entirely to his own profit. The unforeseen chance by which each army outflanked the other was not in itself more favourable to one party than to the other: it merely tested the relative ability of the two leaders. But Edward's care in providing a reserve rendered the defeat of his left wing unimportant, while the similar disaster on Warwick's left was turned to such good account that it decided the day.

Warwick himself indeed, if we investigate his whole career, leaves on us the impression rather of the political wire-puller, '*le plus subtil homme de son vivant*,' as Commines called him, than of the great military figure of traditional accounts. Barnet being won, the second half of the campaign began with Edward's march to intercept Queen Margaret before she could open communications with her friends in South Wales. Gloucester was held for the king; his enemies therefore, as they marched north, were compelled to make for Tewkesbury, the first crossing on the Severn which was passable for them.

The Lancastrian feint on Chipping Sodbury was not ill-judged, but Edward rendered its effect nugatory by his rapid movements. Both armies gathered themselves up for a rush towards the all-important passage, but the king—although he had the longer distance to cover,

Lincolnshire Rebellion

and was toiling over the barren rolling country of the Cotswold plateau—outmarched his opponents. Men spoke with surprise of the thirty-two miles which his army accomplished in the day, without halting for a meal, and in a district where water was so scarce that the men were able to quench their thirst only once in the twelve hours. (This must have been in the Stroudwater, as Edward marched from Wooton-under-Edge by Stroud and Painswick on Cheltenham.)

By evening the king was within five miles of the Lancastrians, who had halted—utterly worn out—in the town of Tewkesbury. As they had not succeeded in crossing its ferry that night, they were compelled to fight next day, since there was even greater danger in being attacked while their forces were half across the Severn, and half still on the Gloucestershire side, than in turning to meet the king.

Queen Margaret's generals therefore drew up their forces on the rising ground to the south of the town, in a good position, where they had the slope of the hill in their favour, and were well protected by hedges and high banks. Edward, however, made no rash attempts to force his enemies' line: instead of delivering an assault he brought up cannon and concentrated their fire on one of the hostile wings. Somerset, who commanded there, was at last so galled that he came down from his vantage ground to drive off the gunners. His charge was for the moment successful, but left a fatal gap in the Lancastrian line. The centre making no attempt to close this opening, Edward was enabled to thrust his main-*battle* into it, and thus forced the position, and drove his enemies in complete disorder into the *cul-de-sac* of Tewkesbury town, where they were for the most part compelled to surrender.

★★★★★★

Somerset attributed this to treachery on the part of Lord Wenlock, commander of the centre-*battle*, who was a follower of Warwick and not an old Lancastrian. Escaping from the advancing Yorkists he rode up to Wenlock, and, without speaking a word, brained him with his battle-axe.

★★★★★★

It will at once be observed that the king's tactics on this occasion were precisely those which had won for William the Norman the field of Senlac. He repeated the experiment, merely substituting artillery for archery, and put his enemy in a position where he had either to fall back or to charge in order to escape the Yorkist missiles.

King Edward was by no means the only commander of merit whom the war revealed. We should be inclined to rate the Earl of

Salisbury's ability high, after considering his manoeuvre at Bloreheath. Being at the head of inferior forces, he retired for some time before Lord Audley; till continued retreat having made his adversary careless, he suddenly turned on him while his forces were divided by a stream, and inflicted two crushing blows on the two isolated halves of the Lancastrian army.

The operations before Towton also seem to show the existence of considerable enterprise and alertness on both sides. Clifford was successful in his bold attempt to beat up the camp and rout the division of Fitzwalter; but on the other hand, Falconbridge was sufficiently prompt to fall upon the victorious Clifford as he returned towards his main-body, and to efface the Yorkist disaster of the early morning by a success in the afternoon.

The same Falconbridge gave in the great battle of the ensuing day an example of the kind of tactical expedients which sufficed to decide the day, when both armies were employing the same great weapon. A snow-storm rendered the opposing lines only partially visible to each other: he therefore ordered his men to advance barely within extreme range, and let fly a volley of the light and far-reaching 'flight-arrows,' after which he halted.

The Lancastrians, finding the shafts falling among them, drew the natural conclusion that their enemies were well within range, and answered with a continuous discharge of their heavier 'sheaf-arrows,' which fell short of the Yorkists by sixty yards. Half an hour of this work well-nigh exhausted their store of missiles, so that the billmen and men-of-arms of Warwick and King Edward were then able to advance without receiving any appreciable damage from the Lancastrian archery. A stratagem like this could only be used when the adversaries were perfectly conversant with each other's armament and methods of war. In this respect, it may remind us of the device employed by the Romans against their former fellow-soldiers of the Latin League, at the battle of Vesuvius.

That the practice of dismounting large bodies of men-at-arms, which was so prevalent on the continent in this century, was not unknown in England we have ample evidence. The Lancastrian loss at Northampton, we are told, was excessive, 'because the knights had sent their horses to the rear' and could not escape. Similarly, we hear of Warwick dismounting to lead a charge, at Towton, and again—but on less certain authority—at Barnet. This custom explains the importance of the pole-axe in the knightly equipment of the fifteenth century: it was the weapon specially used by the horsemen who had descended to fight on foot. Instances of its use in this way need not be multiplied; we may, however, mention the incident which of all others seems most to have impressed the chroniclers in the fight of Edgecott-by-Banbury. Sir Richard Herbert 'valiantly acquitted himself in that, on foot and with his pole-axe in his hand, he twice by main force passed through the battle of his adversaries, and without any mortal wound returned.'

The engagement at which this feat of arms was performed was one notable as a renewed attempt of spearmen to stand against a mixed force of archers and cavalry. The Yorkists were utterly destitute of light troops, their bowmen having been drawn off by their commander, Lord Stafford, in a fit of pique, so that Pembroke and his North Welsh troops were left unsupported. The natural result followed: in spite of the strong position of the king's men, the rebels 'by force of archery caused them quickly to descend from the hill into the valley,' (Grafton), where they were ridden down as they retreated in disorder by the Northern horse.

Throughout the whole of the war artillery was in common use by both parties. Its employment was decisive at the fights of Tewkesbury and 'Lose-coat Field.' We also hear of it at Barnet and Northampton, as also in the sieges of the Northern fortresses in 1462-63. Its efficiency was recognised far more than that of smaller fire-arms, of which we find very scant mention.

******

Edward IV is said to have had in his employment in 1470 a small corps of Germans with 'hand-guns.' Better known is the band of 2000 hackbut-men which the Earl of Lincoln brought to Stoke in 1487. The name of their leader, Martin Schwart, survives in the ballads of the day.

******

The long-bow still retained its supremacy over the arquebus, and had yet famous fields to win, notably that of Flodden, where the old manoeuvres of Falkirk were repeated by both parties, and the pikemen of the Lowlands were once more shot down by the archers of Cheshire and Lancashire. As late as the reign of Edward VI we find Kett's insurgents beating, by the rapidity of their archery-fire, a corps of German hackbut-men whom the government had sent against them. Nor was the bow entirely extinct as a national weapon even in the days of Queen Elizabeth. Further, however, than the end of the great English Civil War of the fifteenth century, it is not our task to trace its use.

The direct influence of English methods of warfare on the general current of European military science ends with the final loss of dominion in France in the years 1450-53. From that period the occasions of contact which had once been so frequent become rare and unimportant. The Wars of the Roses kept the English soldier at home, and after their end the pacific policy of Henry VII tended to the same result. Henry VIII exerted an influence on Continental politics by diplomacy and subsidies rather than by his barren and infrequent expeditions, while in the second half of the century the peculiar characteristics of the English army of the fourteenth and fifteenth century had passed away, in the general change and transformation of the forms of the Art of War.

CHAPTER 7

Conclusion

We have now discussed at length the two systems of tactics which played the chief part in revolutionising the Art of War in Europe. The one has been traced from Morgarten to Bicocca, the other from Falkirk to Formigny, and it has been shown how the ascendancy of each was at last checked by the development of new forms of military efficiency among those against whom it was directed. While ascribing to the pikemen of Switzerland and the English archery the chief part in the overthrow of feudal cavalry—and to no small extent in that of feudalism itself—we must not forget that the same work was simultaneously being wrought out by other methods in other quarters of Europe.

Prominent among the experiments directed to this end was that of Zisca and his captains, in the great Hussite wars of the first half of the fifteenth century. In Bohemia, the new military departure was the result of social and religious convulsions. A gallant nation had risen in arms, stirred at once by outraged patriotism and by spiritual zeal; moved by a desire to drive the intruding German beyond the Erzgebirge, but moved even more by dreams of universal brotherhood, and of a kingdom of righteousness to be established by the sword. All Bohemia was ready to march, but still it was not apparent how the overwhelming strength of Germany was to be met.

If the fate of the struggle had depended on the lances of the Tzech nobility it would have been hopeless: they could put into the field only tens to oppose to the thousands of German feudalism. The undisciplined masses of peasants and *burghers* who accompanied them would, under the old tactical arrangements, have fared no better than the infantry of Flanders had fared at Rosbecque. But the problem of utilising those strong and willing arms fell into the hands of a man of genius. John Zisca of Trocnov had acquired military experience and hatred of Germany while fighting in the ranks of the Poles against the Teutonic knights. He saw clearly that to lead into the field men wholly untrained, and rudely armed with iron-shod staves, flails, and scythes fixed to poles, would be madness.

The Bohemians had neither a uniform equipment nor a national system of tactics: their only force lay in their religious and national enthusiasm, which was strong enough to make all differences vanish on the day of battle, so that the wildest fanatics were content to combine and to obey when once the foe came in sight. It was evident that the only chance for the Hussites was to stand upon the defensive, till they had gauged their enemies' military efficiency and learnt to handle their own arms.

Accordingly, we hear of entrenchments being everywhere thrown up, and towns being put in a state of defence during the first months of the war. But this was not all; in his Eastern campaigns Zisca had seen a military device which he thought might be developed and turned to account. There prevailed among the Russians and Lithuanians a custom of surrounding every encampment by a portable barricade of beams and stakes, which could be taken to pieces and transferred from position to position. The Russian princes habitually utilised in their wars such a structure, which they called a *goliaigorod* or moving fortress. Zisca's development of this system consisted in substituting for the beams and stakes a line of waggons, at first merely such as the country-side supplied, but afterwards constructed specially for military purposes, and fitted with hooks and chains by which they were fastened one to another. (See Denis, *Hus et la Guerre des Hussites* for description of Hussite tactics.)

It was evident that these war-waggons, when once placed in order, would be impregnable to a cavalry charge: however vigorous the impetus of the mail-clad knight might be, it would not carry him through oaken planks and iron links. The onset of the German horseman being the chief thing which the Hussites had to dread, the battle was half won when a method of resisting it had been devised. With the German infantry, they were competent to deal without any elaborate preparation.

It might be thought that Zisca's invention would have condemned the Bohemians to adhere strictly to the defensive in the whole campaign, as well as in each engagement in it: this, however, was not the case. When fully worked out, the system assumed a remarkable shape.

There was organised a special corps of waggoners, on whose efficiency everything depended: they were continually drilled, and taught to manoeuvre their vehicles with accuracy and promptness. At the word of command, we are told, they would form a circle, a square, or a triangle, and then rapidly disengage their teams, thus leaving the waggons in proper position, and only needing to be chained together. This done, they took up their position in the centre of the enclosure.

The organisation of the whole army was grounded on the waggon as a unit: to each was told off, besides the driver, a band of about twenty men, of whom part were pike-men and flail-men, while the remainder were armed with missile weapons. The former ranged themselves behind the chains which joined waggon to waggon, the latter stood in the vehicles and fired down on the enemy. From the first Zisca set himself to introduce fire-arms among the Bohemians: at length, nearly a third of them were armed with 'handguns,' while a strong train of artillery accompanied every force. A Hussite Army in movement had its regular order of march. Wherever the country was open enough it formed five parallel columns.

In the centre marched the cavalry and artillery, to each side of them two divisions of waggons accompanied by their complements of infantry. The two outer divisions were longer than the two which marched next the horsemen and the guns. The latter were intended—in the case of a sudden attack—to form the front and rear of a great oblong, of which the longer divisions were to compose the sides. To enable the shorter columns to wheel, one forward and the other backward, no great time would be required, and if the few necessary minutes were obtained, the Hussite order of battle stood complete.

To such perfection and accuracy was the execution of this manoeuvre brought, that we are assured that a Bohemian Army would march right into the middle of a German host, so as to separate division from division, and yet find time to throw itself into its normal formation just as the critical moment arrived. The only real danger was from artillery fire, which might shatter the line of carts: but the Hussites were themselves so well provided with cannon that they could usually silence the opposing batteries. Never assuredly were the tactics of the *laager* carried to such perfection; were the records of the Hussite victories not before us, we should have hesitated to believe that the middle ages could have produced a system whose success depended so entirely on that power of orderly movement which is usually claimed as the peculiar characteristic of modern armies.

KNIGHTS OF THE TEUTONIC PERIOD

But in the Bohemia of the fifteenth century, just as in the England of the seventeenth, fanaticism led to rigid discipline, not to disorder. The whole country, we are assured, was divided into two lists of parishes, which alternately put their entire adult population in the field. While the one half fought, the other remained at home, charged with the cultivation of their own and their neighbours' lands. A conscription law of the most sweeping kind, which made every man a soldier, was thus in force, and it becomes possible to understand the large numbers of the armies put into the field by a state of no great extent.

Zisca's first victories were to his enemies so unexpected and so marvellous, that they inspired a feeling of consternation. The disproportion of numbers and the inexperience of the Hussites being taken into consideration, they were indeed surprising. But instead of abandoning their stereotyped feudal tactics, to whose inability to cope with any new form of military efficiency the defeats were really due, the Germans merely tried to raise larger armies, and sent them to incur the same fate as the first host which Sigismund had led against Prague.

But the engagements only grew more decisive as Zisca fully developed his tactical methods. Invasion after invasion was a failure, because, when once the Bohemians came in sight, the German leaders could not induce their troops to stand firm. The men utterly declined to face the flails and pikes of their enemies, even when the latter advanced far beyond their rampart of waggons, and assumed the offensive. The Hussites were consequently so exalted with the confidence of their own invincibility, that they undertook, and often successfully carried out, actions of the most extraordinary temerity. Relying on the terror which they inspired, small bodies would attack superior numbers when every military consideration was against them, and yet would win the day.

Bands only a few thousand strong sallied forth from the natural fortress formed by the Bohemian mountains, and wasted Bavaria, Meissen, Thuringia, and Silesia, almost without hindrance. They returned in safety, their war-waggons laden with the spoil of Eastern Germany, and leaving a broad track of desolation behind them. Long after Zisca's death the prestige of his tactics remained undiminished, and his successors were able to accomplish feats of war which would have appeared incredible in the first years of the war.

When at last the defeat of the Taborites took place, it resulted from the dissensions of the Bohemians themselves, not from the increased

HUSSITES

efficiency of their enemies. The Battle of Lipan, where Procopius fell and the extreme party were crushed, was a victory won not by the Germans, but by the more moderate sections of the Tzech nation. The event of the fight indicates at once the weak spot of Hussite tactics, and the tremendous self-confidence of the Taborites.

After Procopius had repelled the first assaults on his circle of waggons, his men—forgetting that they had to do not with the panic-stricken hosts of their old enemies, but with their own former comrades,—left their defences and charged the retreating masses. They were accustomed to see the manoeuvre succeed against the terrorised Germans, and forgot that it was only good when turned against adversaries whose spirit was entirely broken. In itself an advance meant the sacrifice of all the benefits of a system of tactics which was essentially defensive. The weakness in fact of the device of the waggon-fortress was that, although securing the repulse of the enemy, it gave no opportunity for following up that success, if he was wary and retreated in good order.

This however was not a reproach to the inventor of the system, for Zisca had originally to seek not for the way to win decisive victories, but for the way to avoid crushing defeats. At Lipan, the moderate party had been beaten back but not routed. Accordingly, when the Taborites came out into the open field, the retreating masses turned to fight, while a cavalry reserve which far outnumbered the horsemen of Procopius, rode in between the circle of waggons and the troops which had left it. Thus, three-quarters of the Taborite Army were caught and surrounded in the plain, where they were cut to pieces by the superior numbers of the enemy. Only the few thousands who had remained behind within the waggon-fortress succeeded in escaping. Thus, was demonstrated the incompleteness for military purposes of a system which had been devised as a political necessity, not as an infallible recipe for victory.

The moral of the fight of Lipan was indeed the same as the moral of the fight of Hastings. Purely defensive tactics are hopeless when opposed by a commander of ability and resource, who is provided with steady troops. If the German princes had been generals and the German troops well-disciplined, the careers of Zisca and Procopius would have been impossible. Bad strategy and panic combined to make the Hussites seem invincible. When, however, they were met by rational tactics they were found to be no less liable to the logic of war than other men.

Long before the flails and hand-guns of Zisca's infantry had turned to rout the chivalry of Germany, another body of foot-soldiers had won the respect of Eastern Europe. On the battlefields of the Balkan Peninsula the Slav and the Magyar had learned to dread the slave-soldiery of the Ottoman *Sultans*. Kossova had suggested and Nicopolis had proved that the day of the unquestioned supremacy of the horseman was gone in the East as much as in the West. The *janissaries* of Murad and Bayezid had stood firm before desperate cavalry charges, and beaten them off with loss.

It is curious to recognise in the East the tactics which had won the Battles of Creçy and Agincourt. The *janissaries* owed their successes to precisely the same causes as the English archer. Their great weapon was the bow, not indeed the long-bow of the West, but nevertheless a very efficient arm. Still more notable is it that they carried the stakes which formed part of the equipment of the English bowman, and planted them before their line whenever an assault by cavalry was expected. Again and again—notably at Nicopolis and Varna—do we hear of the impetuous charge which had ridden down the rest of the Turkish array, failing at last before the 'palisade' of the *janissaries*, and the deadly fire of arrows from behind it.

The rest of the *janissary's* equipment was very simple: he carried no defensive arms, and wore only a pointed felt cap and a flowing grey tunic reaching to the knees. Besides his bow and quiver he bore a scimitar at his side and a *handjar* or long knife in his waist-cloth. Though their disciplined fanaticism made them formidable foes in close combat, it was not for that kind of fighting that the *janissaries* were designed. When we find them storming a breach or leading a charge, they were going beyond their own province. Their entire want of armour would alone have sufficed to show that they were not designed for hand-to-hand contests, and it is a noteworthy fact that they could never be induced to take to the use of the pike.

Like the English archery, they were used either in defensive positions or to supplement the employment of cavalry. Eastern hosts ever since the days of the Parthians had consisted of great masses of horsemen, and their weakness had always lain in the want of some steadier force to form the nucleus of resistance and the core of the army. Cavalry can only act on the offensive, yet every general is occasionally compelled to take the defensive.

The Ottomans, however, were enabled to solve the problem of producing an army efficient for both alike, when once Orchan had armed and trained the *janissaries*. The Timariot horsemen who formed the bulk of the Turkish army differed little from the cavalry of other Oriental states. Not unfrequently they suffered defeats; Shah Ismail's Persian cavaliers rode them down at Tchaldiran, and the Mamelukes broke them at Radama. If it had been with his feudal horse alone that the Turkish *Sultan* had faced the chivalry of the West, there is little reason to suppose that the conquest of the Balkan Peninsula would ever have been effected. Attacked in its own home the Hungarian—perhaps even the Servian—state could in the fourteenth century put into the field armies equal in numbers and individually superior to the Ottoman horsemen. (At the first Battle of Kossova we know that the allied Servians and Bosnians outnumbered the Turks.)

But the Servian and the Hungarian, like the Persian and the Mameluke, did not possess any solid and trustworthy body of infantry. To face the disciplined array of the *janissaries* they had only the chaotic and half-armed hordes of the national levy. To this we must ascribe the splendid successes of the *Sultans*: however, the tide of battle might fluctuate, the *janissaries* would stand like a rock behind their stakes, and it was almost unknown that they should be broken. Again, and again they saved the fortune of the day: at those few fights where they could not, they at least died in their ranks, and saved the honour of their corps. At the disaster of Angora, they continued to struggle long after the rest of the Turkish Army had dispersed, and were at last exterminated rather than beaten. No steadier troops could have been found in any part of Europe.

Perhaps the most interesting of Ottoman fights from the tactician's point of view was the second Battle of Kossova (1448). This was not—like Varna or Mohacs—an ill-advised attempt to break the Turkish line by a headlong onset. John Huniades, whom long experience had made familiar with the tactics of his enemy, endeavoured to turn against Sultan Murad his own usual scheme. To face the *janissaries,* he drew up in his centre a strong force of German infantry, armed with the hand-guns whose use the Hussites had introduced. On the wings the chivalry of Hungary were destined to cope with the masses of the Timariot cavalry. In consequence of this arrangement, the two centres faced each other for long hours, neither advancing, but each occupied in thinning the enemy's ranks, the one with the arbalest-bolt, the other with the bullet.

Meanwhile on the wings desperate cavalry charges succeeded each other, till on the second day the Wallachian allies of Huniades gave way before the superior numbers of the Ottomans and the Christian centre had to draw off and retire. So desperate had the fighting been, that half the Hungarian Army and a third of that of Murad was left upon the field. The tactical meaning of the engagement was plain: good infantry could make a long resistance to the Ottoman arms, even if they could not secure the victory. The lesson however was not fully realised, and it was not till the military revolution of the sixteenth century that infantry was destined to take the prominent part in withstanding the Ottoman. The *landsknechts* and hackbut-men of Charles V and Ferdinand of Austria proved much more formidable foes to the Sultans than the gallant but undisciplined light cavalry, (since the middle of the 15th century known as 'Hussars'), of Hungary. This was to a great extent due to the perfection of pike-tactics in the West. The Turks, whose infantry could never be induced to adopt that weapon, relied entirely on their firearms, and were checked by the combination of pike and hackbut. (Montecuculi notes that even in his day far into the 17th century, the Turk had not yet taken to the pike.)

It is noticeable that the *janissaries* took to the use of the firelock at a comparatively early date. It may have been in consequence of the effectiveness of Huniades' hand-guns at Kossova, that we find them discarding the arbalest in favour of the newer weapon. But at any rate the Ottoman had fully accomplished the change long before it had been finally carried out in Europe, and nearly a century earlier than the nations of the further East. (The arquebus and cannon were novelties to the Mamelukes as late as 1517, if we are to trust the story of Kait Bey.)

In recognising the full importance of cannon the *Sultans* were equally in advance of their times. The capture of Constantinople by Mahomet II was probably the first event of supreme importance whose result was determined by the power of artillery. The lighter guns of previous years had never accomplished any feat comparable in its results to that which was achieved by the siege-train of the Conqueror. Some decades later we find the *janissaries'* line of arquebuses supported by the fire of field-pieces, often brought forward in great numbers, and chained together so as to prevent cavalry charging down the intervals between the guns. (Richard III of England is said to have adopted this expedient at Bosworth.) This device is said to have been employed with great success against an enemy superior in the numbers of his horsemen, alike at Dolbek and Tchaldiran.

The ascendency of the Turkish arms was finally terminated by the conjunction of several causes. Of these the chief was the rise in central

LANDSKNECHTS

Europe of standing armies composed for the most part of disciplined infantry. But it is no less undoubted that much was due to the fact that the Ottomans after the reign of Soliman fell behind their contemporaries in readiness to keep up with the advance of military skill, a change which may be connected with the gradual transformation of the *janissaries* from a corps into a caste.

It should also be remembered that the frontier of Christendom was now covered not by one isolated fortress of supreme importance, such as Belgrade had been, but by a double and triple line of strong towns, whose existence made it hard for the Turks to advance with rapidity, or to reap any such results from success in a single battle or siege as had been possible in the previous century.

On the warfare of the other nations of Eastern Europe it will not be necessary to dwell. The military history of Russia, though interesting in itself, exercised no influence on the general progress of the Art of War. With the more important development of new tactical methods in South-Western Europe we have already dealt, when describing the Spanish infantry in the chapter devoted to the Swiss and their enemies.

All the systems of real weight and consideration have now been discussed. In the overthrow of the supremacy of feudal cavalry the tactics of the shock and the tactics of the missile had each played their part: which had been the more effective it would be hard to say. Between them however the task had been successfully accomplished. The military strength of that system which had embraced all Europe in its cramping fetters, had been shattered to atoms. Warlike efficiency was the attribute no longer of a class but of whole nations; and war had ceased to be an occupation in which feudal chivalry found its pleasure, and the rest of society its ruin.

The 'Art of War' had become once more a living reality, a matter not of tradition but of experiment, and the vigorous sixteenth century was rapidly adding to it new forms and variations. The middle ages were at last over, and the stirring and scientific spirit of the modern world was working a transformation in military matters, which was to make the methods of mediaeval war seem even further removed from the strategy of our own century, than are the operations of the ancients in the great days of Greece and Rome.

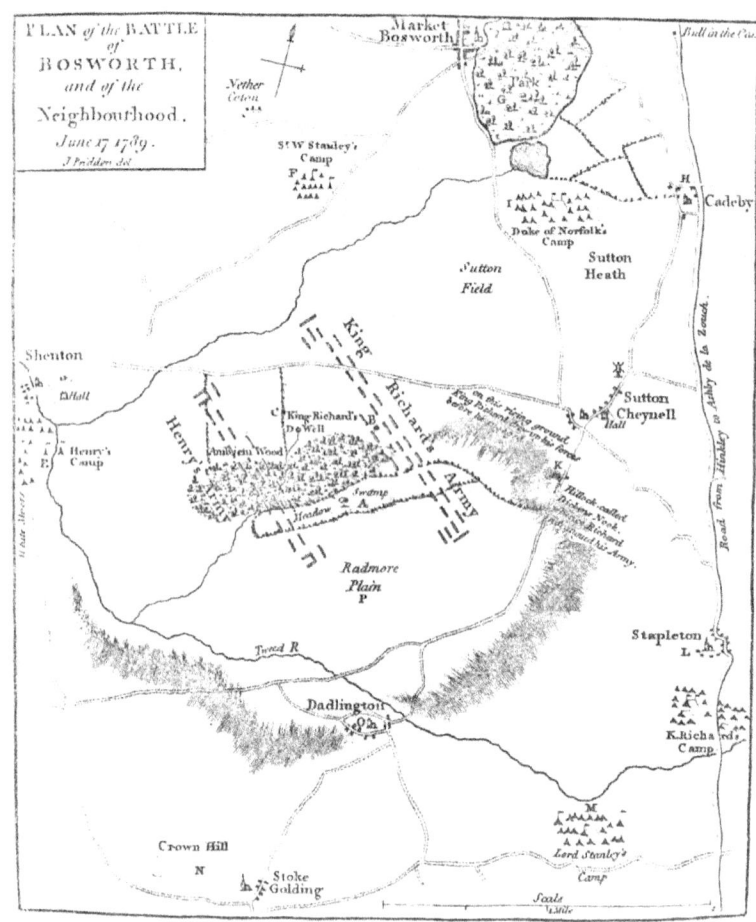

England and the Hundred Years War
1327-1485

Contents

From the Accession of Edward III. to the Fall of
Mortimer, 1327-1331   169

From the Fall of Mortimer to the Outbreak of the
Struggle with France and the Scottish War, 1330-1337   176

The First Stage of the Hundred Years' War, 1337-1349   185

From the Black Death to the Peace of Bretigny,
1349-1360   204

England under Edward III., 1360-1369   214

The Last Years of Edward III. 1369-1377   225

Richard II. the Years of the Minority 1377-1388   235

Richard II. 1388-1399   244

Henry IV. 1399-1413   251

Henry V. 1413-1422   260

Henry VI. 1422-1450   270

The Wars of the Roses 1450-1464   279

Richard the King-Maker and Edward the King
1464-1483   294

Richard III. 1483-1485   304

Chapter 1

From the Accession of Edward III. to the Fall of Mortimer, 1327-1331

On the seventh of January, 1327, the Parliament England, duly assembled at Westminster, declared that their king, Edward of Carnarvon, was deposed, and that they had chosen in his stead his eldest son, Edward Prince of Wales, to fill the vacant throne. In all the long annals of the nation no reign has ever commenced under such shameful auspices as the fifty years' rule of King Edward III. His miserable shiftless father had been deposed not so much by the will of the nation as by the private enmity of an unfaithful wife and a faction of disloyal barons. He had perhaps deserved to lose his crown, but not by such means, nor at the hands of such enemies.

Moreover, heavy as is the guilt which rests on the conspirators who dethroned him, the nation must take share in the blame. The mass of the baronage and the people stood aside while Queen Isabella and her adherents worked their wicked will on the king and his friends, and hardly a voice was raised to protest against the violence and cruelty which accompanied the revolution. The mob of London made itself the accomplice of the traitors by tearing to pieces Bishop Stapleton of Exeter, one of the late monarch's few faithful followers.

No complaint was made in Parliament concerning his murder, nor concerning the equally illegal execution of the Earl of Arundel and the two Despensers, whom the queen had slain without due process of law. No one protested, save four courageous prelates, when the wretched time-serving Archbishop Reynolds cried aloud that "the voice of the people was the voice of God", and pretending to take the cries of a noisy faction for the fiat of heaven, saluted the young Edward of Windsor as his king. So, with surroundings of the basest cruelty, hypocrisy, and cowardice, the new reign began.

Of those whose names appear in the shameful business of the fall of Edward II., the young boy in whose behalf the transaction was nominally carried out must bear the least blame. The new king was only fourteen years and two months old at his accession, having been born on November 13th, 1312. He had been neglected by his father, and had been of late in his mother's hands. There is no reason to believe that he suspected the cause which lay at the bottom of her actions, the hatred which she felt for her husband since she had become infatuated with the handsome, unscrupulous exile, Roger of Mortimer.

In after years we know that he felt bitter shame for the way in which he had been made the tool of his mother and her *paramour*. Meanwhile he accepted the situation, and freely set his hand to all the documents and deeds which they laid before him. He seems to have shown no anxiety about the fate of his father, when the dethroned king was removed from Kenilworth to Berkeley Castle, and put under gaolers who were bent on compassing his death. Of the sinister purpose of the transference he had no suspicion.

To guide the steps of the young king the Parliament, in January, 1327, appointed a Council of Regency of four earls, four bishops, and six barons. But from the first the real power lay in the hands of Queen Isabella; whose word was all-powerful with her son. Behind Isabella, unseen at first, but growing more and more evident as the months rolled on, was the will and influence of her favourite Mortimer. They kept the young Edward in their hands, secluded him as much as possible from intercourse with those who were not of their own faction, and endeavoured to the best of their ability to distract him from affairs of state. It was long before the baronage and the nation realized the true condition of affairs, and longer still before the king awoke to a consciousness of the shameful tutelage in which he was living.

At first public affairs were conducted with some decent semblance of constitutional government. The old charters of the realm were confirmed, lavish promises of good government were made to Parliament, and the persons who had been attainted in the reign of Edward II. were restored to their honours and estates. Mortimer's power was not yet openly shown, and moreover a new danger soon arose to distract the nation's attention. Less than three months after the young king's accession the Scots broke the truce which had been concluded with them in the year 1323, and came flooding over the border into Northumberland and Durham, savagely wasting the whole countryside as far as the Wear and the Tees.

King Robert Bruce was no longer at their head he was already stricken down by the leprosy of which he afterwards died; but two of his old companions in arms, Sir James Douglas and Randolf Earl of Murray, were leading the raiders—twenty thousand moss-troopers mounted on light Galloway nags—and showed themselves quite capable of carrying out their master's usual tactics.

To repel this invasion the young king himself took the field; Mortimer accompanied him, for he never let Edward stir far from his side. The whole feudal host and shire-levies of England followed them, but no good fortune attended their march. The Scots were found waiting behind the Tyne in a post too strong to be attacked in front; when the English by a toilsome march turned their flank, the agile enemy was found to have already decamped, and to have fallen back on a second position as strong as the first Mortimer would not risk an attempt to storm it—the memory of Bannockburn was still fresh in English memories—and again when he proceeded to move round to cut off the invaders from their retreat, Douglas avoided him by a night march and was in safety long ere his slowly-moving enemy had reached the point of vantage.

So, Edward's army followed the Scots for a time, always arriving too late, and always finding nothing but blazing villages and slaughtered cattle to show where the foe had been. The only striking incident in the campaign was a night attack which Douglas made with a small party on the royal camp. He cut his way far among the tents, and almost captured the young king, whose chaplain was slain in the scuffle; then he turned back and escaped unharmed. When the Scots were far on their way towards the Tweed, the English gave up the pursuit, and returned to Newcastle, utterly foiled and nearly starved by their long wanderings on the Northumbrian moors. Such was the inglorious introduction to war of the future victor of Sluys and Crecy. (Aug.-Sep., 1327.)

It was perhaps in consequence of this shameful failure to cope with the Scots, and in fear of the discontent that it might breed against the new government, that the queen and Mortimer resolved to murder the dethroned king. The strong constitution of Edward II. had resisted the harsh treatment and cruel privations to which he had been exposed in his prison at Berkeley. Finding that he did not show any signs of dying, they resolved to put an end to him. Their creatures were introduced into the castle at night, and secretly slew him (Sep. 21,

1327). His death was long concealed, and when it was divulged was attributed to natural causes, or a broken heart.

Another such campaign as the last, which recalled the worst misadventures of the reign of the late king, would have ruined the credit of the new government. Accordingly, the queen and Mortimer resolved to make peace at any price with the Scots. Negotiations with the Bruce were carried on all through the winter of 1327-8, and, since the English were resolved on coming to terms, reached a successful issue. By the Treaty of Northampton, which men called "The Shameful Peace", the independence of the northern realm was fully conceded (May 4, 1328). Edward was made to sign away all claims of feudal superiority of any kind over Scotland, so that for the first time since Anglo-Saxon days the King of Scots could call himself without dispute a wholly independent sovereign.

The Scottish regalia and royal treasures, together with the records of the realm, which Edward I. had brought to London, were restored: with them would have gone the famous "Stone of Scone", which still lies under the throne in Westminster Abbey, if a mob of Londoners had not fallen upon the workmen who were removing it. The King of England also promised to give his sister Joan, a little girl of seven, in marriage to Bruce's young son David. The Scots, on the other hand, promised to restore to their estates the barons of their realm who had been exiled for adhering to the English party, and to pay £20,000 in three instalments in satisfaction for all claims for damage and compensation for the harm which they had done in their many raids into England.

It was only when the danger from the Scottish war had been thus staved off that Mortimer began to show openly his haughty temper and his disregard of the laws. He got himself created Earl of March, and took upon him such state as no subject of the realm had ever before dared to display. A hundred and eighty men-at-arms followed him wherever he went, and were used to overawe any of the barons who showed a wish to oppose him. At the Parliament of Salisbury, in the autumn of 1328, he came with so many armed followers at his back that most of the other peers, who had been bidden to attend without large retinues, fled away to Winchester, fearing that they were about to be seized and imprisoned. Moreover, men began to take note of his relations with the queen; they were so much together and so familiar in their intercourse that the truth began to be suspected.

Nevertheless, it was to be three years before the favourite was overthrown, and ere his fall he was to do much more evil. Among the young king's nearest relatives were his two half-uncles Edmund Earl of Kent, and Thomas Earl of Norfolk, the sons of the second marriage of Edward I. These two princes joined with Henry Earl of Lancaster, who had done so much to overthrow the late king, in resenting Mortimer's influence. They felt that they, and not this upstart who ruled by the queen's favour, ought to have the final word in the governance of the realm. Kent took the lead, and drew upon himself the main brunt of Mortimer's anger. A disgraceful plot was laid to compass his destruction: he was secretly informed that his brother Edward II. was still alive, kept in strict confinement in Corfe Castle.

Such corroboration to the story was furnished by the governor of the place, that Kent was fully persuaded of its truth, and wrote letters to his supposed brother, in which he proposed to free him and replace him on the throne. The documents were promptly passed on to Mortimer, who, when they were once in his hands, seized Kent's person, tried him for high treason, and had him beheaded the moment that he was condemned. The young king was induced to set his hand to the death-warrant by being told that his uncle's plan included his own murder by poison. Only eight days elapsed between the arrest and the execution, so that Kent's friends had no time to attempt anything in his behalf. (March, 1330.) Mortimer seized upon his victim's lands, which, added to the plunder of the Despensers, which was already in his hands, made him almost the wealthiest personage in the realm.

Kent had been well liked by the baronage and people; he was a courteous, kindly, and liberal prince, against whom no one bore any grudge. Hence his fate provoked bitter murmurings, and awoke the nation to a sense of its disgraceful plight. The guilty relations of the queen and Mortimer were growing daily more evident as long impunity made them less cautious. The true story of the death of Edward II. was also beginning to be bruited about. Hence discontent grew every day more marked, and Mortimer's cruel plot against Kent may be said to have brought about his own ruin. When men began to ask each other whether the late king had been dethroned merely in order that a vicious Frenchwoman and a bloodthirsty upstart might rule England at their will, it was evident that the end was drawing near.

The blow, however, was not to be dealt by any popular rising, but by an unexpected hand. The young himself was at last moved to action. For more than three years he had let himself be led by his mother and Mortimer, but at last he was developing a will of his own. He was now eighteen, had married a wife, the fair and virtuous Philippa of Hainault, and had just become the father of a son—Edward, so well known afterwards as the "Black Prince". He at last began to use his own eyes, and to take counsel of others than his mother's partisans. Gradually he began to realize that he was but the tool of Mortimer. Accordingly, he prepared to make an end of this state of things.

In October, 1330, the Court was staying at Nottingham, and the queen and Mortimer lay in the castle, whose gates were well guarded by their retinue. But the king opened his purpose to the governor, Sir William Eland, who feared to disobey him, and consented to show him a secret passage by which he could enter without rousing Mortimer's followers. At midnight Edward, accompanied by his friend William, Lord Montacute, (afterwards Earl of Salisbury), and a few more armed men, was let into the castle, and made for the apartments of the favourite. Mortimer was surprised as he sat conferring with the Bishop of Lincoln, and seized before he could offer resistance. But a scuffle ensued, swords were drawn, and two knights were slain before the king's party got the upper hand. The queen burst out of her chamber and threw herself at her son's knees, begging him to "spare her gentle Mortimer", but she was dragged away, and the earl was cast into bonds. (October 19, 1330.)

A month later the king called Parliament together, and put the earl on his trial before the peers for murdering Edward II., for overawing the Parliament of Salisbury by armed force, for usurping several royal castles and manors without legal warrant, and for having applied to his own private expenses a large part of the £20,000 paid by the Scots. Without troubling themselves to go through the form of a trial the peers voted that:

> All the charges contained in the articles of accusation were notoriously true, and that the Earl Marshal should take custody of Roger, Earl of March, and execute him as a traitor and enemy of the king and realm.

Accordingly, he was hung, drawn, and quartered at Tyburn, on Nov. 29th, 1330. His chief councillor, Sir Simon Bereford, was also condemned and put to death. John Maltravers and Thomas Gurney, the underlings who had actually murdered King Edward II., were not captured: they were proclaimed traitors, and a price set on their heads. Gurney was soon afterwards apprehended in Spain by King Alfonso of Castile and sent homeward in chains; he died on the way, and thus escaped punishment.

The fate of the guilty queen-dowager remained to be settled. After consideration, Edward III. resolved to do no more than relegate his mother to her manor of Castle-Rising, which she was never allowed to quit. She was granted the ample allowance of 3000 *marks*, and not put in strict confinement. She survived nearly thirty years, and only died in 1358.

Thus, all traces of the shameful misgovernment of the years 1327-1330 were swept away. The heirs of the Earl of Kent and other victims of Mortimer were restored to their honours and lands. Pardons were made out for all who had resisted the favourite, and the officials whom he had appointed were obliged to take out fresh grants of their places. A new leaf in the history of the nation was turned over, and the young king began to rule as well as to reign.

CHAPTER 2

From the Fall of Mortimer to the Outbreak of the Struggle with France and the Scottish War, 1330-1337

When the sinister figures of Roger Mortimer and Isabella of France disappeared from the scene, England entered on a more honourable and fortunate period of her history. Everything was now in favour of the young king, and it was to be many years before he forfeited the popularity which he had won by avenging his father's murder and freeing the realm from its shameful bondage. Edward was a handsome, courteous, and generous prince, largely gifted with all the outward graces that win men's hearts. He was an accomplished knight, as distinguished in the tournament in his youth as on the battlefield in his riper years.

He loved splendour and display, was a mighty builder, a friend of music and the arts, and a patron of literary men. But though he did not show any of his father's weakness, he was deeply tainted with the moral failings of his ancestor Henry III.,—selfishness, and a chronic incapacity to keep his promises or to pay his debts. All through his life he disregarded the noble watchword of his grandfather Edward I.,— *Pactum Serva*, "abide by the plighted word", and displayed an entire want of sensibility of the sanctity of private pledges or public treaties. More than once he proved that he could be cruel when provoked.

In his later years, he was destined to show signs of failing vigour long before his due time, and fell into the power of favourites, male and female, who pandered to his failings, and made him even more untrue to the kingly ideal than he had been in early life. His worst fault as a practical ruler was his entire incapacity for understanding finance; he loved the stir and glory of battle, and could never be brought to see that war is the most expensive of luxuries, that great armies must be fed and paid as well as put into the field.

If he had possessed a sterner soul he would have grown into a tyrant, but though hot-tempered and domineering he was neither vindictive nor capable of long-planned and long-enduring schemes of oppression. He was selfish and thoughtless rather than malevolent, and his love of a chivalrous reputation often served him in default of a conscience. England has had many worse kings, and from the constitutional point of view she fared not unprosperously under him. His ambition and his thriftlessness were always causing him to apply to his loving subjects for new grants of money, and money was not given him till he paid for it by confirming charters and conceding privileges to his Parliament.

In 1330, however, Edward had not developed the baser sides of his character, and his subjects were well satisfied with him. During the early years of his personal rule the realm was settling down and recovering somewhat of its peace and good governance. In Mortimer's time disorders of all kinds had been rife, ranging up to the worst forms of open murder and private war. We read, for example, how in 1328 Sir Thomas Wyther, meeting his enemy Robert Lord Holland, in Henley Wood, near Windsor, fell upon him, slew him, and cut off his head, which he carried off on his spear.

In 1329 William de la Zouche tried to make valid his pretensions to some of the De Clare estates by raising a great band of his retainers and besieging Caerphilly, the strongest and largest castle of South Wales. We hear of heiresses abducted, manors sacked, and blackmail extorted. Such excesses were put down when there was once more a king who ruled, and served as the fountain of justice. The cessation of the Scottish war allowed the much-ravaged northern shires time to recover themselves. Commerce, too, began to revive, though we still hear of many complaints as to the misdoing of French and Flemish pirates on the high seas.

There were, however, two outstanding questions which were destined to lead to trouble at no very distant date. The first was a dispute as to the homage due to the French crown for the English possessions in Aquitaine. The elder branch of the old royal house of France had lately died out in the male line (1328), and Philip of Valois, the representative of a younger stock, now reigned at Paris. Edward was, through his mother, descended from the elder line, and seems from the first to have had some notion of refusing to acknowledge Philip as the rightful tenant of the throne. But he had for the time laid the idea aside, and twice did homage to the new king for his Duchy of Aquitaine and County of Ponthieu.

★★★★★★

Ponthieu, a small county at the mouth of the Somme, had come to Edward II. through his mother Eleanor of Castile, whose mother, Joanna, Queen of Castile, had been Countess of Ponthieu in her own right. But the district had been intermittently overrun and occupied by the French.

★★★★★★

Philip, however, was not satisfied with the terms on which homage had been done to him. He proved a bad neighbour, encroached on border lands, encouraged the Gascon barons to make appeals to Paris, and refused to surrender the county of Agenois, which had been seized from Edward II. a few years before. It seems that he had in his mind the expulsion of the English from Southern France, and was biding his time for putting the scheme into operation. For the present, nothing but small bickerings along the frontier resulted from his ill-will.

A dispute with Scotland was destined to lead to troubles at a much earlier date, and ultimately to involve King Edward in a war with France also. Its origin lay in one of the clauses of the "Shameful Peace" of Northampton. Robert I. had promised to give back their lands to the unfortunate barons of the English party in Scotland, who had adhered to Edward II. even after Bannockburn, and had been entirely driven out of the realm. But the Bruce died in 1329, and the regents who ruled for his young son David II. proved unable or unwilling to carry out this clause of the treaty. The estates had been, for the most part, seized by or granted out to barons of the nationalist party, who had no intention of surrendering them to their previous owners, whom they regarded as traitors and enemies of their own country.

Accordingly, the "Disinherited", as the exiles were called, found themselves excluded from the promised lands, and wandered disconsolately about England. The chief of them were Gilbert Umphraville, Earl of Angus, David of Strathbogie, Earl of Athole, Walter Comyn, and Henry Lord Beaumont, an English baron who had married the heiress of the great earldom of Buchan. Finding themselves permanently deprived of their rights, these nobles plotted to restore themselves by force of arms, and sent to France for Edward Balliol, the son of the unfortunate John Balliol, who had been king of Scotland in 1292-96. He, like them, had much to recover; not only had he a plausible claim to the Scottish crown, but he regretted the broad Balliol lands in Galloway which his father had lost.

Scotland was known to be divided into factions, and ill-ruled by the boy-king's representatives: by a bold and sudden stroke the "Disinherited" hoped to place Balliol on the throne, and win back their old baronies and earldoms. Balliol and his friends, therefore, began secretly to muster their adherents, and to raise mercenary troops. Their action came to King Edward's ears, and he, very properly, refused to allow them to cross the border, and sent orders to his Wardens of the Marches to resist them even by force of arms if they should try to cross the Tweed. Turned back from the land-route, the adventurers hired ships and embarked at Ravenspur, on the Humber, with a little army of 500 men-at-arms and 2000 foot. The rank and file were nearly all English-born, and mainly consisted of archers.

The "Disinherited" landed at Kinghorn, in Fife, and marched on Perth; on their way, they were met at the passage of the Earn by the regent, Donald Earl of Mar, with an army at least five times the strength of their own small force. Nevertheless, they won a surprising victory. Crossing the river by night, they attacked the Scottish camp. The regent came up against them with his host arranged in three heavy columns of pikemen, such as Wallace had led at Falkirk and Bruce at Bannockburn. The invaders ranged themselves on the hillside of Dupplin Muir, with the men-at-arms dismounted in a solid clump in the centre, and the archers in a thin semi-circular line on the flanks.

The Scots climbed the hill and attacked the mailed men who stood beneath Balliol's banner, neglecting the bowmen as unworthy of their notice. But while they were pushing the men-at-arms uphill by force of numbers, the arrow-shower beat so fiercely upon their flanks that they were finally brought to a standstill. The slaughter in the side columns was so great that they fell in upon the main column in disorder, and stopped its advance. Every moment that they stood halted, brought new losses from the pitiless rain of shafts, and at last the great mass broke up and rolled down the hill in rout. The "Disinherited" mounted their horses to pursue, and made a cruel slaughter of the fugitives. Among the slain were the regent, Donald of Mar, three earls, and seventy knights, besides many thousands of foot-soldiers.

The blow inflicted by the defeat of Dupplin was so heavy that Balliol had no difficulty in seizing Perth and Stirling, and getting himself crowned at Scone as king of Scotland, while the young David Bruce fled overseas to France and took refuge with King Philip. Balliol at once wrote to Edward III. announcing that he had won back his realm, and was prepared to hold it as a fief of the English crown as his ancestors had been wont to do. He offered, as an extra inducement to secure King Edward's support, to surrender the important and much-disputed frontier post of Berwick.

The English monarch had summoned his Parliament to discuss the acceptance of these terms, when news came which put a new face upon affairs. Balliol had lost his realm as quickly as he had gained it. Though a good soldier he was not himself a man of much mark or influence, and his followers, the Disinherited Lords, had upset all the internal arrangements of Scotland by violently taking possession of their lost estates. The Bruce's party took advantage of the general unrest and discontent to form a conspiracy. As Balliol lay at Annan, near Dumfries, with but a small guard around him, he was suddenly attacked by John Earl of Murray, and Sir Archibald Douglas. They fell upon him at midnight, scattered or slew his retainers, and chased him to the gates of Carlisle. (Dec. 16, 1332.) Immediately risings set in all over Scotland, and the new king's followers were hunted out of the country. Archibald Douglas was installed as regent for the absent David II., and his authority was everywhere recognised. Plundering parties of Scottish moss-troopers soon began to cross the Cheviots and resumed the raids of the days of Robert Bruce.

Edward III. had now to choose between David II. and Balliol. He was young, enterprising, and ambitious, and much set on avenging the discomfiture he had suffered during the campaign of 1327. Accordingly, he resolved to recognise Balliol as king, to accept his homage and the cession of Berwick, and to restore him to the Scottish throne by force of arms. The recent raids into Northumberland supplied him with a plausible *casus belli*.

Accordingly, in March 1333 he gathered a great army and marched for the border. Balliol and his friends the "Disinherited" joined him with their retainers, and siege was laid to Berwick. For ten weeks, the strong harbour-town held out, but at last food grew scarce within the walls, and the garrison offered to surrender if not relieved by the month of July, and gave hostages for the performance of their promise. Before the appointed day a small body of troops under Sir William

Keith slipped between the besiegers' lines and succeeded in entering the place, though they could do nothing to drive off the English. They brought news, however, that the regent was at hand with the whole armed force of Scotland at his back. The governor held that Keith's appearance relieved him from his obligation to open the gates, and held out when the fixed period had elapsed. The English king saw the matter otherwise, and when entrance was still refused him, cruelly hung the hostages in front of the castle gate.

Some ten days later the army of succour came in sight. Douglas had brought with him a formidable army of 30,000 men, and the English were forced to choose whether they would fight or raise the siege. Edward left part of his army in his lines, to blockade the town, and took post with the rest on Halidon Hill, a rising ground three miles north of Berwick, which commands the road from Dunbar and Edinburgh. It was a good position, with a marshy bottom before it and a line of wood along its brow. The king drew up his army in three corps at the head of the slope: he himself took the centre, his brother, John of Eltham, the right, Edward Balliol the left.

In each division, the men-at-arms sent their horses away and stood on foot in a solid body in the middle, while two wings of archers stretched out on each flank of them. This was the same array that the "Disinherited" had used at Dupplin, and we cannot doubt that the English king chose it on the advice of Balliol and his friends, the victors in the earlier fight.

This order of battle proved as effective on the second occasion as on the first. The Scots were forced to attack, under pain of seeing Berwick succumb in a few days: accordingly, the regent formed his host in three heavy columns, just as Donald of Mar had done at Dupplin, and launched them against the English position. They were much delayed by the marsh, but waded through it and began to ascend the opposite slope. But the arrow-shower beat so fiercely upon them that it took them a long time to climb the hill, each party that forced its way to the head of the column being shot down ere it could close.

Only at one or two points did the Scots succeed in reaching the brow, and getting to hand-strokes with the English men-at-arms. They were repelled on each occasion, for their order was lost, and the main body never reached the battle-front. At last they recoiled back to the marsh, the English following them and making great slaughter of the fugitives. The regent was slain, as were also the Earls of Carrick, Menteith, Lennox, Strathern, and Sutherland, with ten thousand of their followers. This disaster came upon them because they had neglected the wise precepts of Robert Bruce, and attacked a strong position well lined with archers, to whose missiles they had nothing to oppose. (July 19, 1333.)

Berwick surrendered next day, and since no Scottish army was any longer in the field, Edward was able to march into the Lowlands unopposed, and replaced his dependant Balliol on the throne. A permanent pacification might perhaps have followed but for the English king's greed: he bade Balliol sign a treaty ceding to him not only Berwick but all the Border shires of Scotland as far as Edinburgh. (*Viz.*, the three Lothians, Berwick. Roxburgh, Peebles, Selkirk, and Dumfries). The Scots could not tolerate the partition of their realm, and rose again to drive out their new master. Balliol had to fly to Berwick and seek English aid once more; it was given him with an unsparing hand, and he was twice able to reconquer the whole land as far as Perth. (1334-1335.)

Balliol was still maintaining a precarious hold upon the Scottish crown, when a new series of complications began to arise, which were destined to draw English attention away from the Scottish war. Philip of France had never ceased to give trouble on the frontier of the English possessions in Aquitaine. He now began to send aid, at first with some pretence of secrecy, but soon with perfect openness, to the patriotic party in Scotland. French men-at-arms crossed the North Sea to fight against Balliol, and French privateers cruised along the eastern coast of England, capturing merchant vessels and gradually making trade impossible.

David Bruce dwelt at the court of Paris, and sent his partisans in the North promises of continued aid from his ally. At last rumours reached King Edward that considerable squadrons were being prepared at Calais and in the Norman ports for an actual invasion of England. Credibility was lent to the report by piratical raids made by parties of French in Jersey, Guernsey, and the Isle of Wight. It was obvious that if Edward continued to bestow all his attention on Scotland he might ere long find himself attacked in the rear. (1336.)

Accordingly, Edward set to work to face the prospect of war with France, and began to send ambassadors to the Emperor Lewis of Bavaria and the princes of the Netherlands, to secure alliances with them against King Philip. By the promise of great subsidies, he bought the aid of the Dukes of Brabant and Guelders and the Counts of Holland and Hainault. He also negotiated a league with the Flemish cities, who were greatly discontented with their ruler, Louis Count of Flanders, a devoted vassal and supporter of the French king.

The Flemings had no wish to make war on England, with which they transacted an immense trade, buying the fine English wool and making it into cloth, which they sold all over Northern Europe. When Count Louis seized, and imprisoned all the English merchants he could lay hands on (Oct. 1336), his subjects were so enraged with him for stirring up war, that they entered into correspondence with King Edward, and offered to aid him even against their own feudal lord. The lead in the rising was taken by Jacob van Artevelde, the famous brewer of Ghent, a wealthy citizen who had turned demagogue, and ruled the guilds of his native town with a despotic sway by means of his ready tongue and his strong will. The count's power in Flanders was small compared with that of his turbulent subject.

Emboldened by the knowledge that he would not lack allies on the Continent, Edward began to treat the French king much as Philip had been treating him for the last four years. He gave shelter to Robert Count of Artois, a French prince of the royal house who had been driven into exile by his cousin, and began to gather together a fleet in order to pay back the late piratical raids on the English coast. In October, 1337, he made war inevitable by laying formal claim to the crown of France, and denouncing Philip as a usurper. It is said that he took this step at the instigation of the Flemings, who told him that they had sworn allegiance to the King of France, and that if he assumed the title it would of course be due to him and not to the representative of the line of Valois.

Edward's claim was a very poor one. He represented that his mother was sister to Charles IV., the last king of the elder line, and that he therefore should have succeeded to the throne in 1328 rather than Philip, who was but cousin to King Charles.

But there was no instance in French history of right to the crown being transmitted by a female, and the peers of France had ruled that the nearest male heir should succeed. There being no precedent to guide them, they based their decision on a text in the Salic Law, a code of the ancient Franks, which laid down that landed property should go to the male representative of the house. The case had never before arisen in France, for since the house of Capet came to the throne in the 10th century every king had left sons behind him.

Undoubtedly the French had the best right to decide who should reign over them, and their voice had unanimously been given in favour of Philip. Edward had practically surrendered his claim when in 1329 he had done homage to his cousin for the duchy of Aquitaine; it was absurd to exhume it eight years later. Moreover, even if it were granted that rights might pass through a female, his case was a bad one. For his mother's brothers had daughters whose title was better than that of their aunt. On Edward's principles the rightful king of France should have been Charles of Navarre, the son of the daughter of Philip V., his mother's eldest brother. (See table following.)

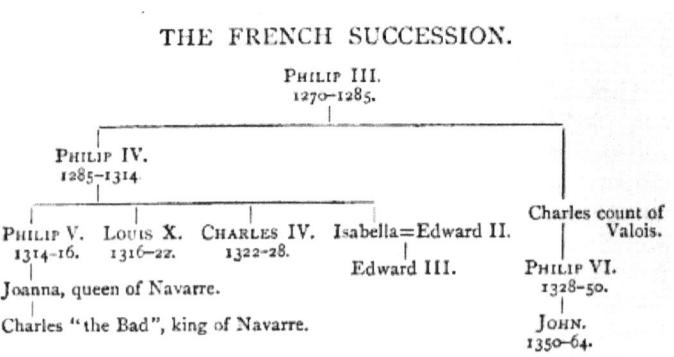

THE FRENCH SUCCESSION.

The claim now asserted was to have the most disastrous results, involving England in a lingering war, whose last blow was not struck till 1453. The vain name of King of France was not surrendered even when the last scrap of territory across the Channel was lost, and continued to be appended to the formal title of the English kings down to the reign of George III.

The commencement of the "Hundred Years' War" had perhaps been rendered inevitable by Philip's persistent intrigues and encroachments. But it was an ill day for England when King Edward formulated his claims to his cousin's crown, and so embittered the strife. The nation had been rapidly recovering from the effects of the reign of Edward II., but it still needed peace and rest: The Scottish war had not much tried its resources, but the bloody and expensive struggle which began in 1337 was to prove a far more serious drain upon its resources. In his reckless and thriftless management of it King Edward was destined to develop all the faults of his character, which had hitherto been hidden from his subjects, who, since Halidon Hill, had worshipped him as the avenger of Bannockburn and the best knight in Christendom.

Chapter 3

The First Stage of the Hundred Years' War, 1337-1349

In the autumn of 1337 the long bickering between England and France, which had hitherto been confined to piratical incursions and unauthorized raids, ended in open war. The Earl of Derby, son of Henry Earl of Lancaster, was sent over to Flanders to raise the king's Netherlandish allies. He came ashore on the isle of Cadzand, where he found the troops of the Flemish count prepared to oppose him, though the majority of the people of the land welcomed the advent of the invaders. Derby beat off the count's men-at-arms with ease, for they could make no head against the English archers; they fled in all directions, leaving their leader Guy, the count's bastard brother, a prisoner in the earl's hands. (Oct. 1337.)

Edward himself was not able to follow so soon as he had hoped, for he found himself unable easily to collect the money needed for raising a large army. Parliament granted him the means of procuring a great sum by the expedient of permitting him to buy 20,000 sacks of wool at £3 a sack from the wool-growers, and to sell it abroad at the best profit that he could make, while other exporters of the commodity, if natives, were to be taxed forty shillings a sack, and if foreigners sixty shillings. In addition, the barons and knights gave him a tax of "a fifteenth", and the town and clergy one of "a tenth" on their property. (The latter grants were made by the Parliament of Sept.-Oct. 1337, the former by that of February, 1338).

These liberal votes were to prove quite insufficient for the king's thriftless hand. Edward sailed in July, 1338, from Orwell with 1600 men-at-arms and 10,000 archers, but their maintenance was only a small part of his expenses. He took into his pay all the princes of the

Netherlands, who were far more anxious to get the English money than to set their troops in the field. He also went to Coblenz and wasted vast sums in a magnificent conference with the emperor, Lewis the Bavarian, who granted him in return for cash the empty title of Vicar-General of the Empire for the parts west of the Rhine.

Edward soon found that this dignity gave him no more power than he had before, and he had the greatest difficulty in inducing the Duke of Brabant and his other allies to join him with their vassals. He could not get them mustered till the spring of the following year; meanwhile he, with his court and his army, lay at Antwerp spending much money to no profit.

The king's enforced idleness seemed all the more exasperating when news came that King Philip had gathered a great fleet of Norman and Picard ships, strengthened by a squadron hired from the Genoese, and had sent them forth to ravage the south coast of England. They landed at Southampton "on a Sunday when all the people were at mass", and sacked and burned the place. Next they passed on to Portsmouth and did the like with it and the neighbouring villages. Then they returned to France with their plunder quite unmolested.

This expedition deserves memory for the fact that the French fleet carried the first cannon which the English had ever seen; they were little pieces described as "iron pots throwing iron bolts by the force of gunpowder", and did nothing effective. But their appearance marks the first beginnings of a new stage in the art of war. (Late autumn of 1338.)

In the following summer, (1339), King Edward at last got his refractory allies together, and marched into France with an army which is said to have amounted to nearly 100,000 men. But this great host effected nothing; they laid siege to Cambray, but failed to take it, and then marched through the Cambrésis and Vermandois ravaging the land. King Philip came out against them with an army as large as their own, but he acted most cautiously, posting himself behind woods and marshes, where he could not easily be assailed. It was to no purpose that Edward drew up his army and offered battle more than once; the French would not leave their position and could not be attacked in it. At last, when his provisions were exhausted and his foreign allies began to steal home, Edward was forced to retire ingloriously into Brabant, having accomplished absolutely nothing by his mighty display of force.

Meanwhile all the parliamentary grants were spent, and the king found himself in dire poverty. He wrote urgently to ask for more money, for he was already £30,000 in debt, though he had had the handling of £300,000, a sum which seemed almost incredible to the men of the fourteenth century. He had even pawned his crown of to the Archbishop of Trier for 60,000 florins. He was forced to come home to raise more funds in the spring of 1340, and obtained the very liberal grant from parliament of "the ninth lamb, the ninth fleece, and the ninth sheaf for the two years next to come". But this was not conceded to him without conditions; he was made to swear to redress many grievances, such as the extortions of his sheriffs and purveyors. Moreover, he was made to promise never again to raise a "tallage", *i.e.* an arbitrary tax on the towns and manors which lay in the royal demesne.

Having once more some money in his purse, Edward resolved to set out again for Flanders. But he received news, which turned out to be quite correct, that the French fleet which had ravaged the south coast in the previous year was again at sea, and intended to intercept his passage. It was necessary at all costs to gain command of the narrow seas, and all the ports of England were ordered to equip vessels and send them to the harbour of Orwell, in Suffolk, from which the king was to sail. On June 22nd 1340, nearly 200 ships, small and great, weighed anchor for Flanders. The French were not met on the open water, but when the Flemish coast drew near it was seen that a perfect forest of masts lay in the port of Sluys. The enemy was waiting there with a fleet about the same in number as that of King Edward—it was said there were 190 sail—but 19 of them were "so great that the like of them had never before been seen." These appear to have been the Genoese vessels, which were true ships of war, and not mere armed merchantmen like the rest of the two fleets.

The enemy was moored in three lines, with ship laid close to ship and barricades built across them, so that it was impossible to force a passage between them. But Edward, by feigning to fly, induced them to cast off and pursue him. He then turned and plunged in among the hostile ships. The battle was a confused medley without any manoeuvring, for the fleets lay wedged together broadside to broadside, and most of the work was done by boarding. The English archers gradually shot down the hostile crossbowmen, who could not stand firm against them for long.

Then the knights clambered from ship to ship and swept the decks of the enemy. Edward himself was in the thickest of the fight, and won

BATTLE OF SLUYS, 1340.
Defeat of the French by the English fleet under KING EDWARD III.

the admiration of all men by his audacious courage. By the afternoon the French fleet was completely crushed, two-thirds of the ships were captured, and more than 20,000 men were drowned or slain. This great fight, the second naval victory in the English annals, put an end to any attempt of the French to dispute the dominion of the seas. For the rest of the war the English went where they would, and always made the sea their base of attack. (24th June, 1340.)

But splendid as was the victory of Sluys, it had but a negative effect on the general fortune of the war. It prevented any chance of the invasion of England by the French, but it did not give King Edward any help in prosecuting his plans for overrunning Northern France at the head of his Netherlandish allies. Soon after his arrival in Flanders he mustered them, and led them to besiege Tournay. (July, 1340.) But he found himself as wholly unable to take the place as he had been to reduce Cambray in his last expedition. After lying before it for two months, he found that his cash was all spent, and that his allies were melting away from him.

Meanwhile King Philip had appeared at the head of a large army, and was watching the leaguer from a distance, though he utterly refused to in offer any opportunity for a battle. Edward found that he could do nothing; the rains of autumn were beginning, no more money came in from England, and vexatious news arrived that the French were winning castle after castle on the borders of Aquitaine, and that the Scots had once more driven out Edward Balliol, and sent their plundering bands across the Tweed. Depressed in spirits, and conscious of his helplessness, the king stooped to propose a truce to his enemy. Philip, who had secret intelligence that Tournay was suffering terribly from famine and might surrender at any moment, gladly listened to the offer, and an armistice, to last for nine months, and to extend to Scotland and Aquitaine, was signed. (Sep., 1340.) Edward promptly disbanded his army, and returned to England in great wrath, blaming every one rather than himself for the failure of his campaign.

The moment that he reached London the king gave vent to his wrath by the wholesale dismissal or arrest of his ministers, whom he unjustly accused of having wrecked his plan of campaign by embezzling or dissipating the money which Parliament had voted him. He deprived his chancellor, Robert Stratford, Bishop of Chichester, of the seals, put the treasurer, Northburgh Bishop of Lichfield, in custody, and imprisoned Stonor, the chief justice, with some of his colleagues, the chief clerk of the chancery, the mayor of London, and many more.

BATTLE OF SLUYS

But Archbishop Stratford (the chancellor's brother) bore the brunt of his wrath; having been practically acting as prime minister, for some years, he was the person on whom Edward laid most of the blame.

It was attempted to bring him to trial for maladministration, but he claimed the right to be judged only by "his peers", the barons and bishops of the House of Lords. Stratford met with general support, and Edward was compelled to yield when a committee of the Lords reported in favour of the archbishop's contention, and laid down the doctrine that "peers cannot be arrested, judged, or outlawed save in full Parliament before their peers." The king's wrath soon burned out, and he acknowledged himself to be in the wrong by reconciling himself to Stratford, releasing his prisoners, and humbly suing Parliament for fresh supplies. These were only granted him after he had conceded three very important constitutional privileges.

The first was that he should recognise the right of the peers which had just been asserted by the archbishop, the second that his ministers should in future be appointed in Parliament and sworn to obey all the laws of the realm, and the third that Parliament should appoint commissioners to audit all the accounts of money voted for the king's service. Thus, the Lords and Commons obtained two most important means of checking the king's rash actions: they were to have a hand in the appointing of his ministers and in the auditing of his revenues. (May, 1341.) But Edward had the shameful duplicity to make a private protest that he did not hold himself bound by his word, and some months later openly declared that:

> He had dissembled, as he was justified in doing, in allowing the pretended statute to be sealed for that time, for all acts done in prejudice of his royal prerogative were null and void. (Oct., 1341.)

For two years after this scandalous trick Edward did not dare to call a Parliament. Meanwhile the war languished, mainly for want of money, but also because the Emperor Lewis and most of the other useless allies of England dropped away and made separate truces with France. On the Scottish border things went from bad to worse; Stirling and Edinburgh fell into the hands of the patriots in 1341, and Balliol's hold on his uneasy throne was so completely lost that he had to take up his permanent residence in England.

It would now have been best to make peace with both France and Scotland, and acknowledge that the war was a failure. But Edward's energies were not yet exhausted, and he was just about to be presented with a new opportunity of vexing King Philip. A bitter war of succession broke out in Brittany, the second most important fief of the French crown; its cause had some similarity to the dispute which was already raging between Philip and Edward for the crown of France.

When Duke John III. died in 1341 the duchy was claimed both by his eldest brother's daughter, Jeanne Countess of Blois, as nearest of kin, and by his younger brother, John of Montfort, as nearest heir male. There was some irony in the fact that King Philip, whose crown had come to him as heir male of Charles IV., supported the Countess of Blois, while Edward, whose French claim rested on the theory that rights could be transmitted by a female, became the advocate of Montfort, who was urging the doctrine of the Salic Law. (See table following.)

THE BRETON SUCCESSION.

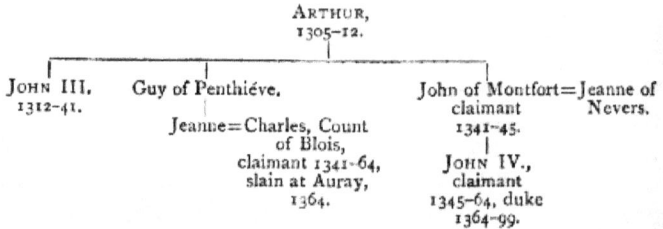

At first the party of the countess had the best of the civil war in Brittany. Aided by French troops they took Nantes, the capital of the duchy, and made prisoner John of Montfort, who had shut himself up within its walls. But the courageous Jeanne de Nevers, Montfort's wife, maintained the cause of her captive spouse, and held out in the strong castle of Hennebont till she was relieved by the arrival of English troops under Sir Walter Manny, a great mercenary captain from Hainault, who was one of the most trusted officers of King Edward. Shortly afterwards the king himself arrived with a considerable army, and cleared Western Brittany of the French and the partisans of Blois. But he failed to take Nantes and Rennes, and all the eastern parts of the duchy remained in the hands of the enemy. (1342.)

The campaign had been a success for neither party, and was ended by a truce which might have turned into a peace but for the inveterate personal hostility between Truce for Philip and Edward. (Jan., 1343.) It was three years, difficult, too, to come to a satisfactory conclusion about the Breton matter, as neither claimant had got possession of the whole duchy. Philip, contrary to his agreement, kept Montfort in prison till he escaped in 1345 and got back to Hennebont. The truce lasted for three years, though border fighting never wholly ceased either in Brittany or in Aquitaine.

In 1343 Edward, had again called a Parliament, which confirmed the truce, and advised him to make a peace also, if good terms could be obtained, or, if not, to make open war. But the unsatisfactory suspension of hostilities was all that could be gained. Meanwhile the national council engaged in a sharp dispute with the pope, a matter in which they had for once their master's full sympathy. The pope was now dwelling at Avignon, whither Clement V. had migrated in 1310, and was wholly under the influence and domination of the French king. The main subject of grievance against him was his inordinate greed in appointing "Provisors" to English sees and benefices. He kept nominating foreigners to rich preferments whenever they fell vacant, in utter disregard of the rights of the king and other patrons.

The clerics so named drew their revenues, but seldom or never came near their cures, to the great injury of the church. As the English complaint ran:

> Clement VI. appointed foreigners, most of them scandalous persons, who do not reside on their benefices, nor know the faces of the flocks intrusted to them, who do not understand their speech, but neglecting the cure of souls, seek, as hirelings, only temporal lucre. The Successor of the Apostles was surely appointed to feed and not to shear the Lord's sheep.

The king had the full approval of the nation when, in 1344, he issued a mandate forbidding any person to bring Papal bulls or any such documents into England except by his leave. This was a reassertion of an old prohibition: as long ago as the eleventh century William the Conqueror had published a similar edict; but now it needed to be once more clearly set forth. It was not, however, till 1352 that Parliament passed the "Statute of Provisors", which rendered liable to arrest and imprisonment all clerics who endeavoured to make use of Papal documents contrary to the interest of the king and the realm.

By the end of 1345 it was quite clear that no permanent peace with France could be procured, and the king resolved to recommence the series of invasions which had hitherto been so fruitless. This time he did not make the Netherlands his base; his allies in that direction

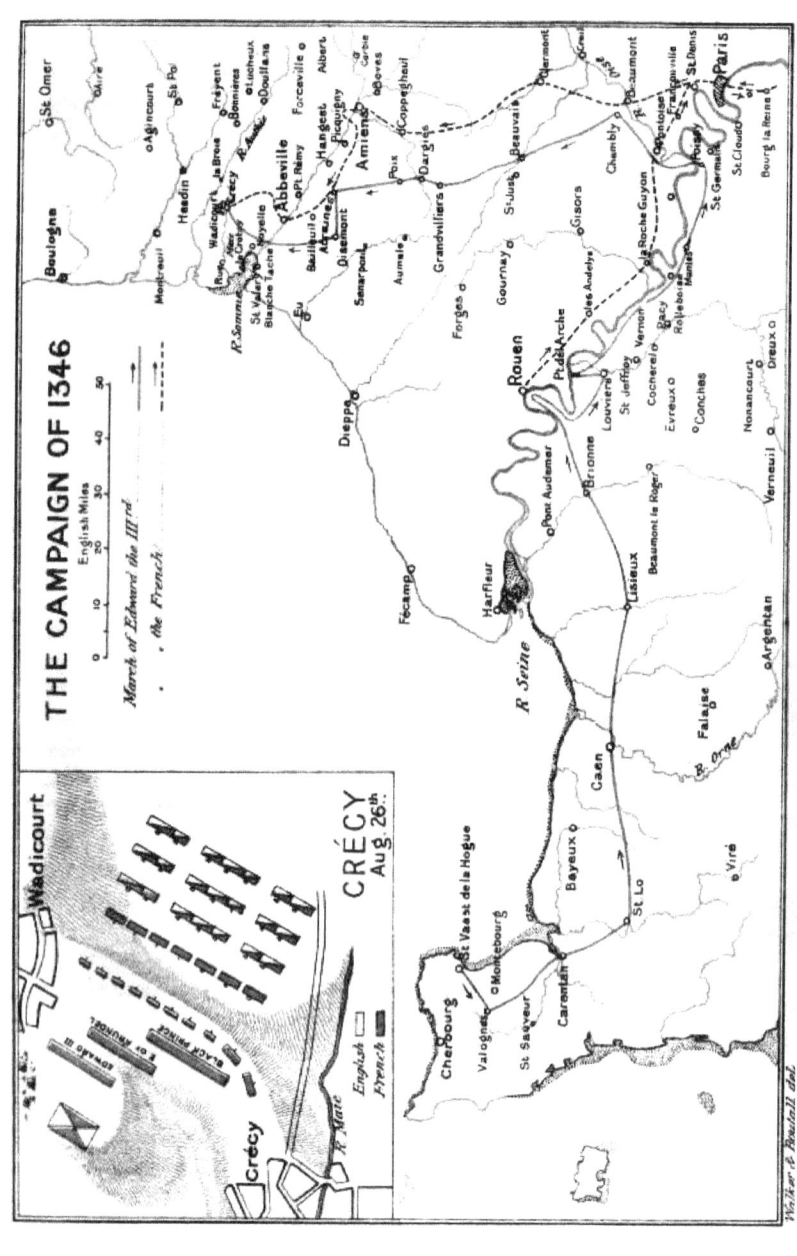

had proved faithless, and his chief supporter, Jacob van Artevelde, had 'lately been murdered in a riot. Though the Flemish towns still continued attached to England, nearly all the neighbouring states had made agreements with King Philip. Nor was Brittany chosen as the starting-point of the attack: Edward had determined to aim at the heart of France, by landing in Normandy and striking at Paris. He sent Henry of Lancaster, Earl of Derby, with a small army to defend Aquitaine, but reserved the main force for his own command. Derby, it may be mentioned, proved as good a soldier in Guyenne as he had already shown himself at the Battle of Cadzand, and gave the enemy a sound beating at Auberoche (Oct. 23, 1345). He drew down to the south a great French Army under Philip's son John, which was still engaged in operations on the Garonne when Edward made his great assault on the lands around the Seine.

On July 11, 1346, the king landed at Cape La Hogue with an army entirely composed of native English, and therefore much smaller than the host of Confederates which had taken the field in Flanders in 1338 and 1341. It included about 4000 men-at-arms, 12,000 English archers, 6000 Welsh light troops, and also a small contingent of Irish. The landing in Normandy was quite unexpected: Edward had concealed his purpose, and everyone had thought that the army was intended to aid the Earl of Derby in Guyenne. The French were wholly unprepared for an assault in this quarter, and Edward was able to march through Normandy for many days without meeting with much opposition; he ravaged the countryside and took several open towns—Barfleur, Valognes, Carentan, and St. Lo, one after the other.

At Caen, he first met with a hostile force, but easily routed the Norman militia, and took prisoner their leaders, the Counts of Tancarville and Eu, the Chamberlain and Constable of France. After plundering the rich town he struck at Rouen, but could not reach it, for the French had broken all the bridges of the lower Seine. Then Edward turned his invasion into a hazardous adventure: he sent his fleet home to England loaded with the spoils of Normandy, and marched on Paris, keeping south of the Seine.

This was a dangerous move, for the French had now begun to assemble in great force, and since Edward had not fortified for himself any post in Normandy, he had no place of refuge or friendly territory nearer than Guyenne or Flanders on to which he could retire. Paris was far too strong to be taken by a sudden attack, and this was so self-evident that it seems probable that the English king was merely carrying out a chivalrous adventure when he marched to beard King Philip in his capital. No opposition of importance was met with on the way, but when the invaders drew near the southern gates of Paris they heard that King Philip had collected 60,000 men or more at St. Denis, and had even been joined by part of his son's army from Guyenne.

The leisurely pace at which Edward had crossed Normandy had permitted his rival to concentrate all his forces. It was impossible to go on, and the English had to choose between a march on Bordeaux and one on Flanders. Nor was the latter alternative easy to take, for the Seine had first to be crossed, and all its bridges were broken. It was nevertheless this choice which Edward determined to make: he hastily moved on the broken bridge of Poissy, ten miles below Paris, and drove off its guards by the force of his archery. Then the army hastily repaired the ruined arches with planks, and succeeded in crossing before King Philip and his host could come up.

Edward now hurried north with all speed, the French king following as hastily a day's march in his rear. They kept their distance till the English vanguard reached the Somme: here Edward found all the bridges broken, and the militia of Picardy drawn up to oppose him on the further side. He made three attempts to cross at various points near Amiens, but was foiled in every one. Meanwhile the pursuers were in close contact with his rear, and it seemed that he might be caught between the French Army and the peat-bogs of the impassable Somme. Things were looking desperate when a peasant pointed out to the king a dangerous ford, named Blanchetaque, the lowest on the river's course, below Abbeville and near the sea. Here the stream was tidal, and at low water the ford was open for four hours at a time.

A body of Picard levies was waiting on the further bank, and the passage was deep, but there was no other chance of saving the army, so the king bade his men-at-arms enter the water and force their way over. Meanwhile the archers kept up a long-range fire across the stream to gall the militia on the opposite bank. After hard fighting the English horsemen drove off the Picards, and the whole army waded after them across the Somme. King Philip came up just in time to find the tide rising and the river once more impassable.

Edward had thus gained a day's start of the pursuers, and had the open road to Flanders before him. He marched on as far as the village of Crecy, and then unexpectedly bade his army halt and announced his intention of offering battle.

He was now in his own rightful inheritance, the county of Ponthieu, and was ready to fight and to take what fortune God should send him.

The fact was that he had found an admirable position in front of Crecy, and that, even if beaten, he had a safe retreat on Flanders.

The host was drawn up on the hillside just east of Crecy, its right flank covered by the brook of the Maye and by a thick forest, while its left rested on the orchards of the village of Wadicourt. There was a valley in front, beyond which lay the rising ground over which the French Army would appear. The English were arrayed in three corps, two in the front line, the third in reserve. The southern wing was put nominally under the charge of the young Edward Prince of Wales, a lad of sixteen now taking his first sight of war: he was placed under the care of the Earls of Warwick and Oxford, two experienced soldiers. The northern or left wing was under the Earls of Northampton and Arundel.

The king himself stood behind, at the top of the hill, with the reserve corps. In each division, the men-at-arms had sent their horses to the rear, and stood on foot in a solid mass, after the manner of Dupplin and Halidon. The archers formed wings, thrown out on each side of the central clumps of spears, and leaning forward on the flanks so as to partly encircle an enemy who should charge directly at the men-at-arms.

King Philip had marched from Abbeville under impression that the English were in full flight for Flanders. Hence it was no small surprise to him to find them drawn up in line of battle on the hill by Crecy. His army was strung out over many miles of road, and the rear was only just setting out from Abbeville when the van was already almost in contact with the English. At first he came to the wise resolve to defer the battle till the next day, but the fiery barons in the front refused to halt, and pushed in so close to the hostile position that fighting became inevitable. Forced by his vassals' want of discipline to attack before he had intended, Philip drew up his army as best he could. His front line was formed by 6000 crossbowmen, mainly Genoese mercenaries, who were bidden to drive back the English archers Behind them rode a great mass of men-at-arms under the Counts of Alençon and Flanders: the other contingents were gradually coming up and taking ground to the rear in successive lines.

The Genoese marched up to the foot of the English slope, and

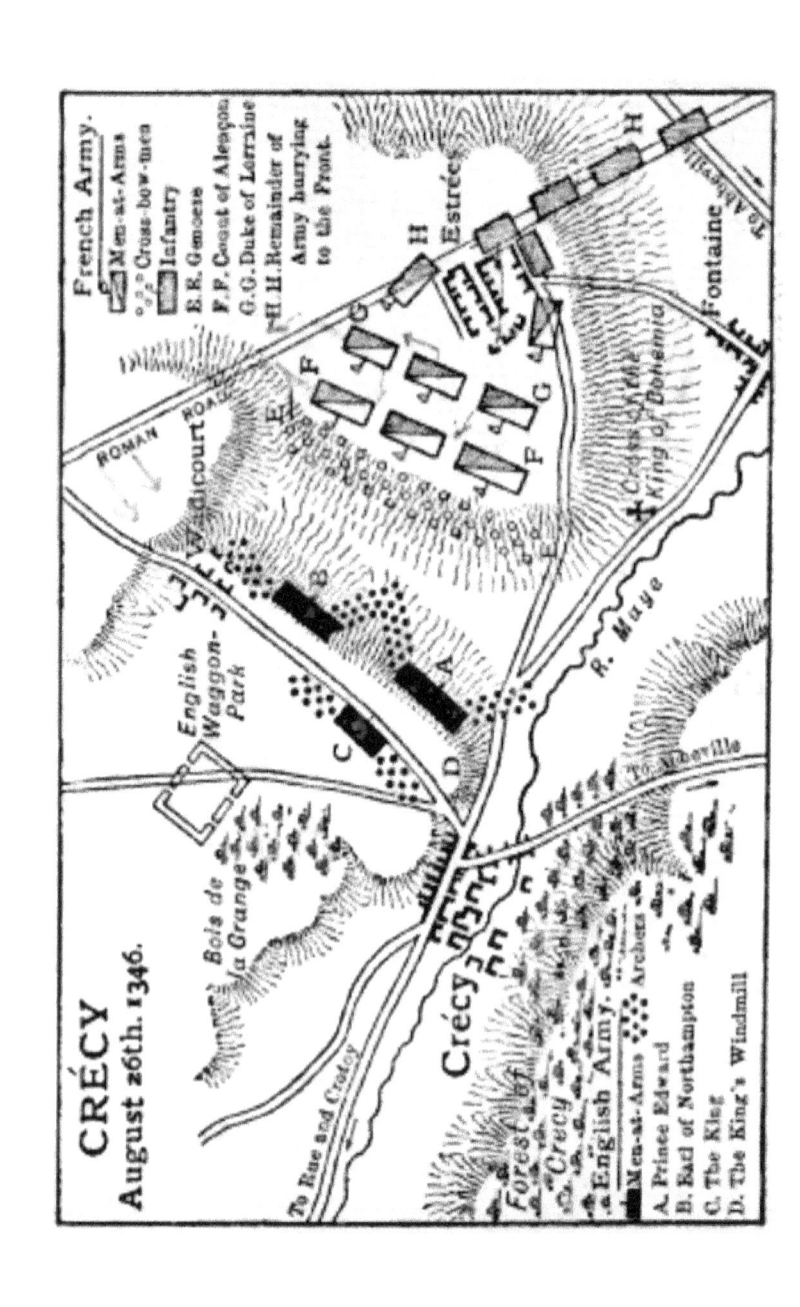

began to let fly, but the moment that they started the engagement the archers "took one step forward, drew the arrows back to the ear, and shot so fast and so thick that it seemed as if it were snowing." Their aim was accurate, and their discharge five or six times as rapid as that of the clumsy crossbow, which required to be wound up after every discharge. In a few minutes the Genoese were hopelessly routed, and fled back towards their own main body. The Count of Alençon, who had no experience of the English archery, cursed them for cowards, and in his rage, bade his men-at-arms ride over them, and make straight for the enemy's front. This act was as mad as it was cruel.

The horsemen trod down many of the wretched infantry, but were hampered by the crowd, and could only push through in small broken parties toward the English. When they came in range they soon found that they had erred in despising their enemy: the archers shot down well-nigh everyone who came near them. Only a very few of the French got to close quarters, and charged in on the dismounted knights of the Prince of Wales and the Earl of Northampton: Alençon and Lewis of Flanders were both slain.

Angered, but not cowed, by this unfortunate opening of the battle, King Philip launched each of his corps as it reached the field against the English line: all had the same fate as the first-comers. But the French *noblesse* was brave and obstinate, and their fruitless attacks did not cease till nightfall. Only once did a large body succeed in closing with the Prince of Wales's corps. King Edward was asked for succour, but refused to bid the reserve charge, observing that "the boy must win his spurs." His action was justified, for the French were beaten off without it being necessary to engage the rear division.

At dusk the French fell into hopeless disorder, and melted away from the field. Edward would not allow any pursuit lest his little army might get broken up in the dark. Next morning the extent of the victory could be gauged: there lay dead in front of the English line at least ten thousand men, of whom no less than 1552 were counts, barons, and knights. The most notable among the dead was John King of Bohemia, an ally of France, who, though he was almost blind, had insisted on leading a charge at the head of the knights of his household. He and they were found all dead together in front of the Prince of Wales's standard. The Duke of Lorraine and ten counts were slain, with half the baronage of Northern France.

Such was the result of the rash attempt of the French chivalry to ride down the dismounted men-at-arms of King Edward, flanked by the deadly archery of the English yeomanry. So complete was the victory that Edward could now choose his own course of action without fear of being further molested. He resolved to besiege and take Calais, the great French port which faces Dover across the narrow strait. If taken it would give England an open door into France: moreover, the English had an old grudge against its seamen, who were noted privateers and pirates, and had often ravaged Kent and Sussex.

While Edward lay before Calais news reached him of a second victory almost as important as that which he had himself won. King David of Scotland had taken advantage of the absence of the English host to invade the northern counties. The Scots, we are told, "thought that no one was left in England save millers and mass-priests", and hoped to find the border ill-guarded. They forced their way nearly as far as Durham, till they were met at Neville's Cross by the militia of the northern counties, headed by the Lords Percy and Neville and by Edward Balliol, their former sovereign, who had now practically relapsed into the condition of an English baron. (He was lord of Barnard Castle and other North Country estates.)

Here King David suffered a sanguinary defeat; once more the archers were too much for the Scottish pikemen, and the tragedy of Halidon Hill was repeated (Oct. 17th, 1346). David himself was taken prisoner, with many of his nobles, and was retained in captivity for ten years. He was not unkindly treated, but one of his companions, John Earl of Menteith, a former partisan of Balliol who had betrayed his master and was specially obnoxious to the English, was beheaded as a traitor a piece of illogical and unnecessary cruelty, since half the Scottish nobility might have fallen under the same accusation.

After Crecy King Edward's arms were successful in all directions. he Earl of Derby (now become Earl of Lancaster by his father's death) thrust the French out of Aquitaine; Sir Thomas Dagworth, placed in command in Brittany, routed the partisans of Charles of Blois at Roche Darien, and in the north, the siege of Calais went steadily on. King Philip collected an army, and came up to endeavour to raise the leaguer, but with the memory of Crecy before him he dared not attack the English lines, and after his departure the place was starved out and yielded on terms (Aug. 3, 1347).

★★★★★★

The story that Edward intended to hang seven of the burgesses, who offered themselves as victims in behalf of the whole town, and that they were only spared at Queen Philippa's intercession, seems an invention. But the leaders "surrendered themselves to the king's mercy", and came out barefoot and with halters round their necks, as a sign that they were wholly in his hands to spare or slay. Hence probably the story. Edward made them hostages, but treated them kindly.

★★★★★★

King Edward permitted those of the *burghers* who would do him homage to retain their houses, but drove out the large majority who preferred to abide by their French allegiance. Their place was filled up by the immigration of several thousand English merchants and seafaring folk, and Calais became for two hundred years a thoroughly English town. On one occasion, it even sent members to the Parliament at Westminster. For the future, all the inroads of the English into Northern France were sent out from this invaluable "open door". The town also developed into a great centre for trade with Flanders. Repeated attempts of the French to recover it by treachery or by open force all came to nothing.

A short time after the fall of Calais another of numerous truces which interrupted the course of the Hundred Years' War was concluded, leaving each party to hold what it was actually in possession of at the moment. It would probably have been short, but for a great calamity which fell on both England and France in the following year. In 1347 a deadly pestilence, coming from India and the Euphrates valley, where malignant disorders are always rife, appeared at Constantinople. In the next year, it swept over Italy and reached the West: by the summer of 1348 it was raging both in England and France.

The "Black Death", as this plague was generally named, seems to have been a kind of eruptive typhoid fever, highly contagious and breaking forth with boils upon the body. In the crowded insanitary towns of mediaeval Europe, among a people utterly ignorant of the simplest laws of health, it spread like wildfire. But the countryside suffered almost as much as the cities. Many districts did not recover for centuries from its effects: the whole Norse population of Greenland died off, so that the very existence of that ancient colony was forgotten. Many depopulated parishes in Sweden relapsed into the forest from which they had been hewn out. The Grand Duke of Moscow and 60,000 of his subjects were cut off: Florence lost 100,000 inhabitants in eight months.

England suffered as much as other regions, for a whole year (Aug. 1348-Sep. 1349) she was labouring under the scourge: the coming of the winter cold brought no relief, and it was noted that rainy weather, which was abnormally prevalent that year, seemed to be particularly favourable to the spread of the plague. The king's daughter Joanna died of it on the eve of her betrothal to Don Pedro of Castile—a fortunate release for her, as he was a cruel and reckless prince, and actually murdered the French lady, Blanche of Bourbon, whom he wedded in her stead. Two Archbishops of Canterbury fell victims to it, John de Ufford and the scholastic philosopher Thomas Bradwardine, whom men called "the *doctor profundus*".

The clergy indeed, owing to their duties at the death-bed, suffered even more than other classes. Some two-thirds of the livings of the diocese of Norwich changed hands during the twelvemonth, as is shown by the bishop's register. In Yorkshire, the mortality, though somewhat lower, yet carried off more than a half of the parish priests. Grass grew in the marketplace of Bristol. London buried some 50,000 corpses in the new cemetery, of thirteen acres in extent, which was consecrated on ground belonging to the Hospital of St. Bartholomew in Spitalfields.

The cattle strayed through the corn and found none to drive them away. Ships were driven ashore on the coast of the North Sea with all their crews lying dead on board. On the whole, it is probable that there was not much exaggeration in the contemporary estimate which calculated that England lost a full half of her population during the terrible thirteen months during which the Black Death raged. All description of local records, such as manor rolls and the like, seem to bear out the statement.

The social and political results of the Black Death were naturally tremendous and widespread. It seems to have generated selfish indifference and demoralisation, and its most prominent consequence was the outbreak of a crisis in the relations of the land-owning and the labouring classes. So large a number of the agricultural class had been swept away, that the lords of the manors could not get their lands tilled, for the survivors demanded wages that seemed extortionate to their employers. The latter fell back on their ancient right to demand the unpaid labour of their villeins during a certain number of days in every year.

This practice had been dropping into disuse for many generations, for the landholders had been commuting forced labour for money, and so allowing their peasants to become rent-paying tenants rather than serfs. The attempt to enforce this half-obsolete practice led to numberless disputes. Many villeins absconded, others formed themselves into secret leagues to resist the lords' claims. It was to no purpose that Parliament, in the interest of the landholders, passed statutes enabling the justices of the peace to fix the rate of wages in each district, and providing for the punishment of the labourer who should ask, or the employer who should offer, more than this maximum. The laws of political economy could not be evaded, and selfish legislation only embittered but could not settle the dispute. This unwise *Statute of Labourers* (1352) was one of the main causes of the violent seditions among the agricultural classes which were to break out thirty years after.

CHAPTER 4

From the Black Death to the Peace of Bretigny, 1349-1360

It was mainly owing to the frightful calamity of the Black Death, which fell with equal severity on France and England, that the war languished for the seven years which followed the appearance of the plague. For the greater part of the time there was a truce between the two countries. The suspension of arms negotiated in June, 1348, was periodically renewed, with an occasional short interval of hostilities. The armistice did not always prevent hostile encounters: while it was prevailing King Philip, late in the year 1349, made a desperate attempt to recover Calais by treachery. He offered Almerigo da Pavia, a mercenary captain who held a position of trust in the garrison, a great sum, 20,000 gold crowns, to admit French troops within the castle by night. But the Italian met craft with craft, and revealed the scheme to King Edward, who hastily crossed from Dover with 900 men and took personal charge of the affair. Part of the French were allowed to enter, when the king and his men-at-arms fell upon them, and after a sharp fight captured or slew the whole body (Dec. 31, 1349).

A few months after this King Philip died (August 22, 1350), but the succession of his son John to the French crown made no change in international politics, for the new monarch would make no permanent peace with England, and continued his father's policy. Before he had been a week on the throne there was heavy fighting in the Narrow Seas. A great squadron of Biscayan ships passed up the Channel, committing many depredations on English commerce. King Philip had interested the King of Castile in his cause, and had induced him to send out his kinsman Charles, Count of La Cerda, at the head of this fleet, whose aims were half warlike, half commercial, for after passing the straits it put into the Flemish ports and loaded itself with merchandise. As it steered homewards King Edward put out from Sandwich with some ships which he had hastily collected, and fell upon it.

The English were outnumbered, and their vessels were much smaller than those of the enemy. At first it seemed that they were likely to fare ill. Both the king's ship and that of his son, Edward Prince of Wales, were sunk by the enemies with whom they had grappled; but the crews clambered up from their sinking craft, and carried the Spaniards by boarding. After much desperate fighting, the strangers made off, leaving twenty-four of their vessels in the hands of the English. This fight, generally known by the name of *Espagnols-sur-Mer*, took place off Winchelsea on Aug. 29, 1350.

The period before the renewed outbreak of open war with France was not unimportant in constitutional history. Besides the unwise *Statute of Labourers*, to which we have already alluded, and the *Statute of Provisors*, which resulted from the long quarrel with the pope which had opened in 1344, several other important pieces of legislation belong to the years 1350-1355. Among them were the Statute of the Staple, which provided that wool, leather, and fleeces, tin and lead, the most important English exports, should only be sold in certain towns, ten within the realm, (London, Bristol, Canterbury, Chichester, Exeter, Lincoln, Newcastle, Norwich, York, Caermarthen), four in Ireland, (Dublin, Cork, Drogheda, Waterford), and two, Calais and Bruges, without it.

The main object of this statute designating the staple-towns was to facilitate the levying of the duties on wool, which could be more easily collected if the king's officers had to keep their eyes on a small number of places only. But it harmed the small trading towns for the benefit of the greater ones, and put a dangerous monopoly in the hands of the "Merchants of the Staple", who were the only persons licensed to traffic in the designated places. Another important step was the passing of the *Statute of Treasons*, which defined more accurately than of old what offences fell under the head of treason—a necessary piece of work, for the judges of late had been trying to extend the meaning of the word, so as to get more profit from confiscations for the king.

The last of the series of truces which had followed the Black Death ran out on April 1st, 1355. In the summer of that year the English once more invaded France, hoping to have the aid not only of their old friends, the Montfort party in Brittany, but also of Charles the

Bad, King of Navarre, whose broad estates in Normandy were conveniently placed for the receiving of English succours. But the great armament which Edward was to have taken to Normandy was beaten back by storms, and Charles of Navarre had to make peace with his cousin, King John, in order to avoid destruction.

A small English Army was despatched to Bordeaux under the Prince of Wales, who had now reached his twenty-sixth year, and was intrusted with independent command. This force after landing and being joined by the forces of Gascony, executed a destructive raid into Languedoc. The Black Prince made his way 'past Toulouse, burning and harrying the countryside as far as Narbonne and Carcassonne, both of which places he plundered, till he almost reached the Mediterranean. This foray cut deeper into France than any English invasion before or after. But it had no result but plunder, and served no political or strategical purpose. Meanwhile the king had reorganised his storm-shattered host, and passed the seas to Calais in the late autumn. But as he was ravaging Picardy news was brought him that the Scots had taken Berwick by surprise and entered Northumberland.

Much angered by the news, Edward abandoned his enterprise, and returned to his own realm to chastise the northern enemy. Though winter had come he crossed the border, and ravaged the Marches and Lothian, as far as Edinburgh, with great cruelty. So systematically did he set fire to all places great and small that the Scots remembered his invasion as "the Burnt Candlemas"—Candlemas day (Feb. 2) having fallen into the midst of his destructive march. No open opposition in the field was offered him, but his foraging parties were cut off, and his retreat to Berwick much harassed by the Lowlanders.

In the summer of 1356 the Black Prince, who had earned the confidence of his followers by his successful raid into Languedoc, resolved to repeat his incursion of the previous year, and started from Bordeaux with an army of some 3500 men-at-arms and 4000 or 5000 infantry, of whom rather more than half were English, the rest of the force being composed of the feudal levies of Guyenne. This time he did not strike at southern, but at central France; he passed through the Limousin, Auvergne, and Berry, plundering far and wide till he came to the Loire. Apparently, it was his purpose to co-operate with a smaller army under his younger brother, John of Gaunt, which had started from England on June 1st to land in Brittany. But this secondary expedition completely miscarried, though it was joined by some discontented Norman barons, the partisans of the King of Navarre.

Edward's own march met with no check till he had marched along the Loire almost as far as Tours. Then he heard that King John, with all the levies of northern and central France, was coming against him, and had crossed the river at Blois, with the intention of getting between the invaders and their base at Bordeaux. The prince's army was not a fifth of the strength of that of the French, and was clogged with a vast wagon train loaded with plunder. He did not, therefore, intend to fight, but made the best of his way homewards. The two hosts lost touch of each other for a space, but suddenly met again near Poictiers, where their lines of march crossed each other.

Finding himself so close to the enemy that he could not get off without sacrificing all his booty, Edward halted and drew up his men on the hillside by the village of Maupertuis, with a hedge covering his front, the River Miausson to his left, and a thick wood behind him. He expected to be instantly attacked, but King John wasted a day in reconnoitring the English position and in sending in proposals that his enemies should surrender on terms. These were, of course, declined. Next day the prince thought he might succeed in slipping off to the rear without a fight, and had moved his baggage and his vanguard across the Miausson, when the French were seen advancing in four lines to assault the position. The English hastily got back into line of battle, and the fighting soon began.

King John, remembering the effect of the English arrows at Crecy on the French cavalry, had made the greater part of his men-at-arms dismount and march on foot in serried columns. Only his vanguard, chosen from the best knights in the army, were bidden to keep on their horses and ride in rapidly on the English archery, as a kind of forlorn hope; the rest came up on foot in three lines, each composed of 4000 or 6000 men, headed respectively by the Dauphin, the Duke of Orleans, and the king himself. The devoted squadrons in front were led by Clermont and D'Audrehem, the two Marshals of France.

The Black Prince's force was now about 6000 strong; it was drawn up, as his father's host had been at Crecy, with two corps forming a front line and a third in reserve. The northern wing was headed by the Earls of Suffolk and Salisbury, the southern by the Earls of Warwick and Oxford. They had lined the hedge with their archers, while the men-at-arms stood behind to support them: in the reserve was the prince himself and the best of his Gascon vassals, Jean de Grailly, the Captal de Buch.

When the two marshals charged up to the hedge with their

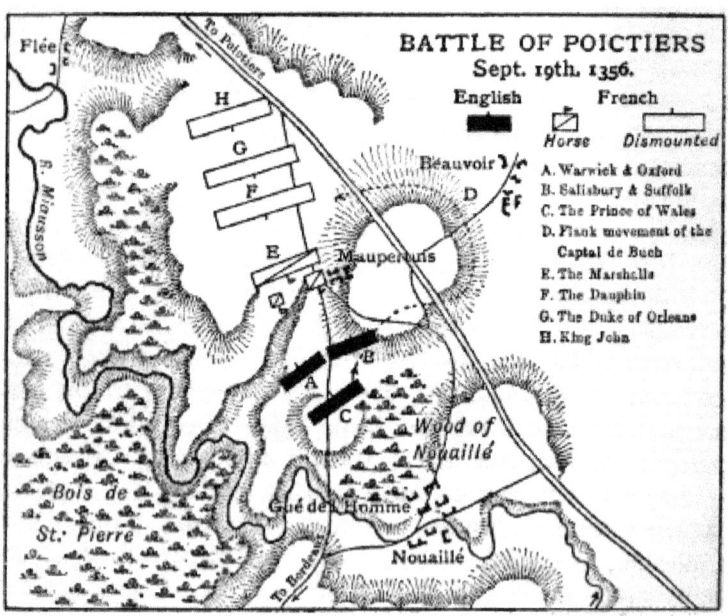

mounted men, almost the whole body were shot down by the bowmen before they could get to hand-strokes. But the *Dauphin's* corps coming up just as the horsemen were disposed of, succeeded in closing with the English and waged a fierce struggle all along the line: the prince had to send forward some of his reserve before they could be beaten off. The fugitives, falling back in utter rout, threw the line headed by the Duke of Orleans into disorder, and, instead of advancing, it left the field in company with the routed van. But King John himself with his last line came forward with great steadiness, and his single corps was equal in numbers to the whole English army.

The Black Prince saw that a desperate effort must be made, for the enemy were fresh, while his own men were almost tired out. Instead, therefore, of waiting to be attacked he put his last reserve into action, and bade the entire host charge downhill upon the French. One more precaution was taken: the Captal de Buch was ordered to take 300 men, to describe a long circuit to the northward, and to fall upon the flank and rear of the enemy when he should see the main battles fairly engaged.

This movement was destined to prove decisive. The French king kept his men together, and made head for a time against the wearied English, whose archers had now used up all their arrows, and were fighting hand to hand among the men-at-arms. But when the Captal's small corps suddenly charged in from the rear, crying "St. George! Guienne!" the French thought themselves surrounded, and broke and fled in panic fear. King John was taken prisoner, along with his youngest son, Prince Philip. Poictiers was not such a bloody field as Crecy, though the Marshal Clermont, the Duke of Bourbon, and many other lords, perished. But it was specially noted for the number of noble captives who fell into the hands of the English: besides the king and his son, fourteen counts and 1900 knights had been obliged to yield themselves to mercy. The prisoners, indeed, were so numerous that their captors preferred to dismiss many of them on parole, when they had promised to ransom themselves, rather than to take the responsibility of keeping guard over them (19th Sep. 1356).

The capture of the king was destined to have the most important political consequences. When her sovereign lay captive in London, France was without a head, and civil troubles broke out on every side. The *Dauphin*, as regent, was unable to keep up the royal authority, and nearly perished himself in a seditious rising of the mob of Paris, who slew the Marshals of Normandy and Champagne before his very face. The mercenaries who had served King John, being no longer paid their hire, turned bandits and went plundering in great bands all over the countryside. Worst of all, the oppressed peasantry, driven wild by the misery of the times, burst out into an anarchic revolt against all constituted authority, and in many regions burnt every castle and manor and slew every man and woman of gentle blood on whom they could lay hands. It was only by a desperate struggle that the *noblesse* finally succeeded in putting them down.

This bloody revolt is generally called the *Jacquerie*, from *Jacques Bonhomme*, the usual nickname of the French peasant. While the land was suffering from all these woes no opposition could be offered to the English, who ranged at their will through the land, and gained possession of many towns and castles. In short, the years 1356-7-8 were the most miserable that France had known since the old Viking invasions of the ninth century.

Edward III. might perhaps have made further conquests if he had not consented to make a truce of two years with his prisoner, King John, for he wished to give him an opportunity of coming to terms, and making a definitive peace. John, who naturally detested the restraints of captivity, was eager to get free, and would have subscribed to almost any conditions. When a treaty was offered him ceding to

England Normandy, Anjou, Maine, Poitou, and all the other lands which Henry II. had held in France two hundred years before, he was quite ready to grant the exorbitant demand, and set his seal to it.

But his son the Dauphin Charles and the States-general very properly refused their assent (May, 1359). It was not worthwhile, even in the desperate state to which France was reduced, to buy back an indifferent king at the cost of so many fair provinces. The English had gained no secure foothold, save Calais, in northern France, and it was preposterous to require the cession of regions where they had proved altogether unable to establish themselves.

To put pressure on the regent Edward III. determined to launch a new invading army into France. His military reputation gathered around his standard many thousands of veteran mercenaries, and these, added to the strong English host which he brought over to Calais, composed an army double or treble the size of that which had fought at Crecy. It was, estimated by the chronicles at 100,000 strong, but this figure is of course a gross exaggeration.

In October, 1359, the king broke up from Calais, and marched through Picardy and Champagne, wasting the land, till he came to Rheims. He laid siege to the town, intending, it is said, to have himself anointed in its cathedral, where the kings of France had been wont to celebrate their coronation for many centuries. But Rheims held out, and Edward then made a sweep through northern Burgundy, and then turned westward towards Paris. He laid waste the suburbs of the capital, but did not sit down before it, the season and the weather being unfavourable.

Next he announced his resolve to march into the fertile lands about the Loire, and there to rest his army, deferring the siege of Paris till the summer should have returned, Meanwhile the *Dauphin* had forbidden his followers to make any attempt to meet the English in the open, and had contented himself with holding the walled towns. But the country was suffering so frightfully that he and his counsellors resolved to make one more attempt to obtain terms from King Edward. His envoys met the invader at Bretigny, near Chartres, and there was signed the famous treaty which put an end to the first stage of the Hundred Years' War (May 8, 1360).

The terms which Edward now granted were more lenient than those which he had demanded in the preceding year, but they were still very heavy. Edward consented to give up his claim to the French throne, and to recognise John as its rightful occupant, but the compen-

FRANCE in 1360 shewing the results of the Peace of Bretigny.

The Boundaries of the English Possessions are shewn by a shaded line sation which he received was enormous. He was to obtain almost the whole of the ancient Duchy of Aquitaine, including the parts which had been lost by John and Henry III., and it was to be granted to him as a free state, not as land owing feudal homage to the French crown.

The English king was already in possession of Guyenne and Gascony: he now added to his portion Poitou, Aunis, Saintonge, Angoumois, the Limousin, Perigord, Quercy, and Rouergue, besides the feudal superiority over the counts of Foix and Armagnac. Nor was this all: in the north Ponthieu, the old heritage of Eleanor of Castille, was restored to him, and the tract round Calais was enlarged so as to include the whole of the small county of Guisnes. Moreover, King John was to pay for his personal ransom the enormous sum of 3,000,000 gold crowns, of which 600,000 were to be given over at once, and the rest paid up by annual instalments of 400,000 spread over six years. The Breton succession was to be settled by equitable arbitration.

Probably the French were wise in accepting the treaty: they needed peace at any price in order to save the realm from the frightful anarchy in which it was plunged. On the other hand, it is certain that Edward would have done better to moderate his claims. He only obtained, by the vast territorial cessions which he exacted, some millions of disloyal and unwilling subjects, who were certain to rebel at the first opportunity. He should have been contented with the ancient English holding in Guyenne, where the towns and most of the nobles were well affected to the house of Plantagenet; his hold on southern France was really weakened rather than strengthened by the new additions. Thus, the treaty bore within itself the seeds of future trouble; but for the moment it appeared to put a splendid and successful conclusion to the long war which had been raging since 1336.

For the moment, the general aspect of affairs seemed satisfactory, for the Scottish war had also been brought to a close. Edward Balliol, who had no son, had ceded his rights on the Scottish crown to the English monarch in 1356, and in the following year Edward III. acknowledged his prisoner David II. as rightful king of Scotland, and set him free on condition of his paying a ransom of 100,000 *marks*, (£66,666, 6s. 8d), which payment was to be spread over ten years (Oct., 1357). The long-disputed town of Berwick remained in the hands of the English, but no attempt was made to insist on the cession of the Eastern Lowlands, which had been made by Balliol in 1333.

Altogether this treaty was a far more statesmanlike achievement than that of Bretigny. On the one hand, Scotland obtained a much-needed repose after her long troubles, and was not again engaged in open war with England for nearly thirty years. Border affrays between the moss-troopers of the two countries could not be wholly prevented, but led to no serious conflict. Edward, on the other hand, was freed from the danger of Scottish attacks on his rear during his subsequent wars with France. But the friendly feeling which had prevailed between the two nations in the thirteenth century, before the invasions of Edward I., could not be renewed after sixty years of almost continuous war.

Chapter 5
England under Edward III., 1360-1369

The Peace of Bretigny forms the high-water mark of King Edward's prosperity. He had still seventeen years to reign, but they were to be a period of growing troubles and gradual decline, corresponding to the decay of the king's own vigour and health. In 1360 Edward, had reached the age of forty-eight, but he was already beginning to show signs of the wear and tear of his busy life: men grew old ere their time in those hard days. He was now the father of a very large family—he had eleven children, of whom five sons and three daughters survived.

One of his main desires was to strengthen the crown by marrying his sons to the heiresses of the great baronial families, so as to concentrate as much of the feudal strength of England as he could in the hands of the royal family. His eldest son and heir, Edward, Prince of Wales, had reached the age of thirty before he entered into wedlock; he chose as his wife a lady of his own age, his cousin, Joanna Countess of Kent, who inherited the estates of her father, Earl Edmund, the victim of Mortimer.

She was a widow, having previously married Sir John Holland, by whom she had two sons, destined to be prominent figures in the next reign. The Black Prince's marriage seems to have been one of inclination—his wife had been known as "the fair maid of Kent", and all authorities unite to sing her praises. The matches into which his younger brothers entered seem to have been of their father's making rather than their own; several of them were wedded before they were well out of their boyhood.

Lionel, the second surviving son of the king, was married to Elizabeth de Burgh, the greatest heiress in Ireland, who held in her own right the county of Ulster. After her early death, he espoused as his second wife Yolande Visconti, daughter of the Lord of Milan. John of

Gaunt, the next brother, made the most wealthy match of the whole family; when only nineteen he married Blanche of Lancaster, the heiress of Henry of Lancaster, the victor of Cadzand and Auberoche. She was in her own right Countess of Lancaster, Derby, Lincoln, and Leicester, and the estates which she brought to her husband were the broadest heritage in England. Edmund of Langley, the fourth surviving son of Edward III., married as his first wife a Spanish princess, as his second his eldest brother's stepdaughter, Joanna Holland.

Lastly, Thomas of Woodstock, the youngest of the princes, obtained as his bride Eleanor Bohun, one of the two co-heiresses of the ancient earldom of Hereford. At different times Edward conferred on each of his sons the title of duke—a dignity hitherto unknown in England. The Prince of Wales was made Duke of Cornwall, Lionel Duke of Clarence, John Duke of Lancaster, Edmund Duke of York, and Thomas Duke of Gloucester.

Of the three daughters of Edward III. who reached adult years Mary married John V., the Montfort claimant to the duchy of Brittany, Margaret was wedded to John Hastings, Earl of Pembroke, and Isabella to Ingelram de Coucy, a French baron who served her father as a great captain of mercenaries: he was created Earl of Bedford.

During Edward's own lifetime the concentration of so many of the richest fiefs in the hands of his sons undoubtedly strengthened the crown and enfeebled the baronage to a corresponding extent. But he does not seem to have reflected that he was leaving an unenviable future to his successor, destined to have to deal with uncles and cousins who were not only very powerful territorial nobles, but also princes of the blood, with possible claims on the crown. In endowing his younger sons with such enormous power he was contributing his part towards making the Wars of the Roses possible. It was the excessive strength of the house of Lancaster which proved the ruin of Richard II., and in a later generation it was the over-greatness of the heir of the united lines of York, Clarence, and Mortimer which brought down the house of Lancaster to its bloody end. Edward does not seem in the least to have foreseen that though his own sons would obey and support him, the patriarch of their race, yet his grandsons would have no such feelings of loyalty to his eldest son's heir.

Meanwhile these dangers were still in the far future, and Edward seemed in 1360 the most successful sovereign of his age. His fame as a soldier was spread all over Europe, and the English, who before his time enjoyed no special military repute, became the models of all

Western Christendom. The soldiers trained in his wars, Sir John Chandos, Knolles, Manny, Thomas and William Felton, and the Gascon Jean de Grailly, the Captal de Buch, were reckoned the best knights of their day. Sir John Hawkwood, who had risen from the ranks to become a captain of adventurers, passed on into Italy with his band and carried the balance of power in the peninsula with him, as he served one state or another with the famous "White Company".

SIR JOHN HAWKWOOD

This ascendency of the English in the field implied the predominance of infantry as the chief power in war, to the detriment of the feudal chivalry which had ruled Europe for the last five centuries. In the new system, whose first victories had been seen at Dupplin and Halidon Hill, the knights descended from their steeds and formed a solid centre of resistance, while the yeomen with their deadly archery took the more active share in the repulse of the hostile attack. Edward III. must have the credit of applying this order of battle, which had originally been devised against the Scottish spearmen, to the discomfiture of the French feudal horse. The effect of Crecy and Poictiers was so great that the art of war in Western Europe was wholly revolutionised, and the French, Germans, and Italians took to dismounting and fighting on foot like the English.

This loss of military ascendency by the *noblesse* was still further developed by another military change of the fourteenth century. Firearms, whose feeble beginnings go back to the first decade of Edward's reign, were slowly improving and coming into more general use all through the succeeding generation. Though their size was still small and their discharge slow, they proved almost as deadly to the feudal castle as the yeoman's arrow had been to the feudal horseman. It began to be possible to breach by the use of cannon strongholds which had hitherto been reckoned impregnable.

This gave the king, the only person in the realm who possessed a competent train of artillery, an advantage in dealing with unruly barons such as he had never before enjoyed. Rebels could no longer rely on holding out behind their walls for many months, nor count starvation the only form of attack that they need dread. But the power of cannon to break up feudalism was only just beginning to be realised in the later days of Edward III.; it was not fully developed till the fifteenth century.

Edward III. did almost as much to advance the growth of English trade and commerce as to increase English military prestige. But his work in this province was not wholly intentional; when encouraging close commercial intercourse with Flanders he was thinking mainly of the political advantages of the connection with the Flemings, and also hoping to draw financial profits from the taxes on increased exports and imports. But there can be no doubt that his Netherlandish and German alliances took Englishmen further afield than they had been wont to go before, and had favourable results on the national trade. Its volume increased so rapidly during the reign that Edward, first of all English kings, was able to introduce a gold currency into the realm.

✶✶✶✶✶✶

Henry III. had tried to introduce a "gold penny", worth 20 silver pence, into circulation, but his subjects refused to take it—being apparently in no need of a coin of such high value, and the issue had to be withdrawn.

✶✶✶✶✶✶

Before his time the silver penny had been the largest monetary unit, but he succeeded in issuing with general approval a large gold coin called the Rose-noble, one of which exchanged for eighty pence. This broad, handsome piece secured such general acceptance that it circulated freely in the Netherlands and western Germany, and many of the lords and towns of the Low Countries took to striking money exactly imitating the noble in type and size.

This extension of the English currency is closely connected with the fact that from the time of Edward III. onward the English were beginning to send their own merchants abroad, and no longer were content to receive all continental goods at the home ports from foreign ships. Down to the fourteenth century the greater part of the sea-borne merchandise which England consumed was brought her by the Italians or the traders of the Hanseatic league. Edward very properly encouraged his subjects to sail abroad themselves, so as to get rid of the "middleman" and the charges which he exacted for transporting commodities to England. To compete with the powerful foreign trading societies the native merchants were bound together in the Company of "the Staple", whose institution we have already had occasion to notice.

Though monopolies are generally harmful, yet in this case it was almost necessary to secure strength by combination, as the individual trader would have been helpless if he tried to oppose himself to the interests of the corporations of aliens whose markets he was invading. By the end of the century the limits of English seafaring trade were Lisbon and Hamburg; into the Mediterranean it did not yet penetrate, and the Baltic was almost entirely in the hands of the zealous Hanseatic league. But Chaucer's typical "shipman", as it will be remembered, knew all havens

From Gothland to the Cape of Finisterre,

i.e. from north-western Spain to the coast of Sweden.

Manufactures were developing no less than trade. King Edward never did a wiser deed than when he invited the Flemish weavers to settle in Norwich, and make up on the spot the fine English wool which used formerly to be taken over to the Netherlands in order to be woven into cloth. In the true protectionist spirit a law of 1337 prohibited the wearing of any but English cloth by all persons save the royal family. Weaving was not the only craft which took a new start in the fourteenth century from the introduction of foreign teachers; metal work was much improved, and the use of glass in domestic architecture grew much more common.

The influence of the Black Death on trade and prices deserves notice. It not only raised the wages of the agricultural classes—in despite of the Statute of Labourers—but increased the selling value of all manufactured goods. While corn and other natural products of the soil remained at their old level of price, and while sheep and oxen rose only slightly in value, all things produced by skilled manual labour cost from 40 to 60 *per cent* more than they did before the great plague. This came, of course, from the fact that the artisans had been seriously reduced in numbers, so that the survivors were able to demand much higher prices for their handiwork.

Since the cost of food remained the same as it had been before, the labouring classes were able to buy it of better quality and in greater quantity than of old, and their standard of comfort appreciably went up. The merchant profited as much, or more, from the enhanced selling value of his wares as he lost through having to pay higher wages to the artisans who manufactured them. On the other hand, the capitalist land-owner was in a worse position than in the days before the Black Death, since his farm produce cost more in the item of labour, and yet sold for much the same money that it had in the first half of the century.

Hence two tendencies had their rise: the landholder who had been wont to cultivate a large part of his estate himself as a home-farm under a bailiff—"*in demesne*" as the term then was—either abandoned the practice and let the demesne land at a rent to tenant farmers, or tried to turn his arable fields into pasture. For a greater profit was to be had from rearing sheep for their wool, the great staple product of England, than by growing any sort of corn. These changes, however, were only beginning to make themselves felt in King Edward's time; it takes many years to turn a simple race of conservative habits into new methods of life and husbandry.

The actual loss of population by the Black Death took many generations to repair; it seems to have been felt far more in some districts than in others. The southern and eastern counties suffered more in proportion than the western, and probably lost in consequence somewhat of the enormous superiority in wealth and importance which they had hitherto possessed. They still remained, however, the preponderant part of the realm.

Nine years were destined to elapse between the conclusion of the Treaty of Bretigny and the renewal of the war with France. They were on the whole a time of peace and prosperity for England; and, as is generally the case during such periods, there is little of importance to record in the domestic annals during their course. The intermittent quarrel with the papacy which had been going on for many years caused the renewal of the *Statute of Provisors*, and the confirmation of a *Statute of Præmunire*, so called because by it persons who took appeals to the pope at Avignon were warned beforehand (*præmuniti*) that they made themselves liable to be brought before the king's courts for showing contempt of his exclusive right of jurisdiction in England

(1365).

The writs addressed against such offenders began with the words *præmunire facias*, and hence came the name of the statute. Some curious legislation against the wearing of clothing too good for their condition by the lower and middle classes bears witness to their growth in prosperity since the Black Death. Like all "sumptuary" laws it had no effect, and had soon to be abandoned. It is perhaps worth noting also that in 1362 English was made the official language of the law-courts, where Norman-French had hitherto prevailed.

The foreign affairs of the realm are of importance, and from the first made it evident that the Treaty of Bretigny was to be a truce and not a permanent pacification. Its terms were never fully carried out. King John failed to raise his enormous ransom, and when he found that it could not be collected, loyally returned to England and surrendered his person, since he had failed to keep his promise. He died at the palace of the Savoy, in the Strand, on April 8th, 1364.

When he had passed away his son Charles V., a very crafty and unscrupulous prince, refused to listen to any complaints as to the non-observance of the treaty. But he was as yet too busy in pacifying his own realm to stir against the English. He was not even firmly set upon the throne till the claims of his turbulent cousin, Charles the Bad of Navarre, were crushed by the defeat of Cocherel, and disposed of by a treaty signed in May, 1365.

The Breton war of succession, which had been raging ever since 1341, at last reached its termination in 1364. The younger John of Montfort, the ally of the English, at last succeeded in winning complete possession of his duchy by slaying his rival Charles of Blois at the Battle of Auray, a fight gained by the valour and tactical skill of Sir John Chandos and the other English knights who served under his banner (September 29, 1364).

But another war in which England was interested was to lead to less happy results. It was the work of Edward the Black Prince, who had been ruling in Aquitaine almost as an independent prince since his father handed it over to him and gave him the ducal title in 1362. To his court at Bordeaux there came as a suppliant an exiled Spanish prince, Pedro, King of Castile, whom his subjects surnamed "the Cruel". He was a stern and high-handed prince, whose harsh and wicked rule—he had murdered his wife and one of his half-brothers among countless other victims—had driven the Castilians into revolt. The insurrection had been headed by his bastard brother, Henry, Count

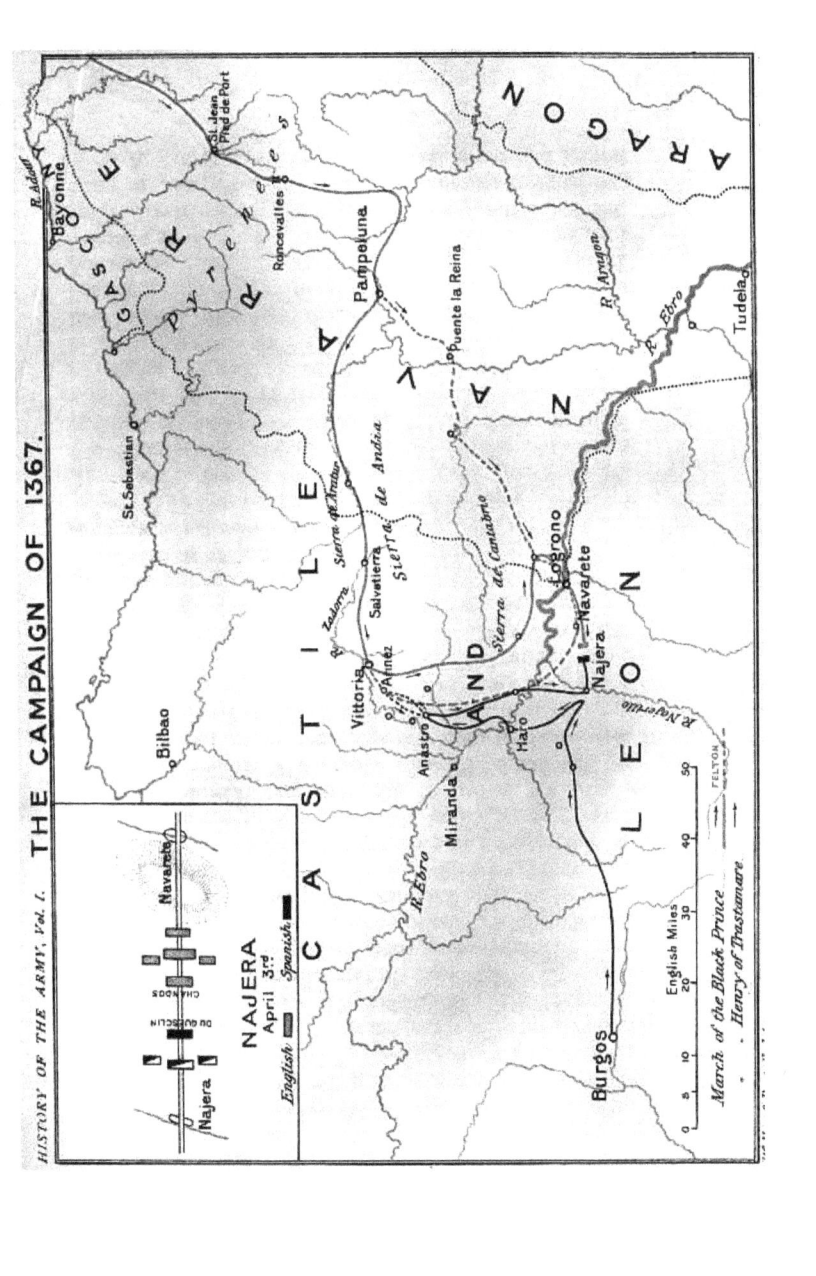

of Trastamara, who had called in to his aid a great host of French mercenaries led by Bertrand du Guesclin, a famous Breton captain of adventurers.

Henry with the help of these allies easily expelled Pedro from his realm, and had himself crowned as king (1366). The exile urged on the Black Prince that his situation in Aquitaine would be perilous if he let the neighbouring Spanish lands pass under the control of a dependant of the French. He promised to repay all the expenses of the war if Edward would restore him to his throne, and to bind himself the closer to the English offered to leave his two daughters, Constance and Isabel, in the Black Prince's hands as hostages. After some hesitation Edward resolved to give the king his aid; the political advantages of the move influenced him much, but he was moved even more by a chivalrous impulse. He hated the idea of turning away a suppliant, and loving war for its own sake he was burning to add new laurels to those of Poictiers and Espagnols-sur-Mer.

Accordingly, he accepted Pedro's offer: and the nobles of Aquitaine were bidden to prepare for a Spanish war in the next spring. John of Gaunt brought over a small contingent from England, but the bulk of the army of invasion was made up of the Gascon *noblesse*, and the veteran mercenaries who flocked in from all quarters to join the prince's banner. So great was his warlike fame in Europe that more adventurers came to proffer him their aid than he could possibly feed or pay. He had to send away thousands of them, after having picked out the best of the men-at-arms to serve him. Thus, his army was composed of none but choice troops, and far exceeded in military value the Spanish feudal levies against which it was to be pitted.

Edward crossed the Pyrenees by the pass of Roncesvalles—famous in history and in song for the defeat of the Emperor Charles the Great in 778, and for the death of Count Roland, the hero of the oldest legend of chivalry. Charles the Bad gave him a free passage through Navarre, and he did not see the enemy till he reached the hills above Vittoria, where Wellington was to win the crowning victory of the Peninsular War four and a half centuries later. Henry of Trastamara and his French allies had raised a great host which blocked the passes over the hills of Alava.

But the prince outgeneralled them, slipped round their flank, and crossing the Ebro entered Old Castile. The Spaniards hurried back to place themselves between Edward's host and Burgos, the capital of the realm. The shock between the two armies took place in a broad level plain between the towns of Najera and Navarette. The result was never for a moment doubtful: though the Castilians were somewhat superior in numbers they were mostly raw troops; moreover, they were accustomed to the skirmishing tactics of the Moors, not to facing the embattled line of dismounted men-at-arms flanked by archery.

The great masses of light horsemen armed with buckler and javelin, which formed the most numerous part of Don Henry's host, broke and fled away in utter rout a few minutes after they came under the deadly shower of arrows. The French auxiliaries, who had sent away their horses and fought on foot (as at Poictiers), were surrounded, and slain or captured to the last man. The bastard, who had tried in vain to rally his scattered horsemen, fled away in haste and escaped into France (April 3, 1367).

Thus, Don Pedro recovered his kingdom at a single blow: he celebrated the victory by beheading such of the prisoners as fell into his hands, to the utter disgust of his chivalrous ally. Edward marched with him as far as Burgos and replaced him in his palace, but dissensions at once began between them. Pedro could not or would not repay the vast sums which the prince had spent in raising and paying his army. The English host was kept cantoned round Burgos all through the summer, suffering severely from the unaccustomed heat, and from a lack of supplies. Sickness broke out among them, and Edward himself was prostrated by an attack of fever.

Meanwhile the Castilian king had gone away to Andalusia, and sent evasive letters instead of remittances of money. At last the prince, in high disgust, marched back unpaid to Aquitaine, leaving his faithless ally to shift for himself. By displaying again his old cruelty and recklessness Pedro soon provoked a second rebellion of his subjects. Henry of Trastamara returned, defeated him in battle, and finally took him prisoner. The bastard then settled the succession question by brutally murdering his brother with his own hands (March, 1369).

Thus, the only result of the victory of Navarette was that an implacable enemy of England was now firmly set upon the Castilian throne, while the duchy of Aquitaine was overwhelmed with the enormous debt incurred in restoring Don Pedro. The prince, honestly desiring to pay what he owed, sold his silver plate, surrendered to his followers the ransoms of his French and Castilian prisoners, and tried to make up the balance by raising money from his subjects. But his proposal to impose on every house in Aquitaine a hearth-tax of one *franc* provoked bitter opposition.

The Poitevins and other newly-annexed vassals of the duchy were thoroughly discontented and disloyal, and took the first opportunity of withstanding their master. The estates of Aquitaine refused to vote the impost, and when Edward persevered in his plan, a body of barons, headed by the lords of Albret and Armagnac, announced their intention of appealing to the king at Paris. This was utterly contrary to the terms of the Treaty of Bretigny, by which Aquitaine had been freed for ever from all feudal dependence on the French crown. The Gascon nobles therefore had no right to call in Charles V.; but legality counted for little, and the one point of importance was to discover whether the king would dare to involve himself in a new English war, after the unhappy experiences of his father and grandfather.

Charles V. resolved to take the risk. He had got his realm into something like order during the five years which had elapsed since he had crushed the king of Navarre, and he was well acquainted with the fact that more than half of Edward's subjects in Aquitaine were ready to rebel and join him. Charles first sent a summons to the Black Prince to appear at Paris and answer before his *suzerain* for wrongs done to the barons of the south, and when this preposterous order was ignored, commenced hostilities. It is said that, as a mark of contempt, he sent the final declaration of war not by a herald, as was the custom, but by the hands of his master-cook (April 29, 1369).

CHAPTER 6

The Last Years of Edward III. 1369-1377

From the very first moment of the outbreak of war, the struggle with France proved disastrous for England. Almost before the designs of Charles V. were realised news came that the isolated county of Ponthieu had been overrun by the enemy, and that Abbeville and its other towns and castles had surrendered. The state of affairs in Aquitaine was not much better: in many parts of Poitou, Perigord, and Rouergue powerful barons disavowed their allegiance, and took up arms in behalf of the French king.

In the war which followed the English lacked the advantage which they had enjoyed in the earlier struggle, of being guided by a single leader: King Edward never again took the field: though only in his fifty-eighth year, he was worn out as much in mind as in body. The direction of affairs ought to have passed to his eldest son, a man in the prime of life verging on his fortieth year. But the Black Prince had never recovered from the effects of the fever which had stricken him down during his Spanish campaign. For the rest of his life he was a confirmed invalid, and every exertion which he made was immediately followed by a relapse, which sent him back to his sick-bed.

For the first two years of the war he endeavoured to stay at the helm, but the want of vigour and combination which attended the movements of the English troops showed that he was not himself. When he finally was obliged to retire from the scene of action in 1370, the main part of the responsibility fell to his next surviving brother, John of Gaunt, a busy and ambitious but not a capable prince. He had made many enemies, and was never able to command the same unhesitating obedience which had been shown to Edward III. and the Black Prince.

As long as the younger Edward still kept his court at Bordeaux the

English continued to defend Aquitaine, with moderate success. But Sir John Chandos, the prince's right-hand man, was killed in a petty skirmish in Poitou, on December 31st, 1369, and after his death things took a turn for the worse. In 1370 the French struck deep into the duchy of Aquitaine, and captured first the strong town of Aiguillon in Agenois, and then the important city of Limoges, whose citizens treacherously opened their gates to the invaders.

The prince took the field for the last time to recover Limoges, though he was so weak that he could not sit his war-horse, and had to be borne on a litter. He took the place after an obstinate defence, by throwing down part of the wall by a mine filled with gunpowder. When his men entered the breach, he bade them cut down everyone they met, for he was much enraged with his rebellious subjects. Thus, his hitherto spotless career was sullied by a massacre in its last moments (October, 1370). Three months later his health grew so much worse that he took ship for England, expecting every moment to be his last. But he survived the passage, and lingered on for more than five years at his castle of Berkhampstead, a helpless invalid, unable to take any part either in war or domestic governance.

With the departure of the prince things in France went from bad to worse. The French could not be kept back from overrunning Aquitaine, though two considerable expeditions had been sent out from Calais to endeavour to distract them from their prey. But by the orders of their king the nobles of northern France utterly refused battle, shut themselves up in their castles, and allowed the English to march past them unmolested. These unchivalrous but effective tactics caused John of Gaunt, in 1369, and Sir Robert Knolles, in 1370, to march across Picardy without effecting anything of note, for they had no leisure to engage in sieges, and they could not get the battle that they desired.

But in 1372 England made a serious effort to reinforce Aquitaine. The Parliament had granted the king a subsidy of £50,000, and with it a considerable army and fleet was collected, and placed under the orders of John Earl of Pembroke, the king's son-in-law. He crossed the Bay of Biscay safely, but as he drew near La Rochelle, the port for which he was aiming, found his path beset by a large Spanish fleet. Henry of Trastamara was bent on revenging Navarette, and he had just found another reason for taking strong measures against the English.

John of Gaunt and his younger brother Edmund of Langley had in the winter of 1371-72 wedded the two daughters and heiresses of Pedro the Cruel, who had been dwelling as hostages at Bordeaux ever since their father broke his word in 1367. In virtue of this marriage John gave himself out as the rightful king of Castile. Henry was much enraged, and had sent forth to aid the French all the ships that he could gather together. A fierce fight ensued off La Rochelle, in which the English were totally defeated, many of their light vessels being sunk by the great stones and masses of iron which the Biscayans cast down into them from their taller ships (June 22, 1372). Pembroke and many scores of knights were taken prisoners.

The defence of Aquitaine, now that the army of succour had been destroyed, fell upon the shoulders of the Captal de Buch, the loyal Gascon baron who had so much distinguished himself at Poictiers sixteen years before. He made a gallant fight, but was utterly unable to stem the advancing flood of French invasion. His forces were too small, and the discontented people of the land would give him no help. Poictiers, Niort, and La Rochelle fell into the hands of the enemy, betrayed by their citizens, and with them went almost the whole of Poitou, Saintonge, and the Angoumois.

At last the Captal was surprised and taken prisoner in a skirmish near Soubise, and with him departed the last hope of maintaining the English dominion north of the Garonne. About the same time John V. of Brittany, the one faithful ally of King Edward, saw the greater part of his duchy overrun by the French, whose forces were led by his own born subject, the great *Condottiere* Bertrand du Guesclin, who had now been made Constable of France (1372-73).

In 1373 England made her last effort to turn the fortune of war. John of Gaunt was sent over the water with 3000 men-at-arms and 6000 bowmen; at Calais, he was joined by a great body of mercenaries raised in the Netherlands and Germany. We hear to our surprise that he had even enlisted 300 Scottish lances to serve against the French. Thus, a formidable army was mustered, but it was led by an incompetent general, and was directed on the wrong lines. It would have been better to start from Bordeaux, and clear Perigord and Saintonge of the enemy, instead of starting on a mere destructive raid into northern France.

The experience of 1369 and 1370 had already shown that such operations had no effect against a king like Charles V., who did not intend to fight, and could not be stirred to indiscretion even by seeing the barns and cottages of his subjects blazing up on every side. John of Gaunt was allowed to push his way across Picardy and Champagne as far as the Loire: the French hung about his route and cut off his stragglers, but would not offer battle. Then he moved on into Berri, and went on ravaging the land on his way to Bordeaux.

The autumn had now set in, and among the rugged mountains of Auvergne the army suffered terrible privations: nearly all the horses died of starvation, and many men fell by the way from cold and overfatigue. At last they reached Bordeaux ragged and famished, after having accomplished no useful end whatever: they had inflicted untold misery on the peasantry of central France, but had brought no pressure to bear on Charles V., nor even retaken one of the lost towns of northern Aquitaine. In April, 1374, Lancaster disbanded the remnants of his host, since he could no longer pay them, and returned to England.

The failure of his ill-managed expedition was followed by the loss of the greater part of Guyenne and Gascony. The inhabitants felt that the King of England's last bolt was shot, and that there was no object in fighting any longer for a lost cause. One after another all the towns along the Garonne and Dordogne gave themselves up to the French after feeble and perfunctory resistances. By the end of 1374 all that was left to King Edward was the cities of Bordeaux and Bayonne, and the narrow slip of Gascon coast-land connecting them: all the inland was gone. That the two great seaports still held out was mainly due to the fact that their trading interests were closely bound up with the English connection, and that they knew that they were getting better and more orderly government from their actual lord than would be granted them by Charles V. It must be remembered too that they had been in the hands of the Plantagenets ever since Henry II. had married Eleanor of Aquitaine two hundred years before, and had no historical nor sentimental ties with the house of Valois.

Considering the utter ruin of the English cause in Aquitaine, Edward III. must be considered to have been fortunate when in the June of the following year (1375) he succeeded in concluding a suspension of hostilities with the enemy. The truce was for a year, but it was renewed for a second twelvemonth in June 1376, and actually lasted for the whole of the short remainder of the old king's reign.

The five years during which Aquitaine was gradually passing into the hands of the French were very important in the constitutional history of England. All through their course a bitter struggle was going on in Parliament, caused by the discontent of the nation at the unfortunate issue of the war. Its first sign was an outbreak against the king's ministers in 1371. It was easy to attribute the successes of the

French to the incapacity of the men whom the king had chosen to carry on the administration: of these the most important were two prelates, William of Wykeham bishop of Winchester, the chancellor; and Thomas of Brantingham bishop of Exeter, the treasurer. Both were able and disinterested men: Wykeham, who had first attracted Edward's attention by his skill as an architect, had been found an honest and capable statesman, and has left a good name behind him as the founder of Winchester College, the first great public school, and of the sister foundation of New College, Oxford.

It was wholly unjust to lay the blame of the losses in Aquitaine on the chancellor and treasurer; they were really due to military causes—the want of a single competent general-in-chief, and the squandering of men and money on the unwise raids into northern France. But the Parliament attributed them to the incapacity of ecclesiastics to rule in time of war, and petitioned the king to dismiss them, and to replace them by laymen. Edward yielded, and Sir Robert Thorpe was made chancellor, while Sir Richard Scrope, a follower of John of Gaunt, took over the charge of the treasury.

The new administration proved far more unfortunate than that which it had supplanted. John of Gaunt had now become the true ruling power in the realm: his elder brother was on his sick-bed, and his father was falling into his dotage. Edward III. had lost his wise and faithful wife, Philippa of Hainault, in 1369, and shortly after fell into the hands of a worthless adventuress, Dame Alice Perrers. In his foolish fondness for her he allowed her to tamper with matters of state, and all who wished to advance themselves about the court came to her with bribes. She even contrived to interfere with the administration of justice, and to frighten or corrupt the judges. John of Gaunt left his father in the hands of this harpy, and assumed complete control of foreign affairs. It was on him that the responsibility for the disasters of 1373-4-5 must be laid. After the loss of Guyenne, he was forced to face Parliament with a lamentable report of money wasted, opportunities let slip, and provinces lost to the French.

On the meeting of the "Good Parliament" of 1376 the storm of national discontent, which had been brewing for the last three years, burst upon Lancaster's head. He was accused justly enough of incapacity, but men added unfounded accusations, such as the charge of plotting to seize the throne at his father's death, to the exclusion of his invalid brother, and of the little prince Richard, the Black Prince's nine-year-old son. It was even whispered that he had planned to get the boy poisoned. John himself was too highly placed for the Parliament to dare to attack him openly, but a vigorous assault was made on his friends and associates.

Peter de la Mare, the speaker of the House of Commons, boldly declared that the nation was ready to help the king in his distress, but that they must first remove from about his person those who were making their private profit out of his misfortunes. The three chief offenders pointed out were the chamberlain, William Lord Latimer, Richard Lyons, the king's financial agent, and Dame Alice Perrers. The two first-named had been guilty of disgraceful frauds; they had bought up the king's debts, from poor men who despaired of ever seeing their money, at half their nominal amount or less, and had then paid themselves in full from the treasury.

On one occasion, they had lent the king 20,000 *marks* (£13,333, 6s. 8d.), and got out of him an acknowledgment for £20,000 sterling. Latimer had extorted a great bribe from the Duke of Brittany, England's faithful ally, and had then betrayed him by selling his castles of St. Sauveur and Becherel to the French. Latimer and Lyons were accordingly *impeached, i.e.* formally accused by the Commons and tried by the House of Peers. The Lords found them guilty, and they were sentenced to be fined, imprisoned, and deprived of their offices. Several minor offenders were punished at the same time. As to Dame Alice, the Commons accused her of breaking the law which forbade women to meddle with the administration of justice, and obtained against her an award of banishment. She was made to swear that she would never return to the king's presence, an oath which she very soon broke.

The Prince of Wales died June 8, 1376. Parliament petitioned the king that his little grandson Richard should be at once recognised as heir to the crown, and that a standing council should be appointed to carry on the government. Edward himself was no longer capable of work, and it was felt that John of Gaunt must be prevented from engrossing all the royal powers into his hands. Accordingly, the king consented that Parliament should nominate nine persons as members of the council, of whom at least four were to be always about his person.

At the same time, he promised to consider favourably the demands contained in a vast list of 140 petitions, dealing with all manner of administrative grievances, which the Commons laid before him. Two of the most important of these documents demanded, the one that Parliaments should be annual, the other that the sheriffs and other royal officers should not interfere with the election of knights of the shire, but always allow the return of the persons whom "the better folk of the county" should nominate.

On the 6th of July, the Parliament dispersed, having, as it fondly supposed, crushed Lancaster and provided for the future good governance of the realm. The moment that they had broken up, John of Gaunt took his revenge, and executed a kind of *coup d'état*. He got his doting father into his hands, and then used his name to declare that the "Good Parliament" had been no parliament at all, and that its acts were null and void. He threw the late speaker, Peter de la Mare, into prison, dismissed the nine newly-appointed councillors, and released Lyons and the other culprits who had been condemned. Alice Perrers was allowed quietly to return to court.

A new Parliament was then summoned to meet, and, by employing the royal prerogative in the most unscrupulous fashion, and threatening and overawing the electors, Lancaster succeeded in getting returned a large majority of his supporters (January, 1377). The king had now entered into the fiftieth year of his reign, and to celebrate his jubilee proclaimed a pardon and amnesty to many minor offenders and debtors. At the head of the list, however, appeared the names of Latimer and Lyons and their underlings, who were relieved of all fines, penalties, and disabilities which had been laid upon them in the previous year.

All these actions were scandalous and highly calculated to lead to civil war. If the party which opposed the duke and the court had been headed by a baronial chief of the type of Simon de Montfort, or of the great earls who had withstood Edward I., it is probable that Lancaster would have been overthrown by force of arms. But this was far from being the case: the most prominent leader of the constitutional party was Bishop William of Wykeham, a lover of peace and caution; and the chief lay patron of the cause, the young Earl of March, was also a man of moderate views. No open opposition to Duke John was made at first, even when he proceeded to bring against Wykeham a ridiculous charge of embezzling public funds, as a kind of counterblast to the impeachment of Latimer and Lyons in the preceding year.

Lancaster, though a short-sighted politician, was yet conscious that he must soon be overthrown unless he could manage to enlist a certain amount of popular sympathy on his side. The truce with France being still running he could not appeal to warlike sentiments, but there was one strong current of opinion which he thought that he might direct into channels favourable to himself. This was the antipapal feeling, which was as strong now as in the days when the *Statutes of Provisors* and *Praemunire* had been passed. The court of feeling. Avignon was going from bad to worse, and its shameless demands and exactions deeply irritated every patriotic Englishman. But a great part of the clergy, now as always, thought themselves bound to side with the papacy, and the English Church was itself full of abuses and scandals, which did not tend to grow less.

Bishops who neglected their dioceses, and were more at home in war and diplomacy than in spiritual work, had always existed, but in the fourteenth century their numbers were greater than ever, since the baronage had taken of late to putting their younger sons into the church and pressing them forward for promotion. In earlier centuries, this had been rare, in the fourteenth it was very common. Three of the seven Archbishops of Canterbury between 1348 and 1400 were sons or brothers of peers. The average of episcopal piety and unworldliness was not improved by the change. Among the beneficed clergy there was a good deal of non-residence, an appreciable amount of simony, and a certain proportion of evil-living. The abbeys and friaries were worse: all accounts agree that the monastic bodies were inferior to the secular priests in zeal and moral worth. It is said that the hasty filling-up of the depleted ranks of the clergy with unqualified and unsatisfactory persons after the Black Death had a permanent effect in lowering the moral tone of the whole body.

At the same time the church was richer than ever: it was believed that a third of the land and wealth of the realm were in clerical hands. The clergy always gave liberal grants in convocation for national purposes, but this did not satisfy men who complained that their land escaped all feudal taxation, and so did not pay its fair share towards filling the treasury.

The feeling that something ought to be done to improve the internal condition of the church, as well as to check the encroachments of the pope, had long been prevalent, and was shared by many who were themselves clerics. Among those who were foremost in calling for radical measures of reform was John Wycliffe (sometime Master of Balliol College), a learned Oxford doctor of divinity. He had first made his mark as a deep thinker in philosophy and theology, but was driven into politics by his indignation at the corrupt state of the church and the papacy. He came to the conclusion that most of the clerical scandals of the day had their roots in the over-great wealth and power of the church, and held that the best way to reform it would be to compel the clergy to return to the apostolic poverty of the early centuries.

Against the papacy, as the source of all other evils, he was particularly keen. He had been first introduced to public affairs as a member of a deputation sent to Bruges in 1374 to negotiate terms of agreement between the English Church and the pope. The evil impression which the papal delegates then made on him he never forgot. Ere long we find him protesting in the strongest terms against the spiritual authority which the pope claimed to exercise over the whole church, and asserting that it was blasphemous for him to pose as God's vicegerent on earth, and the mediator between Christ and the individual Christian. He said, employing a familiar metaphor drawn from the feudal system:

> All men are tenants-in-chief under God, responsible directly to him for their souls and their manner of life; the pope is like an intruder who tries to push in as a mesne-tenant between God and man.

Then he added that spiritual authority could only be wielded by a righteous man, and that no obedience was due to the orders of a spiritual ruler whose life was not in consonance with the word of Christ. Not only the pope, but a large number of the English prelates might fairly be said to come under this condemnation. At a later date Wycliffe added to his attack on the governors of the church an attack on some of the characteristic doctrines of Rome, notably on that of Transubstantiation in the Eucharist.

This later development, however, had not begun in 1377, and it was only as preaching insubordination and resistance to Rome that Wycliffe was at this time arraigned and tried by Bishop Courtenay of London, a strong opponent of John of Gaunt. The duke's only sympathy with Wycliffe came from the fact that they both desired to repress the overgrown power of the ecclesiastical authorities, the one from political and personal motives, the other on religious and theoretical grounds. With Wycliffe's spiritual fervour Lancaster had nothing in common, but he resolved to support him because they owned the same enemies, and because there was always popularity to be gained by opposing Rome.

Accordingly, when Wycliffe was brought before the bishop in St. Paul's for trial (February, 1377) the duke came in person, and threatened Courtenay in such stormy language that after an unseemly altercation the assembly broke up in disorder, and Wycliffe went free. A mob of the bishop's friends and followers went next day and sacked John's palace of the Savoy. Though much enraged he dared not proceed to more violent measures against Courtenay, and contented himself with making his father suspend for a time some of the privileges of the city of London.

Thus, the political strife of the Court party and the Constitutional party had become complicated with the religious dispute between the Reformers and the Romanisers. How much further matters would have gone had John of Gaunt retained his unlimited power and authority we cannot say, for the aspect of affairs was wholly changed a few months later by the death of the old king. Edward died on June 2, 1377, at his palace of Sheen. When his last moments were near his servants stole all they could and fled. The shameless Alice Perrers is said to have stripped the very rings from his hands when she saw him fall into unconsciousness. Of all the numerous train that he had fed only one poor priest was present to minister the offices of the church as he drew his last breath. This miserable death-bed was but the natural termination of a life spent in the pursuit of selfish pleasure and ambition. Such a king was bound to a breed race of heartless courtiers and thankless dependants.

CHAPTER 7

Richard II. the Years of the Minority 1377-1388

The accession to the throne of the late king's grandson, Richard II., a bright promising lad of eleven, put an end to the domination of John of Gaunt. The Princess of Wales and the friends of her deceased husband, who had brought up the young king, had never been allied to Lancaster, and had viewed his movements with suspicion. He had no longer the power to use the royal name for his own profit as he had done for the last few years. Facing the situation with more wisdom than might have been expected, the duke made no attempt .to hold on to the helm, but yielded with a good grace, and entered into a formal reconciliation with Wykeham and the other chiefs of the constitutional party.

Peter de la Mare was released from prison, the Londoners were pardoned for their riot of the preceding February, and it was agreed that old enmities should be forgotten. The governance of the realm was placed in the hands of a council in which both the parties were fairly represented. The first parliament of the new reign passed two important pieces of constitutional legislation: one provided that during a minority the king's ministers should be chosen by the two houses; the other was to the effect that all acts passed by Parliament could be set aside only by the consent of Parliament. This second point was one which was not to be fully established for three hundred years. As late as the time of James II. kings still claimed to have a dispensing power which overrode the statute-book.

Though the danger of domestic troubles was for a time at an end, the condition of politics was yet far from satisfactory. Charles V. of France had refused to renew the truce which ran out in the summer of 1377, and the "Hundred Years' War" had once more passed into an acute stage. The campaigns which followed were neither so disastrous nor so decisive as those of 1373-75, but their results were on the whole unfavourable. Nothing of importance was lost—the whole inland had already fallen into the hands of the French, and the grasp of the English on the coast towns was very firm—but, on the other hand, nothing was regained, and the expenses of the war were ruinous.

In 1380 an expedition under the king's youngest uncle, Thomas of Woodstock, landed at Calais, and cut its way through Picardy, Champagne, and the Orleanois to Brittany. It was a mere repetition of Lancaster's march in 1373: once more the French avoided open battle, and contented themselves with defending their walled towns and cutting off the foragers and stragglers of the invading host. Earl Thomas reached Vannes without any overwhelming disaster, but with an army too much harassed and worn down to accomplish the delivery of Brittany from the French. John V., the faithful ally of England since his accession in 1345, was at last driven to abandon the alliance and make peace with the enemy. He was recognised as duke by the French government in return for his submission, and at last recovered the whole of his dominions (1380).

The abortive expedition to Brittany had been very costly, and heavy taxation was necessary to pay the troops, whose wages were six months in arrears. Accordingly, the chancellor, Simon of Sudbury, Archbishop of Canterbury, laid before the Parliament of Northampton projects for the raising of a sum of £160,000. The method finally adopted for collecting it was a Poll-tax on the whole of the inhabitants of the realm above the age of fifteen: it was graduated upwards from one shilling paid by the poor, to £3 imposed on the richest individuals.

The imposition of this tax, which pressed very heavily on the labouring classes, was the cause of the explosion of a discontent which had been brewing ever since the social troubles that had followed the Black Death and the Statute of Labourers. The Peasant Revolt, or Wat Tyler's Rebellion, as it is sometimes called, was not the result of the Poll-tax only. That imposition, though bitterly resented, was but the occasion and not the cause of the rising just as the greased cartridges in 1857 were not the cause of the Indian Mutiny. The origins of the trouble were many, and varied much in different places.

In London and the towns, the discontent was largely political; the people resented the disastrous results of the French war, and the heavy taxation which resulted from it. They laid the blame on the governing classes, without much distinction of persons and parties, save that John of Gaunt was specially singled out as responsible for the present unhappy situation. In the shires, on the other hand, the explosion was mainly the result of social causes, and especially of the grievances of villeinage. We have had already occasion to remark that the Statute of Labourers had estranged the landholders from their peasants. The attempt to enforce the ancient dues of compulsory labour from the servile tenants had led to much bad blood: everyone wished to hold his land at a moderate money rent, and not to be compelled to give forced labour for his lord's demesne farms.

Wherever the owner of a manor insisted on carrying on the old system discontent was rife. In many parts the peasantry had entered into secret clubs and combinations to resist their masters, and these societies seem to have had much to do with the organization of the rising. But this grievance alone does not suffice to explain the revolt: its outbreak was as violent in Kent, where villeinage no longer existed, as in any other shire. There was a bitter feeling abroad against the tyrannical forest laws, against the tolls and market dues which raised the price of provisions, against the whole tribe of lawyers, whose subtilties and legal fictions were thought to prevent the poor man from obtaining justice.

In some parts, too, the rising was strongly anticlerical: it was very violent in places like St. Albans and Bury St. Edmunds, where the tenants of the church had tried in vain to get from their abbots the charters and privileges which most other small towns enjoyed. Very important also (though it has sometimes been exaggerated) was the influence of Wycliffe's denunciation of the clergy during the last ten years. His teaching had filtered down to the lower strata of society in a form which took the shape of socialism. He had preached that obedience was not due to spiritual superiors of evil life, and that it was expedient that the church should be deprived of the over-great wealth which was corrupting her.

He had founded an order of "poor priests" who went about the country spreading his doctrines, and in the mouths of his more fanatical disciples his teaching took an almost anarchical turn. They denounced all obedience to unrighteous governors, lay or clerical, and spoke as if poverty was the only virtue and riches the sole source of evil. The most violent language of this kind was used by a wandering priest named John Ball, who was well known all over the southern shires. He was not a Wycliffite, since he had been in trouble for his teaching long before Wycliffe's name had been heard outside Oxford, but his addresses pressed to their logical extreme all the ideas which underlay the new doctrine. His famous text:

> *When Adam delved and Eve span,*
> *Who was then the gentleman?*

was the prelude to sermons urging that all men must be made equal, and all property forcibly divided into equal shares. For the most part, however, the men who joined in the revolt were not bent on setting the whole world to rights, but on getting rid each of his own special grievance.

In June, 1381, the rising broke out in all the eastern counties, from Kent as far as Yorkshire, with a simultaneity that shows that it must have been prepared beforehand. Whether the organisation had been made by the secret societies of the labourers or by the travelling agitators is not certain, though we know that John Ball had held a meeting in London, just before the rising, with some of the men who afterwards led the revolt in Norfolk and Suffolk. The first riot broke out, it is said, at Dartford, in Kent, where a certain tiler slew one of the collectors of the poll-tax who had grossly insulted his daughter. Whatever may be the truth of this story, it is certain that all Kent rose in arms as if on a given signal, and a few days afterwards Essex and the eastern counties followed suit (June, 1381).

In all the regions over which the rising spread there was a certain amount of bloodshed and a good deal of plunder. The persons who were slain were mainly justices of the peace, lawyers, and officials connected with the levying of the poll-tax. But local quarrels and grievances led to other murders, such as those of the Prior of Bury St. Edmunds and the Governor of Norwich Castle. Everywhere the manors of unpopular landlords were sacked, and manor rolls and records of taxation sought out and burnt. In Cambridge, where the town and the university had an old quarrel, the mob burst open the university church and burnt all the charters and muniments, crying, "Away with the learning of clerks! away with it!"

After a few days of uproar, the bands of the home counties began to move on London. Those of Kent, under a leader who called himself Wat Tyler, encamped on Blackheath, while the men of Hertfordshire took post at Highbury, and those of Essex at Hampstead. They all agreed in swearing that they were true to the king, and only desired to deliver him from his evil counsellors. The gates of London were shut against them by the Mayor Walworth, but there was no other attempt to resist them, for the government had been taken by surprise, and had no time to collect troops.

But on June 12 the mob of the city rose and opened the gates to the insurgents. They spread themselves through the streets, not indulging in general plunder, but sacking and burning the Savoy, the palace of John of Gaunt, and slaying many foreign merchants and certain persons against whom they had special grievances. The young king, who had retired into the Tower, tried to parley with them. The demands which they sent him were not so wild as might have been expected: they asked for a free pardon, for the abolition of all villeinage, for the removal of many taxes and tolls, and for a permission to all who had formerly held land on a servile tenure to become instead free tenants of their farms at the rent of fourpence an acre.

It is evident that the majority had not been led away by the teaching of John Ball and his fellows. Seeing that their terms were not altogether impossible, the young king, who displayed admirable courage and coolness, though he was but fifteen years of age,—bade them meet him at Mile End, then a great open space, and there discuss their grievances. The majority came to the colloquy; but while it was going on Wat Tyler and John Ball, with about 400 riotous followers, burst into the Tower, and there murdered the Archbishop Simon of Sudbury, who was specially hated as the framer of the poll-tax, and with him Sir Robert Hales, the treasurer, and John Legge, the chief collector of the tax.

While this dreadful scene was going on, the young king had been addressing the main body of the insurgents at Mile End. After some discussion, he agreed to grant their demands, and thirty clerks were set at once to work to draw out charters granting free pardons and the abolition of villeinage for the inhabitants of each town or hundred. That evening the majority of the insurgents went quietly home, having, as they thought, obtained their desires (June 13). But Tyler and many thousands of the rougher and wilder sort remained behind: some of them were fanatics, and others were scenting more plunder and bloodshed.

Next day the king summoned Tyler and his followers to meet him at Smithfield, trusting to make terms with them as he had with their fellows. But the insurgent chief had gone too far to feel himself safe, and was set on keeping up the tumult, lest he should be called to justice for the murders of Sudbury and Hales. He bore himself insolently at the meeting, and began wrangling and insulting the king's attendants. This so excited William Walworth, the mayor, that he drew a cutlass from under his gown and hewed down the rebel from his horse. Thereupon one of the king's squires ran in and struck him dead as he lay.

Richard and his whole party were within an ace of perishing, for the multitude, seeing their leader fall, bent their bows, and were about to let fly. But the courageous young king rode forward among them, crying that he himself would now be their leader, and would see that justice was done to them. They hesitated a moment, and then, won by his noble bearing, followed him to Islington, where, in the open field, he distributed to them charters like those which had been given to their fellows on the previous day. They then dispersed, and he was able to ride back to his mother swearing "that he had this day won back his heritage and the realm of England, which was lost" (June 14).

When the insurgents had gone home the knights and nobles flocked into London, with thousands of armed retainers. The landholding classes were very wroth that their villeins had been freed without their consent, and said that Richard had given away what was not his own. In spite of the free pardon that had been granted, many scores of the leaders of the rebels in Kent and the home counties were seized and hung. Among them were John Ball, and "Jack Straw", who had been captain of the Essex men. In Norfolk, the warlike bishop Despenser took arms and put down the eastern insurgents, slaying their leader, the priest John Wrawe.

Reaction and revenge.

A few months later Parliament met, and voted that all the charters issued by the king were null and void, because they had been issued without the sanction of the two houses. Richard made some attempt to keep his promise to the insurgents, and tried to get his abolition of villeinage confirmed, but the voice of Lords and Commons was given unanimously against him, and he had to yield. The only grace that he obtained was that in January, 1382, on the occasion of his marriage to Anne of Bohemia, the young daughter of the Emperor Charles IV., a general amnesty was published for the surviving insurgents. But all their prominent leaders had already perished.

Nevertheless, it must not be forgotten that in one way the rising had not been without successful results; the land-owning classes had been so thoroughly frightened by the outbreak that they dealt more cautiously with the peasants for the future; for the next century villeinage was silently disappearing, as the lords allowed their men to commute labour for money rents, and to become free tenants. The grievances of villeinage were never again the cause of insurrection, for they gradually disappeared. In the next century, we shall see that the great popular rising of Jack Cade, which in many features recalls that of Wat Tyler, was political and not social in its aims and ends.

Richard was now in his sixteenth year, and had shown that he possessed both courage, ready wit, and a heart that could sympathize with his subjects. But he was not allowed to assume control of the administration; all through his reign he was the victim of a tribe of ambitious uncles and cousins, who were determined to keep him in the background as much as possible. John of Gaunt was now not the only source of trouble; his youngest brother, Thomas of Woodstock, who had become Duke of Gloucester, was a far worse man—domineering, arrogant, selfish, and given to all manner of intrigues.

He and Lancaster fell out, and their quarrels allowed the king some liberty; but in 1385 the elder duke disappeared for some time from the scene. By his marriage with Constance of Castile, mentioned earlier, he had a claim on the inheritance of Pedro the Cruel, and in the hope of making himself a ruler in Spain he went overseas with all the followers he could raise. He allied himself with his son-in-law, the King of Portugal, and at first conquered many towns in the northern provinces of Castile. But his army wasted away: the Castilians hated the memory of Don Pedro too much to submit to his heir, and after long struggles (1385-89) John was to return to England disappointed and grown old before his time.

During his absence Richard, had reached the age of twenty, and at last assumed the governance of his realm. His chosen ministers were Michael de la Pole, and Robert de Vere, Earl of Oxford. The former was a man of a new family: his father had been a wealthy merchant of Hull, but he himself took to war and politics, rose to the front by his ability, and was now, in his middle age, made chancellor, and afterwards Earl of Suffolk. De Vere on the other hand held one of the oldest earldoms in England: he was a young man of the same age as the king, and had become his favourite companion. To raise him to a position above the rest of the barons Richard made him Marquis of Dublin and Duke of Ireland. After these two friends the king placed most confidence in his half-brothers (the sons of the Princess of Wales by her first marriage), Thomas Holland, Earl of Kent, and John Holland, who was afterwards made Earl of Huntingdon.

De la Pole and De Vere could not in any sense be called "favourites" in the objectionable sense of the term. The experience of one and the ancient nobility of the other made them persons whom it was quite fitting that the king should choose as his ministers. It may be that Michael was somewhat avaricious, and Robert somewhat vain and light-headed, but we have only their enemies' word for the accusation. Their rule was certainly no worse than that of their predecessors; the plot which was made against them must accordingly be attributed to jealousy and ambition, and not to patriotism. Thomas of Gloucester, who was set on holding the chief power under his nephew the king, drew into a conspiracy certain discontented nobles, the chief of whom were the Earls of Arundel, Warwick, and Nottingham, and the young Henry of Bolingbroke, the eldest son of the Duke of Lancaster.

In the Parliament of 1386 Gloucester and his friends made a great stir against the ministers, accusing them of embezzling the king's money, mismanaging the war with France (which still dragged on its weary length), and refusing to carry on the government according to the advice of the council and the two houses. De la Pole was impeached and declared guilty, though the accusations were wholly unfair. But the moment that the Parliament had dispersed the king gave him his pardon, and restored him to the office of chancellor.

This action of Richard's gave the conspirators the opportunity which they desired. At Gloucester's call they took arms and called out their retainers; marching on London they found no one to oppose them, and seized the town. They called themselves the "Lords Appellant", because they "appealed (accused) of treason" Suffolk, Oxford, and certain other of the king's advisers. Richard bade his followers take arms, and De Vere gathered some levies in the western counties. But at Radcot Bridge on the Upper Thames, near Lechlade, he was beset by a far greater host which the insurgent barons had sent out against him.

After a brief skirmish the king's men surrendered, De Vere escaping with difficulty by swimming his horse across the river. He fled to France, where he was soon afterwards joined by De la Pole, who had also succeeded in getting away in safety from England. But the greater part of Richard's minor partisans did not leave the realm: they had not foreseen the merciless character of the Lords Appellant. Gloucester had determined to break the spirit of the king, and to deal so harshly with his instruments that no man should ever dare to serve him again.

In February 1388 met the "Merciless Parliament", which was

wholly dominated by the Lords Appellant, who had taken care to pack the Commons with their adherents. Gloucester behaved to his nephew with studied insolence: he brought out the documents which related to the deposition of Edward II., read them to the king before the assembly, and openly told him that there were good reasons for treating him as his great-grandfather had been treated. But for once he should be spared, and placed for the future in the hands of strong and wise counsellors.

The Parliament then proceeded to impeach the king's ministers: Suffolk and Oxford had crossed the seas, so had Neville, archbishop of York, who also was cited as an offender. But there were at hand Tresilian, the chief justice, Sir Simon Burley, an old friend of the Black Prince who had been the king's tutor in his boyhood, and Nicholas Bramber, an ex-mayor of London, all prominent servants of the unfortunate Richard. After the mere mockery of a trial Tresilian and Bramber were hung, and Burley beheaded.

Three knights of the king's household named Beauchamp, Berners, and Salisbury, were subsequently arrested, tried, and executed. The Parliament then voted liberal supplies for the expenses of government, from which the Lords Appellants were not ashamed to take £20,000 "to compensate them for the trouble and expense to which they had been put." Finally, the king was made to renew his coronation oath before the Archbishop of Canterbury in St. Paul's cathedral, and after assisting at the ceremony the "Merciless Parliament" dispersed (June, 1388).

Chapter 8
Richard II. 1388-1399

The Lords Appellant were very much deceived if they imagined that their *coup d'état* was likely to reduce King Richard to a permanent state of dependence. He was no coward or trifler, and devoted the whole of the rest of his life to an elaborate scheme of vengeance against the men who had slain his friends and inflicted such deep humiliation on himself. Warned of the strength of Gloucester's party by the events of 1388, he was resolved to spend years, if necessary, in preparing for a new struggle: the next time he would have armed force at his back, and would not be caught unprepared.

The government of the Lords Appellant lasted no more than a year. It was not more fortunate or capable than that which it had superseded, for Gloucester soon showed that he was an intriguer and not a statesman. Nor was he even consistent in his policy: though he had always been an advocate of vigorous war with France, he now concluded a truce with the young King Charles VI. France was at the time in a condition not unlike that of England, for Charles was the victim of a tribe of domineering uncles, who dealt with him in much the same way that Lancaster and Gloucester dealt with Richard II. He made no objection to the long-needed suspension of hostilities.

In May 1389 King Richard found it possible to take the governance of the realm out of the hands of the Lords Appellants. He surprised those who were present at the council by suddenly asking his uncle, Gloucester, what was his own age. The duke answered that he was now in his twenty-third year. To this Richard replied that since he had so long passed his majority, he was old enough to govern his own realm, and that he would choose his own ministers. He formally thanked the Lords Appellants for their services, but said that he had no further need for them. If he had dared to recall his exiled friends, or to take open measures of vengeance against his oppressors, there is no doubt that civil war would have broken out.

But Richard was now playing a very cautious game: he made his grandfather's old advisers his ministers. The good bishop William of Wykeham became chancellor, and Brantingham of Exeter treasurer, just as they had been in 1371. The Lords Appellants were not driven out of the council, but allowed to keep their seats, though they no longer dominated the whole body. Nothing was done to which any exception could be taken, so the malcontents had no opportunity of appealing to the country or rising in revolt.

The next eight years were by far the most fortunate and prosperous part of King Richard's reign. He governed well and wisely, and won golden opinions on every side. The most statesmanlike of all his measures was the conclusion of a permanent agreement with France. The two countries were to be at peace for thirty years, England retaining Calais and the district round Bordeaux and Bayonne, but surrendering her claim to her other lost possessions. The treaty was made firm by Richard's marriage to Isabella, the eight-year-old daughter of the French king. He had lately lost his first wife, Anne of Bohemia, and so was free to wed again; but peace with it was unwise to choose so young a bride, for France, he had no children by his first marriage, and an heir to the throne was much needed.

As long as Richard was childless his uncles and cousins were tempted to dream of ultimately succeeding to his crown. As a temporary measure of expediency, he recognised as heir-apparent Roger Earl of March, the grandson of Lionel of Clarence, the second son of Edward III. (see table further on). This action was very ill-received by John of Gaunt and his son, the Earl of Derby, who had secret hopes of asserting the preference of the male to the female line of succession.

Among the most prominent features of the middle years of Richard's reign was the growing importance of the Wycliffites, or Lollards as they were now beginning to be called. The reaction which followed the Peasant Revolt had only checked their rise for a short time. The king himself neither identified himself with them, nor took any of the measures against them which the clergy endeavoured to press on him. His wife Anne had been distinctly favourable to them, and her foreign servants and followers took back to their native land the teachings of Wycliffe, which were destined to inspire John Huss, the great Bohemian reformer. Some of the baronage, among whom the Earl of Salisbury was the most prominent person, and a great number of the wealthier members of the citizen class were open supporters of the Wycliffite movement.

The trend of the times was in their favour, for the Papacy was daily growing more scandalous. The "Great Schism" had now begun; and instead of one bad pope at Avignon, there were now two rival pontiffs, one at Avignon and one at Rome, who had excommunicated each other, and were endeavouring to stir up the states of Europe to a general religious war. Wycliffe's teaching had now become doctrinal as well as political. In his old age, he had preached against the invocation of saints, the superstitious adoration of relics and images, the spiritual efficacy of pilgrimages, and the Real Presence in the Eucharist. He persisted in his old denunciation of the over-great wealth of the clergy, and the influence of his followers in the Parliament is shown by their repeated attempts to introduce legislation confiscating monastic lands and church endowments for the benefit of the state.

Richard refused to countenance these proposals, but he was equally firm in refusing to allow the bishops to persecute the Lollards. Wycliffe has died in peace (1384), after having accomplished his great work of translating the Bible into the English tongue. His followers in the next generation were destined to fall upon more troublous times.

Among other characteristic instances of King Richard's wise and careful governance of his realm may be mentioned his endeavour to introduce better order into Ireland, which his predecessors had systematically neglected for two hundred years. The English influence in the sister island had been greatly reduced during the reign of Edward II. by the repeated invasions of Edward Bruce, who had drawn many of the native septs into rebellion. The Scots were finally driven out, but the havoc they had wrought was never repaired, and the area over which the king's authority reached was permanently decreased. Many of the tribal chiefs of the north fell off from their allegiance, and, what was more dangerous still, many of the Anglo-Norman settlers drifted into close alliance with the rebels, adopted Celtic names, and "became more Irish than the Irish themselves".

The assimilation of the new and the old inhabitants would have been advantageous both for themselves and for England if it had tended towards peace and union: but its sole effect was to increase tribal civil war and to diminish the central power of the government. Even the *Pale*, the district round Dublin which had been most thickly colonized by the English, began to fall into disorder. It was in vain that in 1366 King Edward III. caused *the Statute of Kilkenny* to be passed, forbidding the Anglo-Irish from mixing and marrying with the natives and adopting Celtic customs. Such laws can never be kept when the tendency of the times is against them, and the statute raised much bad blood between the settlers and the natives, without having any permanent effect in restoring the power of the king.

In 1394 Richard went over to Ireland to try the effect of his personal presence in setting the land in order: none of his predecessors since King John had visited it. His arrival was not without effect: many of the native chiefs did him homage, and the Lords of the Pale were for a space more obedient. He held a parliament of the whole land at Dublin, and then went home after appointing his heir-apparent, Roger Earl of March, Lord-Deputy of the island.

By 1396 Richard felt himself firmly established on the throne, and knew that he was liked and trusted by the majority of the nation. He felt that it would be no longer possible for a few powerful barons to rise against him and crush him as they had in 1388. Accordingly, he thought that it was time for him to take in hand the punishment of his old enemies, the Lords Appellant. He had even gone to the pains of dividing them, by showing special favour to Thomas Mowbray the Earl of Nottingham, and Henry Earl of Derby, the two who had been least deeply implicated in the rising of 1388.

His real enmity was directed against Gloucester, Arundel, and Warwick. It must be confessed that the duke gave his nephew every opportunity and provocation that he could have desired. He had intrigued against the French peace, insulted the king on his marriage, refused to keep the government of Ireland when it was given him, and caused his partisans in Parliament to make many perverse and unnecessary complaints against Richard's household and ministers. It was even said that he was plotting a second rebellion with the object of again seizing supreme power.

In 1397 Richard suddenly struck down his enemies. Warwick was arrested at a banquet, while Gloucester was captured by the king himself. He rode out to Flashy in Essex, the duke's favourite residence, and personally laid hands on him, telling him that he should "have the same mercy that he had shown to Burley nine years before." Arundel surrendered on promise of a fair trial before his peers. Richard then summoned a Parliament, and announced his intention of trying his three prisoners for treason. Copying their own procedure in 1388, he had them "appealed" by a number of the barons of his own party. Among the new "Lords Appellant" were included the king's half-brothers, Kent and Huntingdon, Mowbray Earl of Nottingham, Edmund of York, Earl of Rutland, and Scrope, a kinsman of the exiled Suffolk.

Arundel and Warwick were duly impeached before their peers, both for their old doings and for the new treason laid to their charge. Both were condemned, and Arundel was beheaded, but Warwick's sentence was commuted to imprisonment for life in the Isle of Man. Gloucester did not appear for trial, but his death was reported to the Parliament. It seems clear that Richard had him secretly put to death in his prison at Calais because he was determined not to spare him, yet shrank from the idea of ordering the public execution of such a near kinsman.

Thus, the king had secured his long-deferred vengeance for the evil doings of the Merciless Parliament. He could not, however, recall his exiled friends Suffolk and Oxford, since both of them had died some time back. During the three years which he had yet to reign he did not delegate his authority to any ministers of such power and influence as De la Pole and De Vere, but carried out a purely personal government, using as his instruments men of no importance who could be trusted to obey his orders. The chief of them were Suffolk's kinsman Scrope, whom he made Earl of Wilts, and Bushey, the speaker of the House of Commons.

In this last period of his reign Richard displayed distinctly unconstitutional tendencies, which gradually estranged from him the popular sympathy which he had gained by his good governance between 1389 and 1396. His conduct was not yet exactly tyrannical, but it made men fear that he might someday grow more violent. He raised some "benevolences", autocratic or forced loans, from rich men whom he wished to keep in his dependence. He made persons whom he distrusted sign blank charters, which he could fill up at his pleasure with whatever terms he liked, if they should happen to displease him. Unlike the kings his predecessors, he always kept a large guard of archers about him.

But most ominous of all was an innovation which he invented in the year 1398; he got Parliament to delegate its powers to a standing committee of ten peers, two bishops, and six commoners, whose consent to a statute or a tax was to have the same power as a parliamentary vote of approval. This was a most dangerous device, for it was obviously easy for the king to dominate such a small body, and to wring from it the approval of things which the two houses themselves would not have been likely to grant.

All these moves on Richard's part were menaces to the constitution, but he cannot be accused of having actually misgoverned the realm. He refrained from oppression, because he hoped to keep the people on his side. But he had already made enemies of a great part of the baronage, and of the clergy whom he had refused to aid in their attempts to attack the Lollards. The mass of the nation were not yet estranged from him, but they were seriously disturbed by his recent autocratic tendencies.

The actual cause of Richard's fall came from a matter of personal revenge. The two surviving Lords Appellant, Mowbray and Henry of Lancaster, fell into a quarrel, and accused each other of treason. Richard allowed them to challenge each other to a judicial duel; but when they appeared to fight it out in the lists at Coventry, he suddenly declared that the combat should not proceed, but that both should be banished the realm—Mowbray for life, Henry of Lancaster for ten years. This was regarded as a very hard decision, for one of the two must surely have been in the right. But there can be little doubt that Richard was merely carrying out to its final stage his vengeance for the acts of 1388. He had now punished all the murderers of Burley and Tresilian (1398).

A year later John of Gaunt died at the age of sixty-one. The vast Lancaster estates and the ducal title fell to his banished son; but Richard very unjustly refused to hand them over to him, or to allow him to draw their revenues, taking them into his own possession. As Henry had not been declared a traitor, or properly convicted of any misdoing, there was obviously no justification for this action. It turned the exile into an open enemy, who was determined to risk anything to get revenge.

In 1399 his opportunity came. The Earl of March, the Lord-Deputy of Ireland, was slain in a skirmish by Irish rebels, and Richard hastily crossed to Ireland to restore order. He was engaged in a difficult campaign amongst the Wicklow mountains when he received the surprising news that Henry of Lancaster had landed at Ravenspur in Yorkshire, having in his company Archbishop Arundel, the brother of the deceased Lord Appellant, and a few other exiles. He proclaimed that he had only come to sue for his duchy of Lancaster, and had no treasonable designs (July, 1399).

He was soon joined by thousands of the retainers of his father, and by many of the northern barons. The charge of the realm had been given during the king's absence to Edmund Duke of York, Richard's last surviving uncle, a simple and unenterprising old man. He gathered an army together, but foolishly disbanded it when Lancaster vowed that he had no treasonable design, and only wished to appeal to a free Parliament and to drive away evil councillors from the king.

Thus, Henry found himself unopposed, and had the realm at his feet, for Richard was detained at Dublin by persistent easterly winds which prevented him from crossing the Irish Channel. He soon showed the bent of his plans, by seizing and executing without fair trial the king's chief ministers, Scrope, Earl of Wiltshire, Bushey, and Green. This roused some of Richard's faithful adherents to take arms, and the Earl of Salisbury got together an army in Wales to meet his master on his expected arrival. But by an unlucky chance the weather still kept Richard storm-bound in Ireland, and he only reached Milford Haven two days after Salisbury's host had disbanded itself and gone home in despair.

The king had arrived almost alone, trusting to find his friends in arms and ready to aid him. He was soon surrounded by a force which Lancaster had sent against him, under Percy the Earl of Northumberland. On a false assurance sworn by the earl that nothing treasonable was designed against his crown or person, Richard surrendered himself. He was at once hurried up to London, where a Parliament had been hastily called together. Having now got his cousin into his hands, Henry showed that he aimed not at changing the ministry but at seizing the throne.

The Parliament voted that Richard had forfeited his crown by breaking his coronation oath and governing unrighteously. On thirty-three separate charges, some of them absurd and all couched in exaggerated language, he was declared to have deserved deposition. Richard, much broken in spirit, yielded and consented to abdicate, whereupon his cousin stepped forward and laid claim to the crown. The deposed monarch was sent to Pontefract Castle, which he was never to leave alive.

CHAPTER 9

Henry IV. 1399-1413

Down to the moment of his accession Henry of Lancaster had been aided by an extraordinary series of chances. The king's absence in Ireland, the feeble action of the Duke of York, the prolonged easterly winds which had kept Richard from returning to England, the supineness shown by his chief partisans, were circumstances on which Henry could not have counted when he landed at Ravenspur. If events had fallen out otherwise, it is probable that he would not have dared to seize the throne, but would have stopped short at his original programme of claiming justice for himself.

But the moment that the usurpation was complete the inherent weakness of the new ruler's position began to display itself. He was in reality no more than the king of a party; his only true supporters were the baronial faction which had been attached to the Lords Appellant, and the churchmen, headed by Archbishop Arundel who had resolved to make him their instrument for the suppression of the Wycliffites. The support of other partisans could only be bought by encouraging a lively sense of favours to come. Meanwhile the deposed king had also a powerful baronial faction adhering to him, though for the moment it seemed crushed, and there were many parts of the country where his name was far more popular than that of Henry.

The house of Lancaster's claim to the crown was in truth dependent solely on the election by Parliament. In strict hereditary right the deposition of Richard II. made the young Earl of March (son of the Roger of March who fell in Ireland in 1398) heir to the throne. By setting him aside Henry committed himself to the theory of popular election to the crown, and he had, therefore, always to remember that Parliament might unmake him even as it had made him. Hence the most prominent characteristic of his domestic policy was a determination to keep the two houses in good temper at all costs, a line of conduct which often led him into a subservience to them which earlier kings would have regarded as degrading. Besides managing Parliament, Henry had to keep together the baronial party which supported him, and to grant the churchmen all that they asked.

Henry had been popular as Earl of Derby, but as king he found that he had no enthusiastic support from the nation. His enemies were many and active, his true friends were few, his interested supporters were greedy but lukewarm, while the bulk of the people cared little for him. It is a great proof of his ability that for fourteen years he kept tight hold on the crown, and finally passed it on to his son. His character was well suited for the task that he had undertaken; though unscrupulous, he was plausible, soft-spoken, and courteous: a proud or hot-tempered man would have ruined himself in a few years. But Henry was pliable, cautious, and wary, though when needful he could strike hard blows without hesitation.

He had only been two months on the throne when the first of the many rebellions with which he was to be plagued broke out. The leaders were, as might have been expected, the partisans of the late king—Richard's half-brother, John Holland, Earl of Huntingdon; his nephew, Thomas Holland, Earl of Kent; Montague, Earl of Salisbury, the best known of the Lollards; and Lord Despenser. Under cover of a tournament they collected several thousand armed men, and suddenly marched on Windsor, intending to catch the king unawares. Henry escaped by a lucky chance—he had only half an hour to spare and fled to London, where he summoned the citizens to arms.

The Hollands and their friends, finding that their first blow had failed, resolved to disperse in order to gather together greater forces the main body began to retire westward, where they hoped to raise the numerous friends of King Richard in Wales and the Welsh border. This delay was their ruin: the king pursued them in haste, and they broke up without a pitched battle. Kent and Salisbury were slain in a skirmish at Cirencester, Huntingdon was caught and beheaded in Essex, Despenser at Bristol, both without any form of trial. Four minor chiefs were hung, drawn, and quartered in London. (Dec. 1399-Jan. 1400).

This ill-concerted rebellion caused the death of the unfortunate King Richard: to prevent further rebellion in his behalf Henry secretly caused him to be starved to death in Pontefract Castle. His agony is said to have endured fifteen days (Jan.-Feb. 1400). His corpse was publicly exposed, but the mystery of his death caused some people to believe that the body shown was not his, and for many years after rumours of his survival were current. An impostor who took his name lived all through Henry's reign at the court of Scotland.

The main event of note in the following year marks Henry's anxiety to secure his unsteady throne by giving guarantees for his fidelity to the church party. At the suggestion of Archbishop Arundel, he induced the Parliament to pass the infamous statute *De Heretico Comburendo*, which condemned to death by fire convicted heretics. No delay was made in commencing the persecution of the Lollards, and before a month was out they counted their first martyr, William Sawtrey, a chaplain of London, who was burnt after steadfastly refusing to recant (Feb. 1401). The persecution went on intermittently for the next twenty years.

Though they obliged the king by countenancing his assault on the followers of Wycliffe, the Parliament took a very high tone with him in dealing with legislation and finance. They endeavoured to bind him down in the matter of expenses, and repeatedly propounded to him a theory that no grants of money ought to be made to the crown till all grievances petitioned against by the houses had been previously redressed. Henry temporised and procrastinated, putting off the evil day when he might be obliged to make this great constitutional concession.

Richard's death had some temporary effect in checking rebellions, for it was difficult to make the child Edmund of March the head of a political cause and to gather a party round his name. Moreover, the long uncertainty as to the deposed king's death kept men from recognising his heir.

The next troubles which Henry had to face were connected not with plots to change the English succession, but with a national rebellion in Wales. For a full century, the principality had been undisturbed by civil strife, and Welsh troops had served Edward III. faithfully in all his wars. A chief of genius arose, in the person of Owen of Glendower. His countrymen had never been partisans of Lancaster, and readily took arms when he called on them to resist the usurper. Owen made some pretence of rising in Richard's behalf, but he was really fighting for his own hand, to restore Welsh independence the rebellion was national and had nothing to do with English dynastic matters.

When Glendower descended from his hills it was not to rally partisans in England, but to ravage the border shires up to the gates of

Shrewsbury and Worcester. Henry sent army after army against the rebels, but he could never catch them; they retired to the mountains till the invader's food was exhausted, and turned to harass his rear-guard when he departed. When a larger expedition, led by the king himself, marched into Wales, it met with such bad weather and suffered so severely, that the English complained that Owen was a wizard and had leagued himself with the powers of the air to discomfit his foes (1402).

The Welsh rebellion gave no signs of spreading into England, but other troubles arose to touch Henry more nearly. The French king armed to avenge his dethroned son-in-law, and threatened invasion: Norman privateers ravaged many of the towns of the southern coast. At the same time the Scots, under the Earl of Douglas, crossed the Border and advanced into England. They suffered, however, a crushing defeat on Homildon Hill at the hands of Henry Percy, son of the Earl of Northumberland, and Douglas himself was taken prisoner with many other Scottish nobles (14th Sept., 1402).

This victory, however, was destined to have dangerous consequences. The king demanded that the captives should be made over to him, since he was desirous of filling his depleted exchequer with their ransoms. But the Percies had looked upon the money as their own, and bitterly resented the order. Northumberland had been Henry's chief supporter at his usurpation, and thought that nothing could be denied him. When peremptorily summoned to obey, he resolved to refuse, and hastily planned a rebellion, for his power was so great in the North that he could put into the field a whole army of his own retainers. The rising was a mere outburst of feudal anarchy, the Percy clan being its sole authors.

Northumberland placed his gallant and reckless son Henry, whom men called Hotspur, at the head of his followers; he released his prisoner Douglas, who consented to espouse his cause, and he called in his brother Thomas Percy, Earl of Worcester, to his aid. They sent messengers to Owen Glendower to secure his co-operation, and resolved to use the name of the little Earl of March to cover their rebellion. They then formally defied Henry, and declared him a perjured usurper and the murderer of his rightful king.

The elder Percy remained in Yorkshire to watch the loyalists of the north, who had taken arms under Ralph Neville, Earl of Westmoreland, the head of a family which had been the local rivals of the Percies. His son Henry ("Hotspur") and the Earls of Worcester and Douglas marched into Cheshire, a district always devoted to Richard

II., and then pressed towards Shrewsbury, where Glendower and the Welsh were to join them. The king, marching hastily from London with a small army, threw himself between the Percies and Wales, and brought them to action at Hately field, two miles outside Shrewsbury. After a fierce battle Hotspur was slain, and his uncle and Douglas captured.

Worcester was immediately beheaded: he deserved no better fate, as he had been one of those who betrayed Richard II., and had received more than £30,000 in gifts from the usurper against whom he now had taken arms (July 21, 1403). Northumberland, hearing that his son was dead, made abject professions of repentance, and was admitted to mercy on promising to surrender his numerous castles in the north.

Less than two years of comparative quiet followed the king's victory at Shrewsbury. Owen Glendower still held his own in Wales, but England was for a short time at peace. In 1405 troubles began again: Henry's suspicions were first roused by an attempt to steal away the young Earl of March from Windsor, where he was kept in safe custody. Insurrection again broke out inbthe north. It was directed by two leaders who had hereditary grudges against the king: Richard Scrope, Archbishop of York, was the brother of that Scrope Earl of Wilts who had been beheaded at Bristol in 1399; Thomas Mowbray, the Earl Marshal, was the son of the Mowbray whom Henry had accused of treason in 1398, and had faced in the lists of Coventry. His father had died in exile, and the son became a bitter enemy of the house of Lancaster. Scrope and Mowbray raised a force at York, and seeing rebellion afoot, the old Earl of Northumberland took arms in his own county to aid them. All three leaders agreed to recognise Edmund of March as king.

But Henry's fortune was still strong. His lieutenant the Earl of Westmoreland broke the back of the rising by capturing the Archbishop and the Earl Marshal by a villainous piece of ill faith. Having invited them to meet him under a flag of truce, he seized them when they came to the conference and put them in chains. Henry hurried northward, and on his arrival at York ordered both the prisoners to be executed. They received no trial before their peers, but were hurriedly condemned by an extemporised court, and beheaded an hour after (June 8, 1405). The death of Scrope caused widespread horror and dismay. No archbishop save Becket had ever been put to death for withstanding his king, and the northern clergy and people saluted Scrope as a martyr. Henry fell grievously ill a few days after, and was

HOTSUR AT SHREWSBURY

never a hale man for the rest of his life: the epileptic fits and leprosy which gradually grew upon him were universally regarded as Heaven's vengeance for the archbishop's cruel end.

The cause of rebellion did not prosper; the king's artillery blew Northumberland's castles to pieces in a few discharges, and the old earl had to flee into Scotland, where he lurked for three years, waiting for another opportunity for a blow at his enemy. Before it came, other troubles had been vexing Henry. His parliaments, with which he dared not quarrel, had learnt to treat him with scant respect. In 1406 they demanded and obtained from him the right to audit his accounts, and made him cut down the expenses of his household; in 1407 he had to acknowledge that the Commons had the sole right of initiating money grants. He was also made to promise to do nothing without first taking advice of his council. The weakness of his position is best understood by the fact that he allowed Parliament to deal with him in such a manner: no king whose throne was safe would have tolerated such interference.

In 1407 the foreign relations of the crown slightly improved. The danger of invasion from France had hitherto been very real: twice great French fleets had been collected in the Channel, and though they had not landed an army on the coast of Kent, yet flying squadrons had sacked many south-country ports, and once a considerable body of troops had been sent to aid Glendower in Wales. The soul of the opposition to Henry IV. had been Louis Duke of Orleans, the king's brother, but in November, 1407, he was murdered by the secret contrivance of his cousin, the Duke of Burgundy. His death was the cause of the outbreak of a long civil war between the party of nobles who had previously followed him and the partisans of Burgundy.

Engrossed in domestic quarrels, the French had no longer any leisure to dream of invading England: their king, Charles VI., was utterly unable to keep his realm together, for he had become subject to fits of melancholy madness, which came on him every summer, and often disabled him for four and five months at a time. Soon, instead of France dreaming of molesting England, it was England which thought of interfering in faction-ridden France.

In 1408 Henry was able to suppress the last of the many insurrections which were raised against him. The old Earl of Northumberland, Lord Bardolf, and the Welsh bishop of Bangor slipped over the Border and raised a considerable force, but they were met and crushed at the Battle of Bramham Moor by Sir Thomas Rokeby, sheriff of Yorkshire.

Both the rebel peers were slain. This was the last trouble which came from the direction of Scotland, where King Henry had of late secured much influence over the government. For King Robert's son and heir, Prince James, was taken at sea as he was crossing to France (1406), and the Duke of Albany, who ruled in his brother's behalf, and wished to keep all the power for himself, made a secret agreement by which Henry undertook to hold the young prince a captive, while the duke covenanted in return not to molest England.

Thus, Henry was freed from the danger on the side both of France and of Scotland, and had only the Welsh rebellion left on his hands. But he had fallen into wretched health, and from 1409 to 1411 was almost a chronic invalid. Most of the functions of government were discharged for him by his promising young son, Henry of Monmouth, the Prince of Wales. When only a boy he had fought at his father's side at Shrewsbury and in Wales; now as a young man of twenty he was already a hard-working statesman and soldier.

There seems little room in his busy life for those curious tales of youthful riot and debauchery and consorting with disreputable companions which popular tradition associated with his name, and which the genius of Shakespeare has immortalised. The greater part of Henry's time was spent in hard soldiering in Wales, where he was constantly chasing Glendower's rebel bands, at first with small success. But as the years rolled on, the final triumph of the great guerilla chief grew less and less probable, since the house of Lancaster was growing more firmly established in England. At last his followers began to desert him, and Prince Henry was able to pacify the greater part of the country, though down to the day of his death Glendower was never wholly subdued.

It is in the end of the period of Henry of Monmouth's administration in behalf of his father (Sept.-Dec., 1411) that the first English interference in France since the peace of 1393 falls. The quarrel of the Burgundian and Orleanist factions being at its height, Henry intervened in behalf of the former, and sent a small force across the Channel which helped the Burgundians to a victory over their enemies at St. Cloud. But this policy was not destined to be carried any further. In 1412 the king's health grew better for a short time, and he was able to take a greater share in public business. He seems to have somewhat resented the way in which his eldest son had monopolized the conduct of affairs during his illness, and showed his displeasure by relegating the Prince of Wales to the background for a time, and employing his second son, Thomas Duke of Clarence, as his chief deputy and agent. In consequence of this change in policy, peace was made with the faction of Orleans, or the "Armagnacs" as they were now called, from their new leader, Bernard Count of Armagnac, who had taken the murdered duke's place.

King Henry was once more smitten down with his old disease, and died rather suddenly at Westminster on March 20, 1413, having been reconciled to his eldest son. After all his troubles and dangers, he expired just as his throne seemed at last secure. But though he had rooted in his dynasty, his reign had not been a success. He left the country poorer than he had found it: civil war had been incessant, the central government was weak, the baronage and nation divided, and the blood feuds had been started that were to last for three generations, and to end in the terrible Wars of the Roses.

Chapter 10
Henry V. 1413–1422

The succession of Henry of Monmouth to his father's throne greatly strengthened the position of the house of Lancaster. The new king had gained the crown by quiet inheritance, not by armed force, and he was not responsible for the cruel death of Richard II. and the Bother crimes by which Henry IV. had climbed to power. Nor was he the man to imperil the position which he had obtained: he had been working hard both as warrior and as administrator since his early boyhood, and had received such a training as fell to the lot of none of his predecessors since Edward I.

Though courteous and even-tempered, Henry could be stern on occasion: he was just according to his lights, but there can be no doubt that his views were often narrow and purely legal. His rigidly orthodox piety left no room in his heart for mercy to heretics. His most unjustifiable renewal of the French war and his persecution of the Lollards mark the unsympathetic side of his character. But he was well loved by the majority of his subjects: a ruler able, orderly, and conscientious, with a strong hand and an infinite capacity for work, was a great boon to the nation.

Henry's first acts after his accession were wise and graceful. He released the young Earl of March and restored him to his estates, though there was obviously some danger in setting at liberty a possible rival. He gave back the earldom of Nottingham to John Mowbray, brother of the Thomas Mowbray who had fallen with Scrope in 1405. He brought the body of Richard II. to London, and had it interred in state beside that of his wife, the "good Queen Anne". But soon after, Henry showed that one section of his subjects must expect no favour from him. He authorised Archbishop Arundel to proceed with greater vigour against the unfortunate Lollards.

The most noted member of the sect was now Sir John Oldcastle, Lord Cobham, who had been an able and trusted lieutenant of the king during the Welsh wars. Oldcastle, when brought to trial, made a vigorous defence, denouncing the efficacy of penances and pilgrimages, the worship of images, the ambition and ill-living of the pope, and the greed of the friars. He was pronounced a heretic and sent back to the Tower, but escaped from it before the day fixed for his execution.

It seems that, in despair for their future, some of the Lollards now engaged in a plot to seize the king's person, and force him to take Oldcastle as his chief minister. It was their design to muster armed men in St. Martin's Fields by night, and make a sudden dash at the palace of Westminster. But the design was betrayed, and Henry, occupying the trysting-place beforehand, caught or scattered each band as it arrived. Nearly sixty Lollards were executed, the chief being a knight named Sir John Acton. But Oldcastle got away, and hid himself on the Welsh border. It was not till some years later that he was captured and executed as both heretic and traitor.

When once firmly set upon his throne King Henry proceeded to turn his attention to foreign politics. Like many other sovereigns in different epochs, he had formed the conclusion that the panacea for internal disorders is successful war abroad. Nothing would strengthen the house of Lancaster more than a vigorous resumption of the old attacks on France, if only they could be carried to a fortunate conclusion.

The state of affairs across the Channel seemed to promise an easy task for the invader: the Burgundian and Armagnac factions were waging open war upon each other throughout the land. The king was a hopeless lunatic; his son, the dauphin Louis, was a dissipated lad of seventeen, who had estranged half the people of the land by becoming a hot partisan of the Armagnacs. The prospect of a war with England was regarded with dismay by the French, and when Henry began to tamper with the Burgundians and to speak of renewing the old claims of Edward III., the dauphin's advisers seemed almost panic-stricken. Before a blow had been struck they offered the King of England the hand of the Princess Catherine, with a dowry of 800,000 crowns, and undertook to restore to him all those parts of Guienne and Gascony which had been lost by England since 1370. The duchy of Aquitaine, as constituted by the treaty of Bretigny, would have been brought back into being, save that Poitou and Saintonge were to remain French.

But Henry was bent on war for war's sake, and had no intention

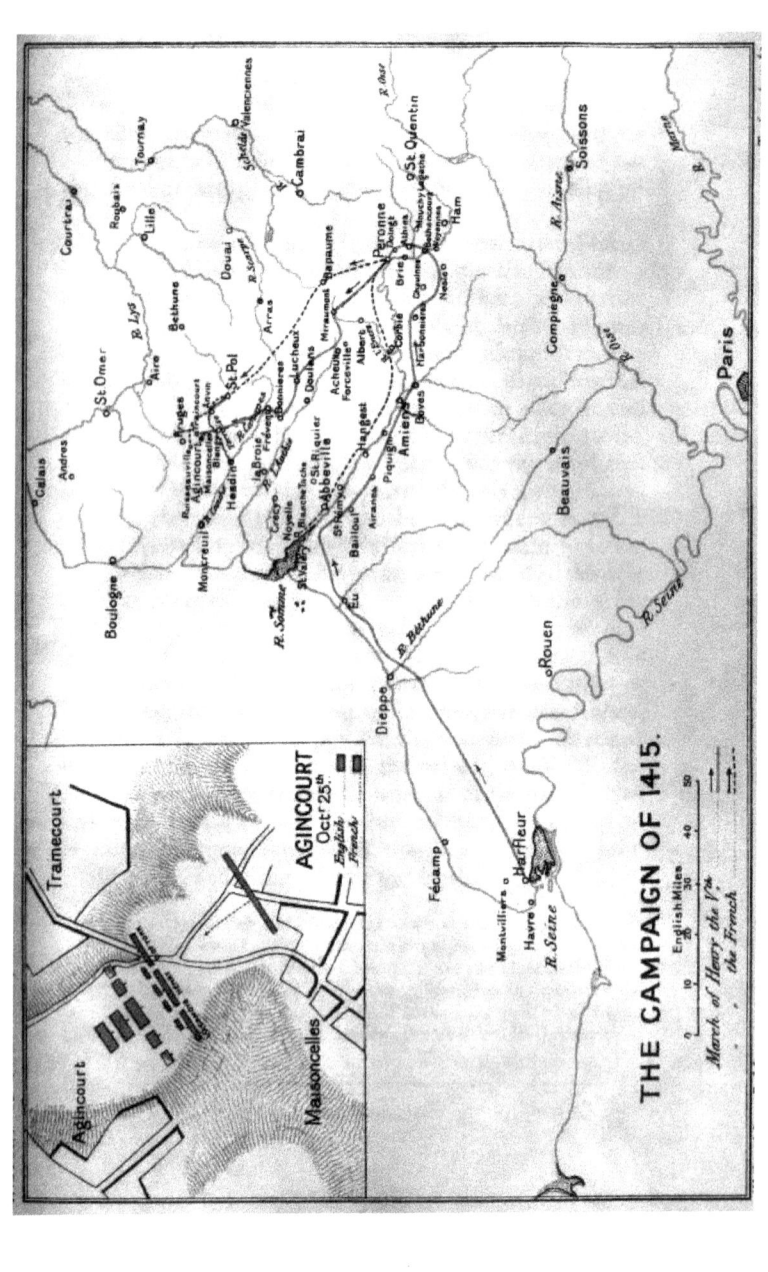

of accepting these liberal offers. In 1415, after many months of negotiation, he broke off all relations with France, and began to make preparations for invading Normandy. No language can be too strong to use in the condemnation of his greed and ambition: for the political gain of the moment he condemned England and France to forty years of misery, and set on foot a war which was to prove the ruin of his own house.

In the summer of 1415 the army of invasion was mustered at Southampton: it was admirably equipped and composed of picked men, but its numbers were not large. Only 2500 men-at-arms and 7000 archers were assembled. They took with them the largest train of artillery that England had yet seen. The host was on the eve of sailing, when the kingdom was startled by the news that a dangerous conspiracy against the king's life had been discovered. It had been formed by Richard of York, Earl of Cambridge, the king's cousin. (Second son of Edmund, Duke of York, who had been regent in 1399. His father was now dead, but his elder brother survived, and was holding the dukedom.)

He had married the sister of the Earl of March, and had planned to place his brother-in-law on the throne and rule under his name. March himself, a harmless and unenterprising young man, had no part in the plot: the chief accomplices of Cambridge were Lord Scrope, a kinsman of the archbishop who had been executed in 1405, and Sir Thomas Grey. They kept their counsel so ill that the king got wind of their designs, and arrested them before they were ready to strike. Full proof of their treason being produced, all three were executed (5 Aug., 1415). This plot was a purely dynastic business, the legitimate continuation of the many movements in favour of the house of March, which had disturbed the reign of Henry IV.

In the middle of August, the army crossed the Channel and landed near Harfleur, to which it laid siege. The place made a gallant resistance, but received no help from without; though the *dauphin* had mustered a large army at Rouen. The English suffered more from the summer heat and from camp fever than from the missiles of their enemies. After a siege of five weeks the artillery of the besiegers had so shaken the walls that the garrison surrendered (Sept. 22, 1415). A good foothold in Normandy had been secured, but meanwhile the season was growing late, and the army was dwindling away.

When 1200 men had been told off to garrison Harfleur, and the numerous sick and wounded had been sent back to England, only

1000 men-at-arms and 4000 archers remained available for service in the field. This body was too small for a march on Paris or a serious attempt to subdue Normandy, and the king resolved to lead them across to Calais and not to advance deeper into France. Such a movement was rather a defiance of the *dauphin* and his host than a serious military movement. It would have been better to bring home the army by sea, for the march placed it in grave peril of destruction.

King Henry crossed Normandy and Picardy till he came to the Somme, which proved as great a barrier to him as it had been to Edward III. in 1346. He was only able to cross it by striking inland as far as Peronne; and while he was making this detour the French army, now commanded by John D'Albret, the Constable of France, outmarched him, and threw itself across his path. Close by the village of Agincourt the English found the way to Calais blocked by a host of six to eight times their own numbers.

It was necessary at all costs to force a passage through them, for the weather had been bad, the army was worn out by long marches, and the provisions were almost exhausted. Henry drew out his little force, and offered battle between the villages of Agincourt and Tramecourt (Oct. 25, 1415). He ranged his handful of men-at-arms in three small bodies, each flanked by two wings of archers, and waited to be attacked. The ground between him and the French was rain-sodden ploughed fields, by no means easy to cross when the knightly armour had grown so heavy that it was no longer a simple matter to march in it. The French, despising the small numbers of their enemies, thought that an easy victory was in their hands. They sent before them, as at Poictiers, two squadrons of mounted men, who were to break in upon the flanks and rout the archers, while the main body followed on foot in three dense lines, each larger than the whole English Army (25 Oct., 1415).

The cavalry in advance struggled through the heavy ground till they came in range of the archery, when they were shot down almost to a man without striking a blow. The masses of dismounted knights lurched heavily on in their wake, but were brought to a stand by their fatigue, and by the deep clay, in which they sank almost to their knees. They halted in exhaustion some distance in front of the English line. Seeing their plight, King Henry made his men advance, and pausing at a convenient distance from the mass bade his bowmen let fly into it for some minutes, and then to close.

The French line of battle, already riddled by the arrow-shower,

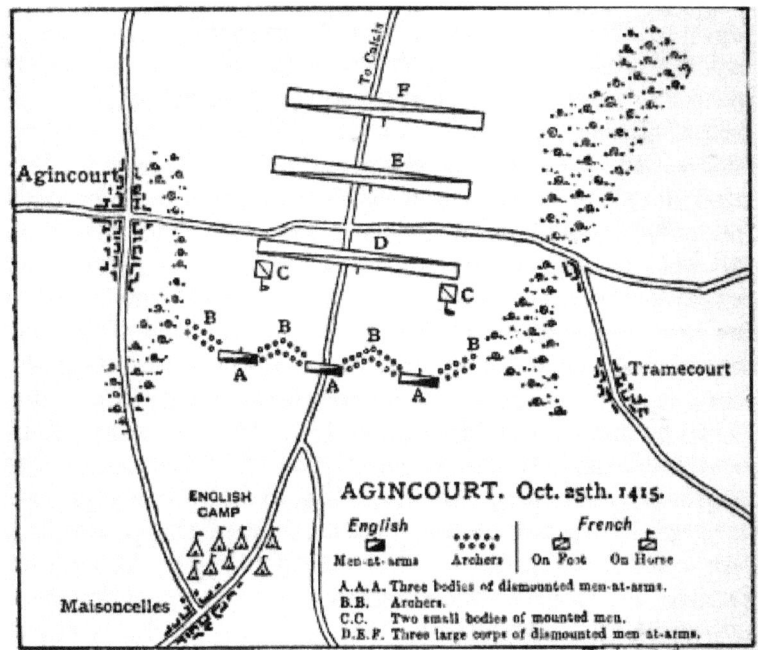

was easily routed by the impact of the charge: the knights were rolled helplessly into heaps, and slain or made prisoners by the lightly-armed bowmen, who proved far more effective than the men-at-arms on such ground. The moment that the first line was disposed of, Henry pushed on against the second, which made a somewhat better resistance, but was finally broken up and slaughtered like the first. The third line melted from the field without fighting, save a few of its chiefs, who refused to fly, and went forward to certain death. While they were being disposed of, an alarm was raised that the English camp was being attacked from the rear, and the king ordered his men to slay their captives, and turn back for a new fight.

But the diversion was caused only by bands of marauders, who fled when they saw the king moving upon them, so that the slaughter of the prisoners, which had been begun, proved wholly unnecessary, and was stopped. When the field was searched by the victors, they found among the slain the Constable and three dukes, Brabant, Bar, and Alençon, with seven counts, ninety barons, and five or six thousand men-at-arms, numbers greater than these of the whole English army. Fifteen hundred prisoners of rank still survived, among them the young Duke of Orleans and the Counts of Vendôme, Eu, and

Richemont.

The English loss was trifling; though two great peers had fallen, Edmund, Duke of York, and Michael, Earl of Suffolk, only thirteen men-at-arms and a hundred archers had perished with them. The heavy armour the French seems to have been fatal to their power of striking effective blows as to their ability to move in the sodden plough-land. The arrows pierced their mail with ease, while in the close fighting they seem to have been at an equal disadvantage, and were dashed down helplessly by the axes and maces wielded by the bare arms of the archers. The victory seemed to justify Henry's rash march across France, and in the actual fighting his tactical skill had been as evident as his personal courage; but if the French had been commanded a cautious and capable general it is hard to see how he could have escaped a disastrous defeat.

Henry's army was so small and so exhausted that he could make no immediate use of the victory, and was obliged to march on to Calais and thence take ship to London. He was received with a splendid triumphal procession, but his victory had been more showy than fruitful, and the possession of Harfleur was the only tangible benefit which had resulted from his campaign. The Armagnac party had not been crushed, even by the carnage at Agincourt, and there was some fear that the Burgundians might be driven into opposing England by a tardy revival of patriotic spirit. Harfleur was beset by the French for the whole of the next year, and had a narrow escape of falling back into their hands.

For the greater part of 1416 Henry was busied with negotiations with the Emperor Sigismund, who visited England, full of great plans for restoring peace to Christendom by putting an end to the "Great Schism" which had been rending the church in twain since 1378. Henry gladly lent himself to this scheme, which had taken shape at the Council of Constance. Two popes having been deposed and a third forced to resign, a universally acknowledged pontiff was secured in the person of Martin V. (1417). But the council is better remembered for the burning of John Huss, the great Bohemian reformer and the spiritual heir of Wycliffe, than for its abortive attempt to reform the debased papacy. In return for Henry's assistance in matters ecclesiastical, Sigismund endeavoured to negotiate a peace with France on terms favourable to England.

But the Armagnacs would not listen to the exorbitant claims of the victor of Agincourt, and the Burgundian duke held aloof, willing to profit by his enemies' misfortunes but afraid to offend the national spirit of France by an open alliance with England. The war had therefore to continue.

Raising an army of about the same size as that-of 1415, the king crossed the sea in August, 1417, and began to overrun Normandy. This time he came not to execute a plundering raid, but to conquer the land piecemeal: one after the other he took Caen, Lisieux, Bayeux, Alençon, and Mortaigne, cutting a huge can tie out of the duchy, in which he established a solid base for further operations. The Armagnacs and Burgundians were fighting hard round Paris, and paid no attention to the invader. In the next year, he steadily pushed his sphere u of operations to right and left, conquering St. Lô, Coutances and Cherbourg in the west, and then turning east to lay siege to the great city of Rouen. He kept stern discipline among his troops, and gave such good government to the conquered districts that it contrasted strongly with the anarchy which had prevailed before.

Meanwhile the struggle at Paris had ended in success for the Duke of Burgundy: the populace had risen against his rivals, massacred the Constable Armagnac with many of his party, and driven the rest away. The duke became by his victory responsible for the conduct of the war with England, but shewed himself as incapable as the Constable had been of checking King Henry. By allowing the gallant defenders of Rouen to remain unsuccoured for six months he drew down upon himself the condemnation of every patriotic Frenchman. In January, 1419, the Norman capital fell, reduced by sheer famine, and Henry entered its gates.

Then at last did John of Burgundy begin to stir, but it was not in order to raise against the English the whole force of France, but to make one last attempt to buy them off by offering more liberal terms than the Armagnacs had proffered. But a conference at Meulan (May, 1419) revealed that-Henry's terms were as exorbitant as ever; he asked for all the lands granted to Edward III. by the treaty of Bretigny, and the whole duchy of Normandy, as well as for the arrears of King John's long unpaid ransom-money of 1360.

In despair at the arrogant demands of the English king, Burgundy resolved to make peace with the Armagnac faction, and unite with them for a last desperate attempt to expel the invader. His enemies were now headed by Charles, the youngest son of the mad king, who had become *dauphin* on the death of his elder brothers. They professed their readiness to come to terms with the Burgundians, but when the two princes met in conference on the bridge of Montereau (10th September, 1419), the *dauphin's* attendants treacherously fell upon the duke and hewed him down as he knelt before his cousin.

This brutal and senseless murder had the natural result: the duke's young son, Philip, and all the partisans of Burgundy, at once went over to the English side, and swore that Charles should never reign over France. Rather than acknowledge the murderer as heir to the throne, they would accept Henry's ill-founded claim and take him as their ruler. All the cities of northern France, where the Burgundians were strong, thus became friendly to the English, and opened their gates to the Treaty of invader. On May 20, 1420, Henry entered Troyes. Troyes with the young duke Philip at his right hand, and there met the Queen of France, her insane spouse, and her daughter Catharine, whose hand had been offered to him as far back as 1414. The unfortunate Charles VI. was made to give his consent to a treaty by which he made Henry regent of France, and gave him the right of succession to the throne on his own death, to the exclusion of the dauphin.

On June 2, the English king married the Princess Catharine, in order to give himself some better claim to the crown than the mad king's bequest. After turning his arms against those towns in the neighbourhood which still held out for the Armagnacs, and reducing them, Henry brought his bride and his father-in-law to Paris, where he celebrated his Christmas festivities in great state.

Early in the spring he returned to England, and made a progress round the whole land with his wife, to receive the homage and congratulations of his admiring subjects. No king of England had ever wrought such feats of arms, and it seemed that he had carried to a successful end the great war which had cost his predecessors so much fruitless expense of life and wealth. Parliament ratified all the provisions of the Treaty of Troyes with alacrity, not noting, we may suspect, the danger which accompanied it that England might ere long become a mere province of France, "for the greater ever draws the less". But it was not long before a jarring note was struck to mar the universal harmony.

In April, 1422, news came to land of a disaster on the Loire. The king had sent his eldest brother, Thomas Duke of Clarence, to chase the Dauphinois out of Anjou and Maine, but the enemy had received a large reinforcement from Scotland under the Earl of Buchan, and for the first time since Agincourt turned to fight in the open. Recklessly pursuing, with his archers far to the rear, Clarence ran into an ambush at Baugé (March 21, 1422), and was there surrounded and slain; his companions, the Earls of Somerset and Huntingdon, were taken prisoners.

The news of this defeat soon drew the king back to France (June, 1422). He marched south and drove the Dauphinois back to Orleans and beyond the Loire, then he turned to reduce their few remaining strongholds in central France. None of them gave him much trouble, save Meaux, whose garrison made a resistance of unparalleled obstinacy. Henry formed the siege in October, and the town did not yield till May; all through a winter of perpetual rain he lay before its walls, obstinately refusing to draw back from his flooded trenches. He and his army were smitten with a terrible plague of ague and dysentery, which thinned their ranks even faster than starvation diminished those of the garrison.

When spring came the town yielded, and Henry, showing the stern cruelty which not unfrequently disfigured his action, hung the governor and four of his companions. He then turned back towards Paris, and ere long his wife, and the infant son whom she had lately borne him, rejoined him. But men saw that he was no longer himself: the hand of death was upon him, for the chills of his winter camp had stricken him with an exhaustion from which he could not rally. He took to his bed in the castle of Vincennes, near Paris, and lingering in a state of utter prostration through the summer heat, died on August 31, 1422, leaving all his great conquests to a weakly child of less than a year old.

CHAPTER 11

Henry VI. 1422-1450

The death of Henry V. was followed in a few weeks by that of his imbecile father-in-law Charles VI. (Oct. 21); thus, the crowns of England and France both fell, according to the provisions of the Treaty of Troyes, to the sickly child, Henry of Windsor. It might have been expected that the domination of the English across the Channel would disappear when the strong personality of the conqueror was removed, and the power which he had wielded passed into many hands. But the Dauphin Charles, the "King of Bourges" as men now called him, was both unpopular and apathetic; his councillors and captains were incapable, and they could make no profit out of the opportunity which was offered them. As long as the young Duke of Burgundy remembered his father's murder and remained the ally of the English, the nationalist party was unable to make any head against the invaders.

Henry V. had left two surviving brothers: John Duke of Bedford, the elder of the pair, was made regent of France, an office which he discharged with great energy and ability, doing his best to carry on the war with very inadequate resources, and conciliating Philip of Burgundy to the best of his power. To bind him yet more closely to the English alliance, John wedded the duke's sister, the Princess Anne. Humphrey of Gloucester was a very different character from his steady and hard-working brother: he was flighty, petulant, quarrelsome, and selfish, though his affable manners, his patronage of learned men, and his cultivation of all the arts of popularity won him the name of "the good Duke Humphrey" from his numerous partisans.

Gloucester had been regent of England at his brother's death, but the Lords of the Council and the Parliament feared his reckless ambition so much that they would only allow him to continue in power under many restrictions. Instead of Regent they made him only "Protector of the Realm and the King's Chief Councillor", and he was to act in all things with the consent of a Council of Regency composed of fifteen members. The chief opponent of the duke was his half-uncle Henry Beaufort, Bishop of Winchester, an able and obstinate man, who thoroughly distrusted his nephew: the majority of the council generally backed the bishop, and Gloucester spent much of his time in fruitless bickerings with them.

It is most astonishing to find that the death of Henry V. was not followed by any shrinkage of the English possessions in northern France. On the contrary, the area of the region which acknowledged his little son as king continued slowly to increase for more than six years. Bedford was zealous and untiring in his exertions, and though help was doled out to him from England with a very sparing hand, he contrived to keep up the war—to a great extent by the use of French money and French mercenaries.

Twice the Dauphinois strove to break into the provinces of the English obedience, but they suffered two bloody defeats at Cravant (July 31, 1423) and Verneuil (Aug. 17, 1424). In the second of these fights fell the Earl of Douglas and nearly all the Dauphin's Scottish auxiliaries. Further aid from Scotland was hard to get, for the English government had just released and restored to his kingdom the long-imprisoned King James I. That prince had married an English wife, Joan Beaufort, the bishop's niece, and adopted a policy of consistent friendliness to his southern neighbours.

The first danger to the English dominion in France came from a freak of Humphrey of Gloucester. He provoked the Duke of Burgundy to great wrath by marrying Philip's cousin Jacquelaine, Countess of Holland and Hainault, who had absconded from her lawful husband, the Duke of Brabant. Obtaining for her a divorce of more than doubtful validity from the Anti-pope Benedict XIII., the duke wedded her, and tried to make himself master of her heritage in Hainault. Burgundy had no desire to see Gloucester established as a neighbour to his county of Flanders, and joined John of Brabant in overrunning Hainault. He might even have broken away from the English alliance if he had not been turned aside by the soft words of his brother-in-law Bedford.

Gloucester meanwhile proved himself an indifferent champion of his wife's claims: he fled back to England, while she fell into the hands of Duke Philip, and was thrown into prison. Instead of pursuing the quarrel further, Humphrey very meanly acknowledged that his marriage had been invalid, and consoled himself by marrying Eleanor Cobham, a Kentish lady who had taken his fickle fancy (1427).

After escaping the dangers to which his reckless brother's conduct had exposed him, Bedford was ere long to be confronted by a far more formidable difficulty. Slowly pushing his operations southward Bedford arrived at the gates of Orleans, the last French stronghold north of the Loire. To besiege this important strategical point the whole available field-army of the Regent was sent forward under the Earl of Salisbury—the son of Richard II.'s Lollard friend.

So limited were the resources of the English that the expedition did not exceed 4000 men. Yet weak as was the attack, the defence was weaker still, and Salisbury was able to blockade the place by erecting a number of forts (*bastilles* as they were called) watching all its gates: he was unable with his inadequate numbers to erect a complete line of circumvallation. The French made several feeble attempts to save Orleans, of which the best known was that foiled at the Battle of the Herrings. A small reinforcement from Paris, guarding a convoy largely composed of salt fish "and other Lenten stuff," was attacked near Rouvray by the Dauphin's forces, but parked its wagons in a square and easily beat off the French by the force of archery (Feb. 12, 1429). Nevertheless, Orleans held out stoutly, and Salisbury soon after was killed by a cannonball as he was reconnoitring its walls.

After the "Battle of the Herrings" Charles seemed to have resigned himself to the prospect of losing Orleans: but in the early spring of 1429 a new factor appeared in the war, and the fortune of the English at last began to wane. Patriotic hearts all over France were deeply stirred by the fact that for fifteen years a foreign enemy had been able to overrun and plunder the whole land, owing to the bitter civil strife which divided its inhabitants into two hostile camps. The English were insignificant in numbers, and could not for a moment have maintained themselves, but for the fact that a disloyal French faction gave them active aid, while the apathetic majority stood aside and allowed the Dauphinois and the Burgundians to fight out their disreputable blood-feud to a miserable end.

Meanwhile the countryside lay desolate, the towns were sinking into decay, and the land groaned for a deliverer from the interminable war. Help came from an unexpected quarter: Jeanne D'Arc, a young country girl from Domrémy on the borders of Lorraine, had been from her youth a dreamer of dreams and a seer of visions. While her mind was brooding over the misery of her country she was visited by a series of ecstatic trances in which she believed that her patron saints, the Virgin, St. Michael, and St. Catharine, appeared to her and bade her save France by preaching unity to all Frenchmen, and setting them an example of vigorous action.

After some doubting she set out to seek the *Dauphin's* court at Chinon, and presented herself before the apathetic prince, bidding him bestir himself and drive out the English by means of the divine aid which she brought him. Her visions promised her that she should relieve Orleans and lead Charles to Rheims, there to crown him king. Convinced by some secret token which Jeanne revealed to him, or perhaps moved only by motives of policy, the *Dauphin* gave his sanction to her mission, and sent her forth with an expedition which was about to attempt to succour the beleaguered garrison of Orleans. She assumed knightly armour, girt on a sword which was said to have been discovered by a miracle in the church of St. Catharine at Fierbois, and bore a white banner.

The French leaders were at first inclined to treat her as a mere impostor or fanatic, but the soldiery eagerly accepted her as an emissary of Heaven, and went forth with a confidence which they had not shown since Agincourt. Jeanne D'Arc entered Orleans in safety (April 30), and then led a series of sorties against the English forts which lay around it, heading the storming parties in person. Such was the enthusiasm with which the garrison followed her that her enterprises were successful, and the besiegers, seeing their line broken, were compelled to raise the leaguer and retire into their nearest strongholds, Jargeau and Beaugency. Rapidly following them up, Jeanne captured both places, and then defeated in the open field at Patay (June 18) the wrecks of the beaten army strengthened by a reinforcement from Paris under Lord Talbot.

This series of astonishing successes gave the French the confidence which they had so long lacked, while the English, amazed at defeats which they could not understand, declared that Jeanne was a witch and an emissary of the devil. A contemporary chronicler wrote:

> Before her day, two hundred English would drive five hundred French before them; but now two hundred French would beat and chase four hundred English.

For the future, the offensive was always taken by the *Dauphin's* troops, and the invaders would only fight on the defensive. After the victory of Patay the Maid escorted Charles to Rheims, as she had promised, and there saw him crowned King of France (July 17 1420). After this triumph she begged leave to withdraw home, but her presence was considered too valuable, and she was begged to stay with the army. Yielding to the request, she then advised an instant attack on Paris: it was carried out, but with such slackness and mismanagement that it failed. Jeanne herself was wounded as she urged on the troops to the storm, and her prestige suffered somewhat from the repulse. But meanwhile Senlis, Beauvais, Laon, and Soissons surrendered to the new king, and as a result of Jeanne's appearance all Champagne and most of the Isle de France had been abandoned by the English: even their hold on Paris and Normandy had been shaken.

Next spring the Maid again took the field, though her ungrateful master sent her forth with a very inadequate force at her back. She declared herself that her career was nearing its end, but persevered gallantly in the task which she had undertaken. After some small successes, she threw herself into Compiegne, which was being beleaguered by a Burgundian Army. Leading a sally of the garrison to beat up the besiegers' camp, she was unhorsed and taken prisoner. Philip of Burgundy sold her to the English for 10,000 crowns, and she was led into captivity. The Regent Bedford was always reckoned a just and wise prince, but in this case, he shamefully belied his reputation: he had no mercy for "the limb of the devil", as he called the unfortunate Jeanne.

She was for some time held in bonds, and subjected to cruel maltreatment in order to induce her to declare that her mission was not from God. Persevering in her belief to the end, she shamed her keepers by her courage and piety. At last Bedford commissioned the Bishop of Beauvais to proceed against her as a witch. After a formal trial before a French ecclesiastical court she was condemned and burnt to ashes at Rouen on May 30, 1431. Charles VII. was only less guilty than the English in this black business: he made no effort whatever to rescue his saviour, though he had in his hands Lord Talbot and many other English prisoners, and could have stopped Jeanne's persecution at any moment by threatening to retaliate on his captives any judgment that might be passed on her.

The Maid died unavenged, but the movement which she had set on foot did not die with her. She had destroyed the self-confidence which had made the English almost invincible. She had also stirred up the heart of the French Nation, and taught them to forget their wretched factions and feuds. From the moment of her appearance the Burgundian partisans of the English began one by one to drop off, and to make their peace with Charles VII. In spite of all his faults they saw that he represented the cause of French independence, and that it was a sin to fight against him in the ranks of the invader.

Bedford did his best to struggle against fate, and his military talents availed for some years to stem the tide, but he felt himself that he was only postponing the inevitable. The fatal blow was struck when at last Philip of Burgundy consented to forget his father's murder, and to make peace with the murderer. At the Congress of Arras he threw up his long alliance with England, and reconciled himself to Charles (Sept. 10, 1435). Four days later the Regent John of Bedford died at Rouen, worn out by his long campaigning. For twelve years, he had hardly been given a moment's rest, and he saw that the ruin of the cause which he had so long maintained was at hand.

Bedford had not been buried seven months when Paris, the last refuge of the English in central France, fell into the hands of the enemy. The *burghers*, once such hot partisans of Burgundy and England, opened the gates to the besiegers, and Lord Willoughby with his small garrison had to fly in haste (April, 1436). Nothing was now left to the English but their old foothold in the duchy of Guienne, around the ever-loyal Bordeaux, and in the north Normandy and part of Maine. It is therefore most extraordinary to find that in these limited regions they were able to maintain themselves for no less than sixteen years more.

The chief heroes of this last and most hopeless stage of the Hundred Years' War were John Lord Talbot, and Richard Duke of York. The latter was the son of that Richard Earl of Cambridge who had conspired against Henry V. in 1415. He had succeeded to the duchy of York when a young boy on the death of his childless uncle, Duke Edmund, at Agincourt. But he became a much more important personage in 1425, when his other uncle, Edmund Mortimer Earl of March, died, and left him his heir. Through his mother Anne Mortimer, Richard now represented the eldest line of Edward III.'s descendants.

He was twice appointed to the command in France, and held it from 1435 to 1437, and again from 1441 to 1445. He kept a tight hold on Normandy, beating off assault after assault upon the duchy, and often pushing raids almost to the gates of Paris. He even recovered from the French in 1437 the important fortress of Pontoise, one of the keys of the Seine, and it was maintained till 1441, being four times relieved and reprovisioned by the indefatigable Talbot. When York was recalled from France in 1445, and replaced by Edmund Beaufort, Duke of

Somerset, a commander of a much lower stamp, the power of resistance of the English in Normandy seemed to collapse, and place after place began to fall into the hands of the enemy,

Meanwhile the internal affairs of England present little that is of importance. A long struggle went on between Humphrey of Gloucester, representing the extreme war party, and Beaufort, now a Cardinal, who led those who were in favour of coming to an agreement with France, and sacrificing the untenable claim to the French throne in return for some territorial concessions. Gloucester gradually lost ground, more especially after 1441, when his wife, Eleanor Cobham, was prosecuted for using sorcery to compass the king's death, and rightly or wrongly condemned to imprisonment for life. Her husband made no attempt to defend her, but whether from cowardice, or from consciousness that she was guilty, it is impossible to tell.

The temporary discredit of the war party led to serious negotiations with France in 1444. The king had now attained his majority, and men trusted that a new era would commence when he took over the conduct of affairs from the hands of the council. He himself was set on peace, and it was hoped that the agreement might be sealed by his marriage with a French princess. Unfortunately, however, the son of the heroic Henry V., and the grandson of the politic Henry IV., turned out to be the weakest sovereign that ever sat upon the English throne. A gentle, pious, incapable young man, he was full of good wishes, but lacked the strength to put them into practice. He was so modest and diffident that he was always ready to defer to the opinion of the nearest adviser; but the next person that had his ear could as easily turn him from his first purpose.

One unfortunate heritage from his ancestors showed itself in him long ere he reached middle age—a touch of the melancholy madness of his grandfather, Charles VI. of France. When it fell upon him he had to be placed in retirement, and the cloud did not pass from his brain for many months. He was entirely well meaning, and his people loved his pious and simple character, but they were at the same time driven to despair by the hopeless incapacity which he showed for affairs of state. Usually he was merely the mouthpiece of those behind the throne.

The full extent of Henry's weakness was not yet known, in 1444, William de la Pole, Earl of Suffolk, a particular of Cardinal Beaufort, signed the Truce of Tours for the king. By this agreement the English retained their foothold about Bordeaux and in the duchy of Normandy, but gave up their fortresses in Maine and other outlying regions. At the same time the king received the hand of Margaret of Anjou, a cousin of Charles VII., daughter of Réné, Duke of Anjou and titular King of Naples. The terms which Suffolk had obtained were very unfavourable; in return for the ceded strongholds, England should have got something more than an uncertain truce and a dowerless bride for her king.

When the details of the Truce of Tours were divulged, Gloucester again raised his head and began to clamour against the cession of Maine. He found plenty of support from the enemies of Suffolk and the Beauforts, and was able to make himself most unpleasant to the young queen. Margaret was a woman of strong passions and considerable ability, who soon learned how to domineer over her meek husband, and was quite reckless in using her power.

She threw herself vehemently into English politics as an enemy of Gloucester and his party, and started her career in England as the leader of a faction. At the Parliament of Bury (Feb. 1447), she and Suffolk concocted a *coup d'état* against Humphrey. He was seized and thrown into prison, where he at once died: there were strong suspicions of foul play, but it seems more likely that apoplexy, caused by a fit of passion, carried off the duke. His old rival Cardinal Beaufort, who had retired from politics a few years before, only survived him for five weeks.

The government of the realm now passed for a space into the hands of Suffolk, the queen, and Edmund Beaufort, Duke of Somerset, who used the king's name at their pleasure. The leadership of the opposition, on the other hand, had devolved on Richard Duke of York, a far more able man than Duke Humphrey; he had never forgiven the way in which his career in Normandy had been brought to an end by his being superseded by Somerset.

At all costs the ministry should have endeavoured to turn the truce with France into a permanent peace. But they were unable to do so, and, what was worse, could not keep their own troops in Normandy in order. A disgraceful raid into Brittany by some mutinous bands, whom Somerset had left unpaid, gave the French an excuse for renewing the war (March, 1449).

The best testimony to the incapacity of the English Government was the extraordinary rapidity with which Normandy was lost. In less than a year Somerset had been driven out of the duchy which York and Talbot had so long maintained against all the strength of France. A small army of relief, sent over from Southampton, was cut to pieces at the Battle of Formigny (April 15, 1450), and four months later Cherbourg, the last fortress held for England, lowered its flag. Nothing now remained to England in northern France save the single stronghold of Calais.

The outburst of wrath which followed Somerset's disgraceful loss of Normandy marks the opening of a new period in English history. Civil strife was about to be added to foreign war, and the Wars of the Roses were close at hand.

CHAPTER 12

The Wars of the Roses 1450-1464

Down to the moment of the loss of Normandy the misfortunes of the French war had provoked no more than a certain amount of clamorous criticism of the king's ministers. The burden of the war had not been very heavily felt; it had been largely maintained with French money, and the parliamentary grants in aid had not been extravagant. The drain of men had been considerable, but it had fallen entirely on volunteers and mercenaries. The hope of conquering all France had long been abandoned, and as long as a broad foothold was kept beyond the Channel, the details of the struggle had not been minutely investigated. It was generally thought that a good deal of mismanagement and maladministration was going on, and grumbling never ceased, but there had as yet been no great explosion of popular wrath. The fact that the opposition was headed by a discredited and reckless busybody like Humphrey of Gloucester had also availed somewhat to weaken its criticism of the ministers.

Now, however, matters were changed. The great Duchy of Normandy had been lost in a few months, and this disaster fell like a thunder-clap on the nation. Moreover, the discontented had now got an able and popular leader in Richard of York, who (as men now began to remember) was very near the throne. Since Gloucester's death the duke was the first prince of the blood, and the king's nearest kinsman. Moreover, Henry had now been five years wedded and yet had no offspring: if he continued childless, Richard would inherit his crown. For this reason, both York himself and his admirers were much incensed that, in spite of his well-known ability, he was excluded as far as possible from public affairs; indeed he had of late been sent into a kind of honourable banishment by being made Lord-deputy of Ireland (1448) for a term of ten years. In the unhappy sister-island he proved to be one of the few successful governors whom England has entrusted with the unenviable post. He and his house were ever after very popular in Ireland.

Nor was Richard powerful by reason of his popularity alone: his following among the baronage was very considerable. He himself, through his father's marriage with Anne Mortimer, sister of the last Earl of March, was one of the greatest landholders in the realm. He had wedded Cicely Neville, a daughter of the greatest baronial house in the England of that day. Her brother Richard Neville Earl of Salisbury, and her nephew Richard Neville Earl of Warwick (the famous "king-maker" of a later day) were always the trusty partisans of the duke.

★★★★★★

The elder Neville had married Alice, heiress of Salisbury, granddaughter of the Lollard earl who fell in 1400. The younger Richard had wedded Anne, heiress of Warwick, and had obtained her great heritage in the western Midlands and on the south Welsh border.

★★★★★★

Three other Neville peers, the Lords Abergavenny, Latimer, and Fauconberg, firmly adhered to the family politics of their race. Another faithful friend was John Mowbray, Duke of Norfolk: he was the nephew of York's wife Cicely Neville, but his opposition to the king's ministers was probably due rather to an ancient blood-feud with the house of Lancaster; for his uncle was the Mowbray who had been beheaded at York in 1405, and his grandfather was the unfortunate opponent of Henry IV. in the lists at Coventry. Three or four other houses of minor note were allied with the Nevilles and Mowbrays, and the whole group constituted a faction of formidable strength.

The baronage of England had been dwindling in numbers for a century and more: there were now not more than thirty or forty lay peers in the House of Lords. Each of the titles of the year 1450 represented three or four of the old baronies of the time of the Edwards. Hence a compact group of a dozen peers now comprised a third of the whole baronage of England. The estates of Mortimer, Mowbray, and Neville were scattered thickly all over England, and gave rallying points in almost every county for the partisans of York.

There is no proof whatever that Duke Richard had personally dabbled in treasonable schemes before he had been banished to Ireland by the king's ministers. His conduct all through Henry's minority had been loyal and correct. It seems that he was first roused to action by the clamours of the nation, and only moved when public opinion demanded that he should take his proper place in the state, and exert the influence to which he was entitled as first prince of the blood. Had King Henry been a man of ability, who could rule his ministers instead of being ruled by them, there seems no reason to think that Duke Richard would have stirred. All through his life he was a man of cautious and moderate measures: but he would have been more than human if he had refrained from using his strength when he was shouldered aside and ignored by the faction led by the Beauforts, Suffolk, and Queen Margaret.

The loss of Normandy was followed by the first popular outbreak in England which had been seen for more than a generation. It was directed against the king's ministers and advisers, and appeared all over the southern shires. Already, before Formigny had been fought, a mob of mutinous soldiers had stoned to death Bishop Moleyns, the keeper of the Privy Seal, at Portsmouth (Jan., 1450). Two months later such a bitter outcry in Parliament was raised against Suffolk that, after he had been impeached, the timid king ordered him to leave the realm for the present. He took ship for Flanders, but was waylaid on the high seas by some vessels from London, and was murdered by the sailors. Who was at the bottom of this act of piracy was never discovered. (May 2, 1450.)

If the queen and Somerset hoped that the unpopularity of the ministry might end with Suffolk's fall they were soon undeceived. The populace was still unsatisfied. In the month of June troubles broke out in many places: Ayscough, Bishop of Salisbury, the king's confessor, was slain by rioters in his own diocese. There were risings in Sussex and Norfolk also, but the main focus of the trouble lay in Kent. It was fomented by a certain John Aylmer or Cade, a soldier of fortune who had served under York both in France and Ireland. He assumed the name of Mortimer, stated that he was a distant relative of Duke Richard, and pretended that he was acting in his interests.

With a great mob of Kentishmen at his back he entered London (July 3, 1450), after beating the hasty levies which the ministers sent out against him. The Londoners joined him, and for a few days he was master of the streets: he used his power to execute Lord Say, the treasurer, and Crowmere, Sheriff of Kent, the chief officials who fell into his power. But Cade soon proved unable to keep his followers in hand: they fell to plundering, and so frightened the citizens that many of them took arms and aided the garrison of the Tower in driving the insurgents out of the city. On being promised a pardon the Kentishmen dispersed, but their leader, refusing to disarm, was hunted down and slain.

Meanwhile Richard of York, hearing of the tumults in England, had left his post at Dublin and crossed St. George's Channel. When he came to land many of his followers flocked to join him, and it seemed likely that a new civil war might break out. But the duke contented himself with issuing manifestoes against the ministry, and setting on his partisans in Parliament to attack them. The Yorkist majority in the House of Commons tendered to the king a petition begging him to dismiss Somerset and his friends, but Henry was entirely in the hands of the Beauforts, and refused to listen to it. When Thomas Young, member for Bristol, spoke of the duke as rightful heir to the crown, he was sent to the Tower.

York still held back from violent measures, but if anything was yet wanting to complete Somerset's discredit with the nation it was the result of the next year's campaign in France. In 1451 the French threw themselves upon Aquitaine, which the government had wholly neglected during the domestic troubles. The Gascons did their best, but one after another all their cities fell before the French artillery. Bordeaux yielded in June and Bayonne in October, without having received any succour from England. Only Calais now remained unconquered of all the broad domain which Henry VI. had inherited on the Continent.

The loss of Aquitaine at last drove York to desperation. Raising his own retainers and those of the Nevilles and Mowbrays he marched on London. The king, at the head of a larger force, faced him at Dartford, in Kent, and there at a conference Henry promised to dismiss his present advisers and change his methods of governance. But when York had disbanded his army Somerset appeared again at the king's right hand, and Duke Richard found that he had been tricked (March, 1452). He was arrested, and only released after pledging himself never again to take arms. This promise he kept, under circumstances of great provocation, for three years (1452-5).

In 1452 the last campaign of the Hundred Years' War was about to begin. The Gascons, sincerely attached to the English connection and oppressed by their new French governors, burst out into insurrection in the summer of 1452. To aid them Lord Talbot, now Earl of Shrewsbury, came over from England at the head of four or five thousand men. Aided by the insurgents he recovered Bordeaux and all the lands around it, and during the winter of 1452-3 held his own with ease. But when summer came round the whole national levy of France marched into Aquitaine and laid siege to Castillon.

Hurrying up to rescue it, the brave old earl resolved to storm the French lines of circumvallation. Forming his men in a deep column, contrary to the English custom, he launched them at the entrenchments. But the hostile artillery blew the head of the mass to pieces, Talbot himself was slain, and after a hard struggle the English and Gascons were cut to pieces (July 17, 1453). This battle settled the fate of Aquitaine, for Somerset could not or would not send out further succours, and Bordeaux capitulated in October, after holding out gallantly for ten weeks.

A few days after the Battle of Castillon, and long before it could be known in England, King Henry fell for the first time into a fit of madness, the result (it is said) of a sudden fright For eighteen months he remained in a state of melancholy apathy, or rather idiocy, and was unable to discharge the simplest functions of royalty. This was in many ways the best thing for England that could have happened, and many years of trouble would have been avoided if he had never recovered.

After a space Parliament met and appointed Duke Richard Protector of the realm, while Somerset was sent to the Tower. But some three months after her husband had gone mad, the Queen, after nine years of childless wedlock, gave birth to a son, a circumstance which changed the aspect of politics by cutting York out of the line of succession to the throne. He behaved, however, with correctness and moderation, acknowledged the infant prince as heir to the crown, and did homage to him. He acted as regent for more than a year, and did his best to bring the internal affairs of the kingdom into order: for the French war, nothing could be done: with the second fall of Bordeaux all hope of retaining a foothold in Aquitaine had vanished.

About mid-winter 1454-5 King Henry suddenly recovered his senses. The moment that he was convalescent his wife induced him to release Somerset from prison, and a few weeks later York and his friends were dismissed from all their offices, which were given back to the Beauforts and their partisans. A parliament was then summoned to meet at Leicester, which was to reverse all the acts of the Protectorate. Now at last Duke Richard lost his temper, and took arms at the head of his faction, after issuing a manifesto which denounced Somerset, not only as a minister of tried incapacity, but as a perjured traitor.

Death of Talbot at Castillon

The king, with a considerable armed following, was moving from London towards the Midlands, when the duke and his partisans fell upon him at St. Albans: there was a short but sharp fray in the streets, which ended in the victory of the Yorkists, due mainly to the hard fighting of the younger Richard Neville, the Earl of Warwick, who first broke through the Lancastrian barricades. Somerset was slain, and with him several peers of his faction: the king fell into the hands of the victors (May 22, 1455).

This insignificant skirmish, in which neither side had more than 2000 men present, cost the lives of only a few scores of fighting men. But it was to be the prelude of a war of the most desperate and bloody kind, which was to mow down half the baronage of England. It came to be known as the "War of the Roses" from the white rose, which was the badge of the house of York, and the red rose, which was afterwards assumed as the token of the house of Lancaster.

At first it seemed possible that the Battle of St. Albans might lead to a mere change of ministry, much desired by the majority of the nation. Duke Richard treated the captive king with all respect, and merely reinstated himself and his friends in power. The excitement of the battle had thrown Henry back into his melancholy madness, in which he lay for some months incapable of all action. The duke's term of power, however, lasted little more than a year: in October, 1456, the king, having recovered his senses once more, fell under the influence of his wife, who now put herself openly forward as head of the Loyalist faction in place of Somerset. By her advice the Yorkists were removed from office.

Three years of unrest and bickering followed (1456-59) before matters again came to a head. Each party meanwhile was preparing for the inevitable strife: the blood shed at St. Albans had made reconciliation impossible, and it was felt that the next struggle must lead to the extermination of one party or the other. Duke Richard saw that it would not avail him to attain once more to office, if he was always liable to be dismissed from it at the queen's pleasure: when forced to take arms again he must make his position secure.

Margaret, on the other hand, was conscious that if she failed in the on-coming struggle the succession of her little son to his father's throne would be more than problematical. She was resolved to fight to the death for his rights, and spent all her time and energy in binding into a compact Lancastrian party those of the baronage who were not allied by blood or ancient friendship with the houses of York, Neville,

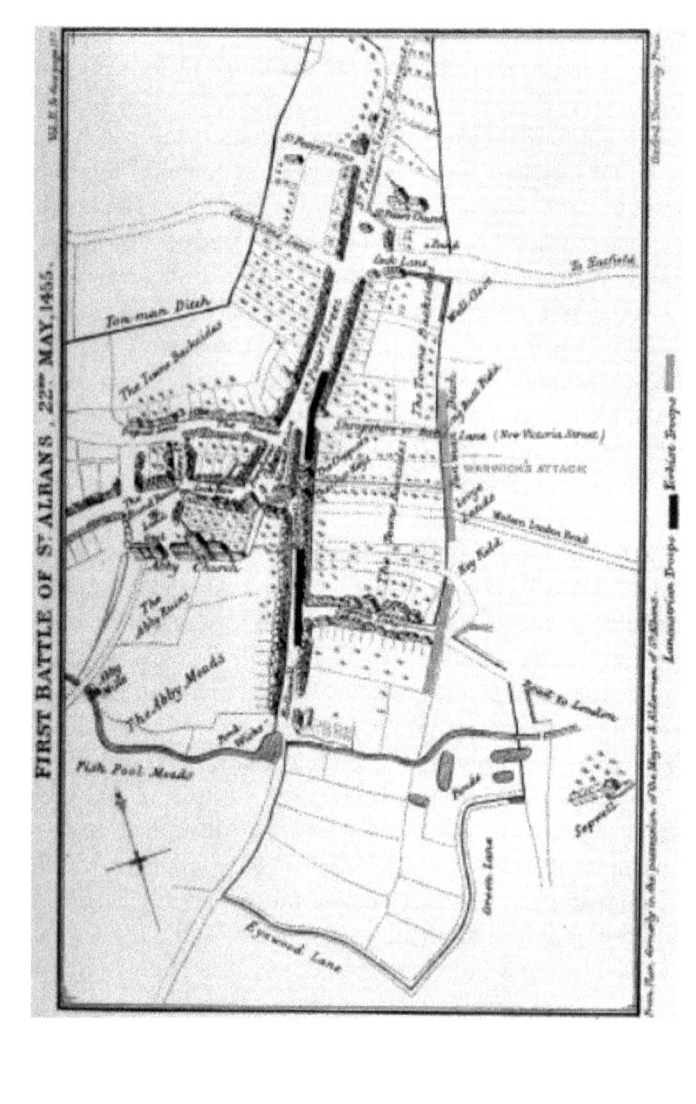

and Mowbray. Beside the Beaufort clan, now headed by Henry, son of the Somerset who had fallen at St. Albans, she could count on the support of the Percies (old rivals of the Nevilles) in the North, of the Courtenays Earls of Devon in the West, of the Dukes of Buckingham and Exeter, and the Earls of Oxford and Shrewsbury, and of a body of barons decidedly more numerous than those who followed Duke Richard, though not individually so powerful.

All through 1458 both Yorkists and Lancastrians had been secretly arming for a new trial of strength. In the summer of 1459 the queen began to issue writs in her husband's name, bidding her partisans be ready to turn out in arms at a moment's notice. It was this fact, followed by a peremptory summons to the Yorkist leaders to present themselves before the king in person, which seems to have provoked the final outburst. In September Duke Richard raised his standard in the Mortimer lands on the Welsh border, while Salisbury called out the Neville tenants in the North Riding, and the young Earl of Warwick hurried over from Calais to join his father.

The two Nevilles made their way to the west to join their kinsman, Warwick without difficulty, but Salisbury only after a sharp fight with the Loyalists of Cheshire and Staffordshire, on whom he inflicted a bloody check at Bloreheath. But the numerous supporters of York in London and the eastern counties had no time to join their chief before the fate of the campaign was settled. The king, showing for once in his life both energy and decision, had placed himself at the head of the levies of central England, and marched on Ludlow, where the insurgents lay. Their armies faced each other at Ludford across the flooded Teme, and a battle on a large scale seemed imminent: but the duke's partisans saw that they were much outnumbered, and many of them felt scruples at resisting their sovereign when he personally led his army to attack them: this time it was no question of opposing a Suffolk or a Somerset; the king himself, and not merely the king's name, was arrayed against them.

When Henry and his host passed the Teme and advanced on the Yorkist camp, the insurgents melted away before his face without fighting, and the Lancastrians were victorious without striking a blow. Duke Richard escaped to Ireland, where he found a warm welcome: the two Neville earls escaped in a fishing-smack to Calais, where the garrison was devoted to Warwick, who had long been their governor (October, 1459)

The "Rout of Ludford" placed the queen in a triumphant posi-

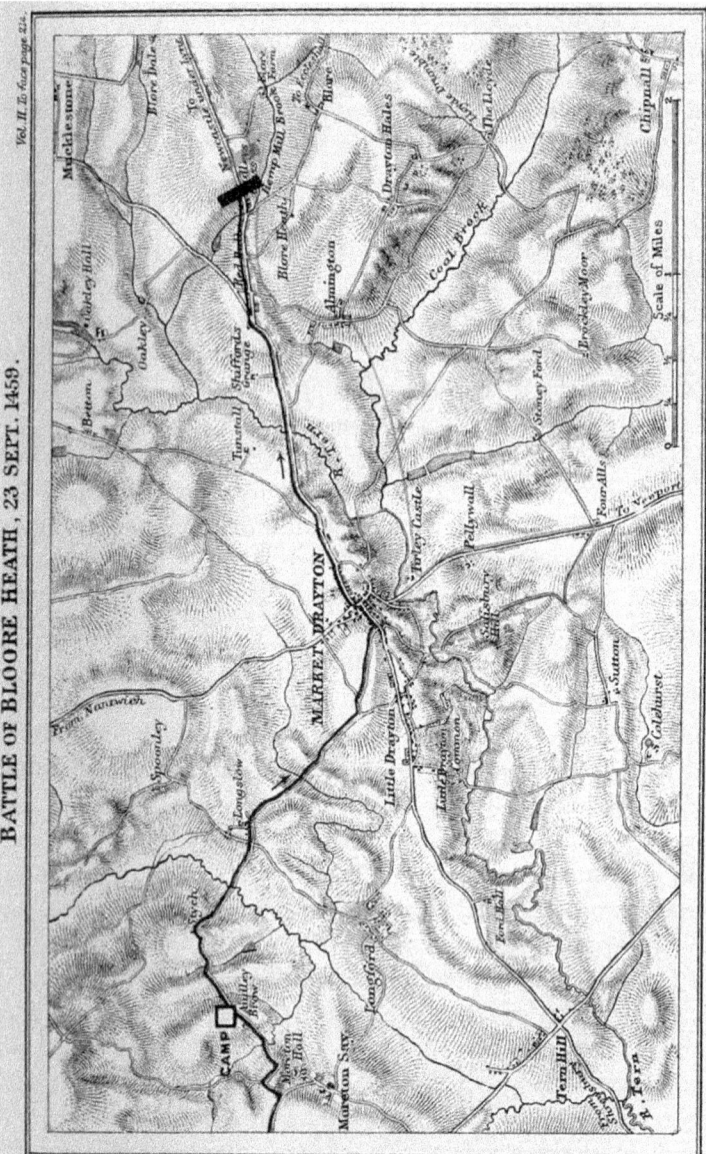

tion: the Yorkists had put themselves in the wrong by their armed rebellion, and it would have been easy to crush them in their two last strongholds. But Margaret showed herself an incompetent ruler: instead of making a vigorous attempt to end the war, she set to work to proscribe and punish her enemies before they were completely disposed of. The duke and his chief followers were attainted, their lands were confiscated, some of their minor adherents were executed, but no assault in strength was made on Calais or on Ireland. The Yorkist party had time to recover from its panic, and the nation was shocked by the queen's violent actions—the most unwise of them was that she had allowed the open town of Newbury to be sacked merely because it belonged to the duke.

In June 1460, Warwick, who showed himself throughout the leading spirit in the Yorkist ranks, landed at Sandwich with a few hundred followers from Calais. The Kentishmen at once rose in arms to aid him: the Londoners opened their gates to him, though a Royalist garrison maintained itself in the Tower; and Archbishop Bourchier, a cousin of York, brought the levies of the eastern counties to his aid. The Queen, taken by surprise, had called together her partisans from the Midland shires at Northampton, where they palisaded a strong entrenched camp. But Warwick hurried forward from London, stormed the fortifications, and routed the Lancastrians. King Henry was taken prisoner, while the captains of his host, the Duke of Buckingham and the Earl of Shrewsbury, were slain (July 10, 1460). The queen and her young son escaped to the North, where they took refuge with the Earl of Northumberland.

Duke Richard arrived from Ireland too late to take part in his nephew's victory, and found the greater part of the realm at his feet. He called together a parliament, in which hot disputes broke out among his partisans as to the way in which the governance of the realm should be arranged. Twice already the plan of retaining King Henry on the throne and making York Protector had been tried and had failed. Many of the duke's advisers were of opinion that he might now set aside Henry, and declare himself king: there was no doubt that from the point of view of strict hereditary right the heir of the house of March and Clarence had a better title than the heir of Lancaster.

Richard himself leaned to this alternative, but Warwick and the Nevilles were for a less violent change. They thought that Richard should be proclaimed Protector for life, and heir to the throne, while Henry should be allowed to reign in name so long as he lived. Personally, the pious king was not unpopular, and no one wished him ill, but it was necessary to disinherit his young son Edward, in order that Queen Margaret might never again interfere in politics. This alternative was ultimately adopted: it bears a strong resemblance to the scheme formulated at the Treaty of Troyes in respect to the crown of France.

York, being named Protector for life, had now to subdue the parts of the realm where his title was not acknowledged. He sent against Wales, where the two Tudors, Jasper and Owen, stepbrother and stepfather of King Henry, were in arms, his eldest son Edward Earl of March, a young man of eighteen, who had seen his first service in the field at Northampton. He himself, and his brother-in-law, Richard Neville Earl of Salisbury, marched into the North.

✶✶✶✶✶✶

Some years after the death of Henry V. his widow, Catharine of France, had wedded Owen Tudor, a plain Welsh gentleman. Her two sons by him, Edmund and Jasper, were made Earls of Richmond and Pembroke by their half-brother the king. The former, who died young, was the father of Henry VII.

✶✶✶✶✶✶

There the Lancastrian interest was very strong: indeed, the Yorkists had little influence north of the Humber save in the Neville estates in the North Riding. The queen, the young Duke of Somerset, and the Percies had raised a considerable army and were bent on fighting. York, undervaluing their numbers and overestimating the extent to which they had been demoralised by the defeat of Northampton, rashly engaged with them at Wakefield, though his forces amounted to only a third of theirs. He was surrounded and cut to pieces with the whole of his army: The Earl of Salisbury and Edmund of York, Richard's second son, a lad of sixteen, were captured and put to death in cold blood by the victors. Their heads, with that of the duke himself, were struck off and placed on spikes over the gate of York (Dec. 30, 1460).

This murder of prisoners and mutilation of the dead was by far the worst outrage which had yet happened in the struggle. It embittered the civil war into a blood-feud, and made the heirs of York and Salisbury pitiless for the future. Hitherto they had given quarter, but now they had the death and dishonour of their fathers to avenge. A change for the worse is at once visible in their action.

After the victory of Wakefield, the Lancastrians flocked in from all sides to join the queen, and she was able to march on London at the head of a formidable host. The task of opposing her fell on Warwick, who, by the deaths of his father and uncle, had become the undisputed head of his party, Edward of March being as yet young and little known. Warwick arrayed the Yorkists of London, Kent, and the eastern counties at St. Albans, and there awaited the hostile attack. It was delivered with great vigour on Feb. 17, 1461, and once more the queen was victorious. Treachery or chance left a gap in the earl's line, through which the Lancastrians penetrated, and the routed host was pushed westward in its flight, leaving the road to London open. The king was recaptured by his friends, and his wife celebrated his deliverance by executing the two chief Yorkist prisoners who fell into her hands.

The fall of London now seemed so sure that the victorious Lancastrians spent eight days in settling the terms of capitulation at their leisure. This delay proved their ruin, and saved the capital. Edward of March had now beaten the Welsh levies of the Tudors at the Battle of Mortimer's Cross (Feb. 2, 1461), and was already on the march for London when the news of the disaster at St. Albans reached him. At Chipping Norton Warwick joined him with the wrecks of his beaten host, and after a short conference they agreed to move on the capital and throw themselves into it, if it was not already in the enemy's power. By a forced march they reached it on the very day when it was to have been surrendered to the queen (Feb. 26).

The sudden arrival of 12,000 Yorkists within the walls changed the aspect of affairs: and the Londoners resolved to hold out. Margaret and her generals were not prepared for a siege: their army was discontented at being denied the sack of London, and was already beginning to melt home with the plunder which it had gathered in the Home counties. After some hesitation, the Lancastrians determined to retire northward to gather reinforcements, and to throw the dangers of the offensive on their enemies. As they moved backward along the road to York they ravaged the country around in the most shameful manner.

It was this misbehaviour of the northern moss-troopers which mainly accounts for the sudden vehemence with which the Midlands now took up the cause of York: hitherto they had been but lukewarm, but smarting under their losses they turned out in great force to join Edward of March and Richard of Warwick. The former, before starting on the campaign, was saluted by his followers as king, under the name of Edward IV. He claimed the crown as heir of Lionel of Clarence, ignoring the Lancastrian usurpation, and dated his reign from March 1461, though his title did not receive Parliamentary sanction till November. Thus, with him triumphed the cause of hereditary right, as opposed to that theory of election by the nation represented in Parliament, under which the Lancastrian house had held she throne.

Allowing only a few days of rest to their army, Warwick and King Edward followed the Lancastrians towards York, gathering up on their way numerous levies from the Eastern and Midland shires. On March 28th, the enemy was found lying behind the River Aire. After driving in his rear-guard by a skirmish at Ferrybridge, the Yorkists crossed the stream and came upon the queen's host drawn up on the hillside of Towton. Next day (Palm Sunday, March 29, 1461) the bloodiest battle of the Wars of the Roses was fought.

Both sides were in great force, and contemporary writers thought that as many as 60,000 Lancastrians and 45,000 Yorkists were engaged,—figures that cannot be trusted for a moment. In a blinding snow-storm the Yorkists climbed the hillside and ranged themselves opposite their foes: after a preliminary discharge of arrows the hosts clashed together all along the line, and remained locked together for many hours of close fighting with sword and axe. Towards evening a flank attack made by the Duke of Norfolk settled the result of the battle, and the queen's army turned to fly.

Besides those who fell in the pursuit great numbers were drowned in the flooded stream of the Cock, which lay just behind their position. The slaughter was very great, especially among the barons and knights, who could not easily fly in their heavy mail. The Earl of Northumberland and four other peers were slain: the Earls of Devon and Wiltshire, and a great number of knights and squires captured in the pursuit, were beheaded, in revenge for the slaying of Salisbury and Prince Edmund after Wakefield.

The queen, with her husband and her young son, fled from York into Scotland the moment that the result of the battle was known. With them went the young Duke of Somerset, almost the only Lancastrian of note who escaped from the field alive. The party was crushed beyond hope of recovery, and though its desperate partisans held out for nearly three years more in Wales and on the Scottish border, they were never able to shake the power of the new king. Indeed, England south of the Tees was free from civil war from the day of Towton onwards.

The lingering struggle in Northumberland was only sustained by two supports, the queen's untiring energy, and the desperate hatred for the Nevilles which filled the hearts of the Percies and the other nobles of the north. Margaret bought aid from Scotland by ceding Berwick to King James III.: she crossed to France and wrung money and auxiliaries from the stingy Louis XI. by promising to give over Calais to him.

But all her efforts came to nought: the great Northumbrian fortresses of Alnwick and Bamborough were taken by the Earl of Warwick (1462). By the aid of her French troops she recovered them for a moment, but this success was only to lead to a second disaster: Warwick returned and blew the great northern strongholds to pieces with his artillery (1463). The Scots grew tired of the war: King Louis would give no more aid when he found that Calais was not likely to come into his hands.

The final desperate rally of the northern Lancastrians was crushed at the fights of Hedgeley Moor (April 15) and Hexham (May 13th, 1464). After this last victory, the few surviving chiefs of the loyalists fell into Warwick's hands, and when he had beheaded the Duke of Somerset and the Lords Roos and Hungerford, the long resistance collapsed for lack of leaders. At last there was no man left in England who did not bow his head before King Edward and his great vicegerent, Richard Neville. King Henry himself, wandering hopelessly in disguise through the realm that had once been his own, was captured and consigned to the Tower, where he lingered for six years in pious melancholy.

CHAPTER 13

Richard the King-Maker and Edward the King 1464-1483

While the struggle with the last survivors of the Lancastrian faction was still in progress, the governance of England had been in the hands of the Neville clan. Richard of Warwick, "the King-maker", the head of the house, and by far its most able representative, had been continually in the field as the leader of King Edward's armies; George Neville, Archbishop of York (Warwick's brother), was chancellor; John Neville Lord Montague (another brother) was regarded as the king's confidential councillor; he had also commanded at Hexham and Hedgeley Moor. William Neville Lord Falconberg had been made Earl of Kent for his services at Towton, and several other members of the family were high in place about the king.

The house and its connections had formed the backbone of the Yorkist party, and its members thought themselves entitled to good payment for their services. If Edward IV. had been a weak ruler the domination of the Nevilles might have continued all through his reign. But the young king was far from being a nonentity: he was able, obstinate, selfish, and ungrateful, the last of men to suffer himself to be made the tool of his mother's relations.

As long as the Lancastrians still made head against him he was content to use the services of Warwick and his brothers, but now that his throne was safe he intended to rule after his own will and inclination. He was quite competent to do so: at Mortimer's Cross and Towton he had already shown that he was a good soldier; he had a clear head, a hard heart, and no scruples. His weak point was a love of pleasure and debauchery, which sometimes led him to waste his time in idleness; but when prompt and decisive action was required he always shed his sloth, and set to work with an energy and ability which startled his enemies.

The first rift between the king and the Nevilles appeared in the year 1464, just after the last hopes of the Lancastrians had been crushed at Hexham. The king was now twenty-three, and it was high time for him to wed: with his apparent consent Warwick commenced a negotiation for his marriage with the sister of the Queen of France. The Neville foreign policy had always been to ally England to France, and to distrust the King of France's rival, Charles the Rash, the great Duke of Burgundy.

Suddenly Edward announced that the French match must be dropped, because he was married already. He had become infatuated with a beautiful widow seven years older than himself. Elizabeth Woodville was the daughter of Lord Rivers, a Lancastrian peer, and her first husband, Sir John Grey, another prominent Lancastrian, had fallen at St. Albans. Caring nothing for the disparity of rank nor for the disloyal traditions of Elizabeth's family, Edward had secretly married her, and kept the matter dark for six months (May-October, 1464). When he vouchsafed to declare what he had done, Warwick had at once to abandon his negotiations with Louis XI., and was much displeased at the manner in which he had been tricked.

The king soon began to display an exaggerated fondness for his wife's numerous relations, to place them about his person, and to seek wealthy marriages for them. We cannot doubt that his conduct was dictated by policy, and not by a real regard for the Woodvilles and Greys, who were a greedy and grasping crew. He wished to surround himself with persons entirely dependent on his favour, as a check on the haughty and self-reliant Neville clan. For the same reason, he created a number of new peers to counterbalance the Neville family group in the House of Lords.

For two years there was no open breach between Edward and Warwick, but in June, 1467, the king dismissed George Neville, the chancellor, openly disavowed Warwick and his policy, and put himself entirely in the hands of his new friends. His change of views was completed by the formation of an alliance with the Duke of Burgundy, to whom he gave his sister Margaret in marriage.

To break so rudely and openly with the Nevilles was unwise: the family was powerful in nearly every part of England, and Warwick had been for so long the figurehead of the Yorkist party that most of its older members looked to him and not to the king for guidance.

Moreover, the Woodvilles were making themselves hated for their pride and shameless greed. A typical instance of their conduct was the marriage of young John Woodville, the queen's brother, to the Dowager Duchess of Norfolk, who was old enough to have been his grandmother, but possessed wealth enough to tempt him into the match.

Noting the unpopularity which was gathering around Edward, Warwick began to make quiet preparations for resuming his old position, even though he might have to use force in the process. He enlisted in his cause the king's brother, George Duke of Clarence, an ambitious and discontented young man, by giving him the hand of his eldest daughter, Isabel Neville, on whom (since the great earl had no male issue) the larger half of his vast estates would someday devolve.

In July, 1469, thinking matters ripe for his interference, Warwick set his followers to work. His nephew Sir Henry Fitzhugh and his cousin Sir Henry Neville took arms in Yorkshire, with a programme much like that which the Lords Appellant had used against Richard II., or the early Yorkists against Suffolk and Somerset. The king must be freed from unworthy favourites, and provided with a respectable and responsible ministry, *i.e.* replaced in his former dependence on the house of Neville. This rising is often called the rebellion of "Robin of Redesdale", an assumed name adopted by one of its leaders, Sir John Conyers. Warwick had passed the word around among his friends and adherents to support the rising, but did not appear himself.

Soon the rebel army swelled to formidable proportions, moved south and routed the troops which the king sent against it, under the Earls of Pembroke and Devon, at Edgecot Field, near Banbury.

★★★★★★

These men are not, of course, the Lancastrian Earls, Jasper Tudor and John Courtenay, but Yorkists (named Herbert and Stafford) to whom the titles of the others had been given.

★★★★★★

Edward after the battle saw his army disperse, and fell into the hands of the rebels. Warwick and Clarence then appeared upon the scene, and assumed the custody of the king's person. Edward was treated with formal courtesy, but placed for a time in safe keeping at Middleham Castle, a Neville stronghold in Yorkshire. His favourites fared much worse: the queen's father Rivers, her brother John Woodville, and the Earls of Devon and Pembroke, were all beheaded by the rebels, with Warwick's full approval. Greedy upstarts as they were, they did not deserve to die without a trial, and their bloody end shocked the whole Yorkist party.

After keeping the king two months under restraint (Aug.-Sept, 1469), Warwick released him, thinking that he had been taught the necessary lesson, and would for the future refrain from offending the Neville clan. As a matter of fact, Edward's spirit was not broken, and his only thought was to revenge himself on the earl and Clarence. Six months later he got his opportunity: a Lancastrian insurrection broke out in Lincolnshire in March, 1470, and to suppress it the king gathered a large army, whose leaders were carefully chosen from among the enemies of the Nevilles. After dispersing the rebels near Stamford, in a fight often called "Lose-Coat field", the king suddenly wheeled about, and marched against Warwick and Clarence, who were coming from Coventry to join him with a small force.

★★★★★★

Lose-Coat field was so called from the haste in which the rebels cast off their cassocks, in order to fly the quicker.

★★★★★★

He was resolved to treat them just as they had treated him in the preceding year: having caught them unprepared he hunted them across England, and finally forced them to embark at Dartmouth, and flee to France (March, 1470).

★★★★★★

Some think that Warwick was really implicated in the Lincolnshire rising, and the king stated so at the time, but it seems more likely that he was not. If he had been organising the business he would not have been caught unprepared, and the leaders of the rebellion were all old Lancastrians.

★★★★★★

The great earl had fallen so easily because he had not been granted time to call together his numerous adherents: if the king had lingered, Warwick's expulsion would have cost him much heavy fighting. He was now master of his realm again, but not for long. His enemy was bent on revenge, and had made up his mind to forget all his old grudges against Margaret of Anjou and the Lancastrians. At the court of Louis XI. the earl met the exiled queen, and made his peace with her. They agreed to join their forces in order to crush Edward IV., and Warwick undertook to replace Henry VI. on the throne: as a pledge of reconciliation, his younger daughter, Anne Neville, was betrothed to Prince Edward, the heir of the Lancastrian house. Warwick soon set to work to use all his powers of intrigue: his emissaries overran the whole of England, bidding his partisans to be prepared for a rising in the autumn; while Queen Margaret sent similar warnings to the survivors of her party.

In September, the plot had been prepared: Lord Fitzhugh, a brother-in-law of Warwick, got up an unimportant rising in the North to attract the king's attention. Edward took the bait, and when he had reached York the earl slipped across the Channel and raised his banner in Devonshire, a district where the Lancastrian party was strong. When the signal was given the retainers of the Nevilles rose in arms in every shire, and the king had to turn southward: he had only reached Nottingham when he found that Warwick's brother Montague had led over to the enemy the whole of the levies of the Midlands which had been gathered together to resist the invasion.

The king's own soldiery began to melt away from him, and in despair he rode hard for the coast and took ship at Lynn with his young brother Richard Duke of Gloucester, Lord Hastings, and a few scores of faithful followers. He reached the Netherlands in safety and was kindly received by Charles the Rash, his brother-in-law. The Duke of Burgundy was anxious to oblige any enemy of his old foe Louis XI. of France.

The power of the Nevilles had been vindicated, and Warwick might indeed call himself the "King-maker" when he drew Henry VI. from his prison in the Tower and replaced him on his long-lost throne. Edward had been beaten without a blow struck, and his wife and young daughters were at the earl's mercy as hostages. He did not, however, disturb them when they took sanctuary at Westminster.

The position of the conqueror was a difficult one: he was distrusted by the Lancastrians, and himself distrusted them: Clarence, his chief supporter, was discontented at the restoration of the old king: he had hoped that his father-in-law would have given him the crown instead of replacing it on the head of Henry. Edward was known to have many partisans, but how many no one could say, since they had been given no opportunity of displaying themselves. Meanwhile a ministry, partly composed of Warwick's friends, partly of Lancastrians, was put in power, and for the moment all was quiet. Queen Margaret and her son very unwisely lingered in France: they should have crossed the Channel when their party had triumphed.

In March, 1471, came the last development of the long strife between the King-maker and his former master. Edward IV. was furnished with 50,000 florins and 1200 mercenaries by the Duke of Burgundy, and railed forth from Holland to try his fortune once more. He landed in Yorkshire, giving out at first that he was only come to claim his father's duchy, and did not ask for the crown or intend civil war. By the inexcusable carelessness of Montague, who was commanding in the North, he was allowed to slip across the Trent and to reach Leicester, where a considerable body of his partisans joined him.

It seemed probable, however, that he would soon be crushed by numbers, for hostile forces began to close around him on all sides, and Warwick himself advanced to Coventry, which had been appointed as the mustering place of his host. From this rather desperate position Edward was rescued by the treachery of his brother George of Clarence. The duke had been commissioned to raise the western Midlands in King Henry's name: but when he approached Coventry he swerved aside and joined the invaders with seven or eight thousand men. This made Edward so strong that Warwick could not fight him till he had received reinforcements. While the earl was waiting, his adversary made a desperate dash for London, and was admitted within its walls by a sudden rising of his partisans (April 11, 1471).

But Warwick was now close at his heels with all his host, and till he was beaten off nothing had really been secured. Accordingly, the Yorkists marched out and met their pursuers at Barnet, where on April 14 a desperate battle took place. It was fought in a dense fog, a circumstance which proved fatal to the great earl, for two corps of his army mistook each other for enemies and came to blows. When they recognised each other, each thought the other had deserted to the king, and both cried "treachery" and fled. The remainder of the Kingmaker's men stood their ground but were overwhelmed by numbers and cut to pieces. Warwick himself and his brother Montague were both left dead upon the field.

On the very day of Barnet, Queen Margaret and her son landed at Weymouth and put themselves at the head of an army which the Beauforts had gathered in Somerset and Devon. Hearing of Warwick's defeat and death they resolved to make their way towards Wales, a great Lancastrian stronghold. But by a forced march King Edward threw himself across their path and forced them to fight at Tewkesbury with the unfordable Severn at their backs.

After a hard struggle the Lancastrians were beaten from their position, and all who could not fly fast were slain, captured, or driven into the river. The young Prince Edward was killed as he cried in vain for quarter and called on the name of "his brother Clarence": with him

Death of Warwick at Barnet

fell the Earl of Devon and Lord Wenlock. Edmund, the last Duke of Somerset of the Beaufort line, was captured and executed with ten other prisoners of rank (May 4, 1471). Queen Margaret also fell into the victor's hands: her life was spared, but with a perfectly gratuitous cruelty Edward ordered her harmless husband to be secretly put to death in the Tower. Now that his only son was dead Henry was no longer valuable as a hostage, and was made away with. His murderer gave out that he died "of pure displeasure and melancholy".

So ended in one common disaster the dynasty of Lancaster and the great house of Neville. The male line of John of Gaunt was extinct: the female line was only represented by the King of Portugal and the Queen of Castile, who descended from two of his daughters, and by the Lady Margaret Beaufort the last of the Somersets. She had a son by her first husband Edmund Tudor, Earl of Richmond, and this young boy was one day to reign under the name of Henry VII. The vast estates of Warwick were divided between his two daughters, the Duchess of Clarence and the Princess Anne the widow of Prince Edward. The latter was forced to marry the king's youngest brother, Richard Duke of Gloucester, so that all the broad Neville, Montacute, and Beauchamp lands passed into the hands of the royal family.

Edward had yet twelve years to reign: they contrast strongly with the troublous times between 1460 and 1471, for their annals are lacking in interest and incident. The king was strong-handed enough to rule as he pleased, and might have become a tyrant had he been more restless and energetic. But habits of sloth grew upon him, and he wasted much of his time on pleasures, lawful and unlawful, and on riotous living. Before he was forty he had ruined his constitution and had grown grossly corpulent and unwieldy.

His rule was far more autocratic than that of the Lancastrian house: between 1478 and 1483 he did not call Parliament together, and he often indulged in the unconstitutional practice of raising "benevolences" or forced loans not sanctioned by parliamentary authority. But he can hardly be called an oppressive ruler: his arbitrary acts did not affect the bulk of his subjects, and his financial exactions were moderate, for he was much wealthier than his predecessors owing to the vast amounts of confiscated land, belonging to the followers of Lancaster and Warwick, which had fallen into his hands.

After 1475 he had another source of revenue. In alliance with Charles of Burgundy he invaded France, and advanced as far as Peronne in Picardy. But the wily Louis XI. offered to buy him off, by paying down a great sum of money and guaranteeing him an annual pension as long as peace should endure. Edward threw over his ally and greedily closed with the offer. By the Treaty of Pecquigny (13th Aug., 1475) he received 75,000 gold crowns in ready money, 50,000 more as a ransom for the unfortunate Margaret of Anjou, and the guarantees for the payment of 50,000 crowns *per annum* as long as he should live. He at once retired from France, and for the rest of his life was paid the subsidy with great regularity.

The main anxiety of Edward during these years arose from the discontent of his brother George of Clarence. The treachery of the duke in the years 1469-70 could never be forgotten, and the king always viewed him with suspicion. Clarence did his best to justify these doubts: his behaviour was captious, insolent, and overbearing. In 1477 he provoked Edward to great wrath by putting to death on his own authority and without a proper trial a lady named Ankaret Twyndow, whom he accused of having caused by sorcery the death of his wife the Duchess Isabel.

On another occasion, he tried to marry Margaret, the heiress of Burgundy, without Edward's leave. In 1478 the brothers had a violent quarrel about the arrest and execution of some of Clarence's followers for treason. It ended in the duke's being sent to the Tower: soon after Edward called together a Parliament and accused his brother in person before the Peers. Clarence was, he said, incorrigible, and "he would not be answerable for the weal, public peace, and tranquillity of the realm if such loathly offences should be pardoned". The Lords could do no less than find the accused guilty, when the king acted as prosecutor. A fortnight later "false, fleeting, perjured Clarence" was put to death in the Tower. A tradition dating back to the very year of his execution declares that he was drowned in a butt of Malmsey wine: but nothing is really known of the details of his end.

Edward survived his brother for five years: his health was steadily growing worse, but he made no attempt to break himself of his evil habits, and as he became less fit for business handed over much of the conduct of affairs to his youngest brother Richard Duke of Gloucester and his chamberlain Lord Hastings, the two faithful partisans who had never shrunk from his side in all the troubles of the evil days in 1469-71.

The last important event in the reign was a short war with Scotland in 1482, caused partly by the raids of the moss-troopers of the Border into Northumberland, partly by the intrigues of the exiled Duke of

Albany, who stirred up England against his brother James III. for his own private ends. Gloucester held the command, since the king was too ill to take the field, and distinguished himself by retaking Berwick, which had been held by the Scots since Margaret of Anjou made it over to them in 1461. He ravaged the Lowlands till the Scottish king sued for peace, but the negotiations were still unfinished when news came that King Edward was dead.

Though only in his forty-second year his constitution was worn out, and he succumbed to an attack of ague of no special virulence (March 30, 1483). Thoroughly selfish, cruel, and debauched, he was one of the worst men who have sat on the English throne, but it cannot be said that he was an inefficient ruler. The country was not unprosperous under his hand, in spite of all the wars and rumours of wars which had passed over it. The nobles and their retainers had been thinned by the sword and axe, but the storm had passed far above the heads of the majority of the nation. Taxation was light, trade and commerce were not unprosperous: England in short has seen much worse days under much better kings.

CHAPTER 14

Richard III. 1483-1485

Edward IV. had been the father of a large family; but he had been cut off at so early an age that the two sons and five daughters whom he left behind him were all very young. Elizabeth, his eldest child, was only seventeen; Edward, Prince of Wales, his heir, was five years younger; Richard of York, his second son, but nine. It was obvious that several years of regency must elapse before the young king could take up the reins of government. Edward IV. had made no arrangements on his death-bed for nominating a regent, but there were only two possible persons who could be thought of for the post. One was the queen dowager, the other Richard of Gloucester, the first prince of the blood. It was at once seen that trouble would come of their rivalry: Elizabeth's success would mean danger to Gloucester, for her kindred, the Greys and Woodvilles, were old enemies of the duke.

But the game seemed at first to be in her hands, for her son was at Ludlow under charge of his uncle, Anthony Woodville Earl Rivers, the chief of the clan. The queen's kindred held the young king's person, and *"possession is nine points of the law"*. A less wily and resolute adversary than Richard of Gloucester would have yielded the game; but the duke was a man of a cunning and ambition unsuspected even by those who knew him best. He had hitherto been known only as a good soldier, a capable administrator, and a most faithful servant of the late king. Unlike his brother, George of Clarence, he was a prince of a sober and cautious demeanour, and made public pretensions to piety which his private life did not altogether bear out. No one dreamed that he would prove the most unscrupulous man of his unscrupulous house, and that he was prepared to wade to power through streams of innocent blood.

Richard was often pictured by Tudor writers as a sort of deformed and unnatural monster: they said that he was dwarfish, hump-backed, and hideous. But though his left arm and shoulder were smaller than his right, and his stature rather small, his exterior was not unpleasing: none of the line of York were wanting in good looks, and Richard's worst drawback was the shifty and suspicious glance which all his portraits display. He had only reached the age of thirty-one when his brother died, but his ability had never been doubted since the day when as a lad of eighteen he commanded the Yorkist right wing at Barnet and Tewkesbury.

When the funeral of Edward IV. had taken place Lord Rivers proceeded to bring the young king up to London. There it was intended that his coronation should take place, and that the council should nominate a regent or a protector to carry on the business of the realm. When the royal cortege arrived at Stoney Stratford it was met by the Duke of Gloucester and his friend and supporter Henry Duke of Buckingham, the lineal representative of Thomas of Woodstock, and the younger line of Edward III.'s descendants. (See table further on.) Rivers must have noted with some alarm that the two dukes had brought with them armed retainers in numbers that were wholly unnecessary for the occasion. But he did not suspect how near was the blow that he dreaded: on the next day, as the cavalcade was starting again for London, Gloucester's retainers laid hands on Rivers and on Sir Richard Grey, the queen's second son, and threw them into bonds (April 30, 1483).

They were hastily sent up to the duke's northern stronghold of Middleham, while the young king was taken on to the capital by his uncle. Queen Elizabeth saw that her cause was ruined, and took sanctuary at Westminster: her eldest son, the Marquis of Dorset, and her brother Edward Woodville fled to France.

Gloucester meanwhile, on arriving at London, dismissed the ministers, and appointed partisans of his own to their places. He then summoned Parliament to meet, proposing (as men thought) to have his nephew duly crowned and himself appointed protector. But soon an incident occurred which showed that his designs were not so simple as had been supposed. There were in the council many magnates who were glad to see the Woodvilles driven away, but wished for no further change. The chief of them was Lord Hastings, an old and faithful friend of Edward IV. Gloucester seems to have spent some days in sounding these men, to see how far they were ready to follow him.

When he was clear upon the point he arranged a dramatic scene.

The council had met in the Tower, and the duke seemed all smiles, when suddenly he withdrew for a moment, and then returning with a changed countenance began to declare that he had discovered a plot against his life. Sorcery was being practised against him, he said, and he asked what should be done to those implicated in the matter—the queen dowager, Jane Shore (the late king's favourite), and certain others, whom he would not name.

Hastings, much surprised and somewhat alarmed, faltered that "*If* they had so done they were worthy of heinous punishment".

"I tell thee they *have* done it, and that I will prove on thy body, traitor!" thundered the duke.

He struck the table, armed men rushed in, and Hastings was dragged down to the courtyard and beheaded on a log. At the same time Lord Stanley, Rotheram Archbishop of York, and Morton Bishop of Ely, were taken into custody (June 13, 1483).

Having purged the council of the young king's true friends, Gloucester was omnipotent. He now proceeded to further measures of ominous significance. Edward's younger brother, the little Duke of York, was taken out of his mother's hands, the queen being half cajoled half frightened into letting him quit the sanctuary and join his brother in the Tower. Thus, Gloucester had both the heirs to the throne in his power. He then began to pack London with armed men drawn from his estates in the North, to whom were added those of his fellow-conspirator, Buckingham. It seems that no one save this young duke, and perhaps John Lord Howard, knew how far Gloucester's designs extended. Their aid had been bought by enormous gifts: the protector had granted to Buckingham the custody of all the royal castles in Wales and the West Country, and promised Howard the duchy of Norfolk, to which he had some claims in right of his mother.

The plea on which Richard had determined to strike at his nephews' right to the throne was that Edward IV.'s marriage with Elizabeth Woodville was invalid. He maintained that it had been celebrated in private, and without the proper ecclesiastical forms (which was partly true), and also that Edward had been previously betrothed to Lady Eleanor Talbot, a statement for which no real corroboration has ever been found. The princes, therefore, he said, were illegitimate children: Clarence had left a son and daughter, but his attainder in 1478 had "corrupted their blood", and they could make no claim through him. Richard himself, therefore, was "the very sure and true crown heir of the house of York".

This preposterous theory was first set forth by the duke's chaplain, Dr. Shaw, in a sermon at St. Paul's on June 22. On the 24th, Buckingham made a harangue to the same effect to the mayor and aldermen of London at the Guildhall: overawed by the armed men about them the citizens made no objection. On the 25th a larger meeting was held, to which all the peers in London and many other men of note were bidden: a petition was laid before them to which they were requested to give their consent; it implored Gloucester to assume the crown as the only true representative of the royal house. To their eternal disgrace the assembly bowed before the display of arms in the streets, and not a voice was raised to refuse the petition. Gloucester, after some hypocritical show of hesitation, assented to the request contained in it: next day he was proclaimed king, and on July 6th was crowned under the name of Richard III.

The moment that he was certain of success the new king had sent orders to the North for the execution of his enemies, Rivers and Grey: they were dead before he was crowned. But their faction was not extinguished: it had only been taken unprepared by the extreme swiftness with which Richard had acted. Before he had been a month on the throne, a conspiracy was already on foot to overthrow him and restore Edward V. Its chiefs were Thomas Grey Marquis of Dorset, Lionel Woodville Bishop of Salisbury, and Thomas St. Leger, who had married the king's sister Anne. Richard got wind of the conspiracy, and thought to frustrate it with ease by the most abominable of expedients. He hastily sent word from Warwick, where he chanced to be at the moment, to order the secret murder of the young princes in the Tower.

The wicked deed was done on or about the 9th of August, 1483: the boys were smothered, and their bodies hurriedly interred under a staircase, where they were found nearly two hundred years after, when some repairs were in progress in 1674. It was soon known that the princes were dead: the feeling throughout the country was one of horror: many atrocities had been committed during the Wars of the Roses, but not one that could vie with this. It may be said that Richard ruined himself by it: no man whose heart and mind retained any regard for righteousness could serve the tyrant faithfully for the future. Usurpation was one thing, the gratuitous murder of innocent children another. From this moment onward Richard felt that every man's hand was against him: not even those on whom he had heaped the most lavish gifts could be trusted.

The best proof of this was that the conspiracy, far from being crushed by the crime in the Tower, gathered force from it, and was joined by many who had hitherto held aloof. Chief of these was the Duke of Buckingham, who had hitherto acted as Richard's right-hand man. Though he had been given all that he asked, he cast in his lot with the rebels, not urging his own claim to the throne (which was not much worse than Richard's) but consenting to back that of another. For the conspirators, hearing of the death of Edward V., had resolved to rise in the names of the houses of York and Lancaster combined. Elizabeth, the eldest daughter of Edward IV., might marry Henry Tudor, son of Margaret, Countess of Richmond, and heir of the Beauforts. His Lancastrian claim was a poor one, but the only one that could be brought forward: no one thought of urging that of the distant Queen of Spain. (See tables further on.)

In October, 1483, the insurrection broke out, Buckingham raising the Welsh border, while Dorset, St. Leger, and the Courtenays mustered their retainers in Devon, and other leaders unfurled their banners at Salisbury and Maidstone. The Earl of Richmond with some mercenaries hired in Brittany was to land at Plymouth and head the rising. For the last time in his life luck favoured Richard: an extraordinary and prolonged downpour of rain checked the communication of the rebels, and so swelled the Severn that Buckingham could not cross it to join his friends.

Richmond was beaten back by storms and was unable to land. The king meanwhile, with such levies as he could raise, struck right and left at his foes. Buckingham's Welshmen dispersed, and he himself was captured and executed (Nov. 2). His failure awed the rebels in the south, who made no stand against Richard: St. Leger was caught and beheaded by his brother-in-law: the rest of the leaders escaped to France. Richmond returned to Brittany without having set his foot ashore.

The failure of this first movement gave the king a short respite of eighteen months. They were a time of trouble, for everyone knew that the attempt would be repeated at the earliest opportunity. Richard lived in a state of miserable suspicion, knowing that there was treachery around him, but generally unable to strike for want of full knowledge. When he could lay hands on a foe he made away with him, even descending so far as to hang the unfortunate Collingbourn, a Wiltshire squire whose offence was that he had composed the rhyme—

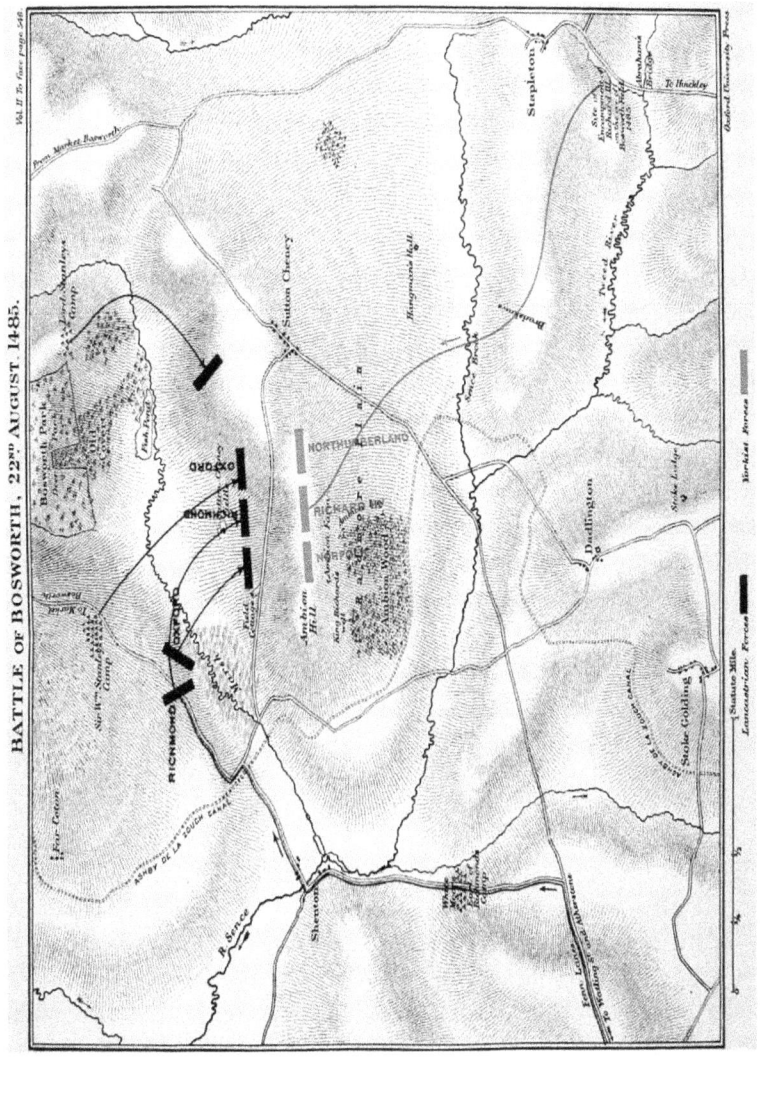

The Cat, the Rat, and Lovel the Dog
Rule all England under the Hog—

in which Richard's ministers William Catesby, Sir Richard Ratcliffe, and Francis Lord Lovel, as well as the king's personal badge of the White Boar, were held up to scorn.

The Parliament met early in 1484 and a considerable parade of benevolent and constitutional legislation was made. But Richard's position was too uncertain to allow him to carry out any real reforms: having, for example, allowed "Benevolences" to be formally abolished, he was a few months later in such dire need of money that he had to have recourse to them again in spite of his handsome promises. Perpetual alarms of rebellion, and the need to retain his supporters in good temper by lavish gifts, conspired to keep his pocket always empty.

In April, 1484, the king's position was notably weakened by the death of his only child Edward, whom he had created Prince of Wales. Compelled to name an heir in his stead, Richard selected his nephew John de la Pole, Earl of Lincoln, the son of his eldest sister. (It may be of interest to point out that this heir-apparent to the English throne was the great-grandson of the poet Chaucer.) He could not fall back on Clarence's son, a more natural choice, as to do so would have falsified his own claim to the crown, which depended on Clarence's attainder.

Not quite a year after Prince Edward's death his mother Queen Anne, the King-maker's daughter, followed him to the grave. Her end is said to have been hastened by her husband's ill-concealed intention of getting rid of her by divorce or otherwise, in order that he might marry a wife who would bring him another heir. When she was dead Richard is said for a moment to have thought of marrying his niece Elizabeth, the elder sister of the victims of the Tower. But the universal horror expressed by the nation, and brought to his notice by his own most trusty followers, caused him to abandon the horrid project.

When the summer of 1485 had come round, the exiles, who had never ceased to weave plans for a second invasion, tried their fortune once more. Henry Earl of Richmond had borrowed a little money from the French government, and with it had raised some 1200 continental mercenaries. He sailed from Harfleur on August 1: with him were the last survivors of the old Lancastrian party, his Uncle Jasper Tudor Earl of Pembroke, and John de Vere Earl of Oxford, as well

King Richard at Bosworth

as the representatives of the Yorkist factions whom Richard III. had crushed, headed by Sir Edward Woodville. It seemed foolhardy to attack England with such a small force, but the invaders knew that their way had been prepared for them, and that aid would be forthcoming from many secret sympathizers.

Landing at Milford Haven they were soon joined by some of the Welsh gentry, who gladly rallied round the red dragon of the Tudors. When they reached the Severn the retainers of the old Lancastrian house of the Talbots, Earls of Shrewsbury, came to their aid. But still when they faced King Richard at Bosworth Field in Leicestershire they could only put 5000 men in line against the 14,000 in the royal host. Nevertheless, the Earl of Oxford marshalled his men in two small columns and led them up hill to attack the king. His confidence was justified: when the clash of battle came, half of Richard's army refused to close and hung back. The rest fought feebly, save where the king himself and his one trusty partisan, John Howard Duke of Norfolk, maintained their ground.

Ere long a fatal blow was struck by two old Yorkists, Lord Stanley and his brother Sir William, who had pledged themselves to aid the invader. At the Battle of Bosworth, coming on the field with fresh levies from Cheshire and Lancashire, they attacked the royalists in the flank. King Richard's army at once broke up, with shouts of "Treason!" Seeing himself betrayed the usurper refused to fly, and setting his face towards Richmond's banner cut his way as far as his adversary's person before he was borne down and hewn to pieces. With him fell the Duke of Norfolk, Lord Ferrers, and Sir Richard Ratcliffe, "the Rat" of poor Collingbourn's rhyme.

Of the victorious army less than a hundred men fell, of the vanquished no very great number more—the whole matter had been settled by treason and not by hard fighting (Aug. 22, 1485). Richard had climbed to power by treachery, and by treachery he met with a righteous retribution. His body, stark naked and pierced by half a dozen wounds, was thrown across a horse and sent back for burial to Leicester, the place from which he had gone forth in royal state on the previous day.

Thus ended the Wars of the Roses, one of the most sordid and depressing epochs in the history of England. They had begun in a justifiable attempt to displace a corrupt and incapable ministry: but soon they had become a mere blood-feud between the great baronial houses. A yet worse stage had been reached in the struggle between

Henry crowned after Bosworth

Warwick and Edward IV., when the personal dislike between a selfish and ungrateful king and an arrogant and unscrupulous subject kept the realm disturbed for year after year. They closed in the most disgraceful scene of all: peers and people had accepted a bloodthirsty and hypocritical usurper as king in a moment of unworthy panic, and only got rid of him by deliberate treachery on the battlefield.

England has suffered more misery in other periods—the Wars of the Roses passed lightly above the heads of citizens and peasants, and were only fatal to the quarrelsome baronage. But she has seldom or never been in a worse moral state than in the years 1455-85. The constant and violent changes of rulers, the unending chain of attainders and executions, the easy swearing of allegiance to one king and another, the enormous part played by treachery and bad faith in politics, had swept away all the old traditions of constitutional order and good governance. To restore the realm to a healthy state there was needed the hard discipline of a century of rule by the stronghanded house of Tudor.

THE WHITE ROSE AND THE NEVILLES.

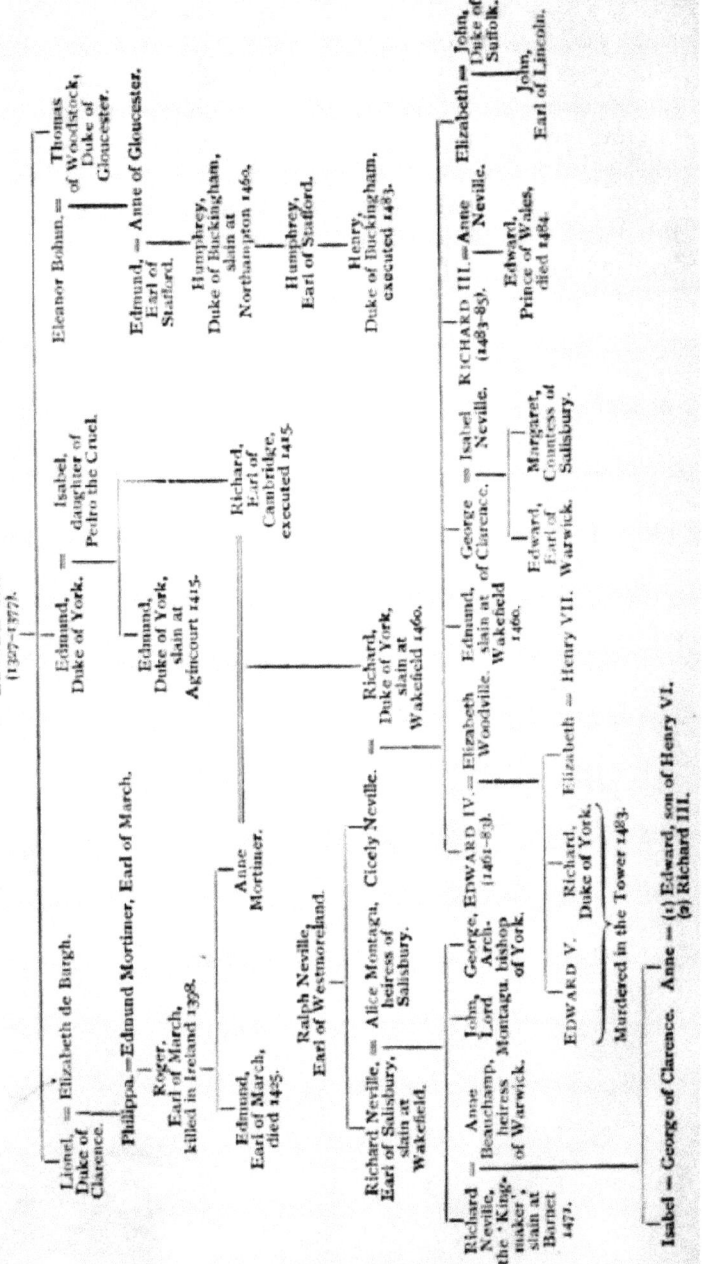

THE RED ROSE.

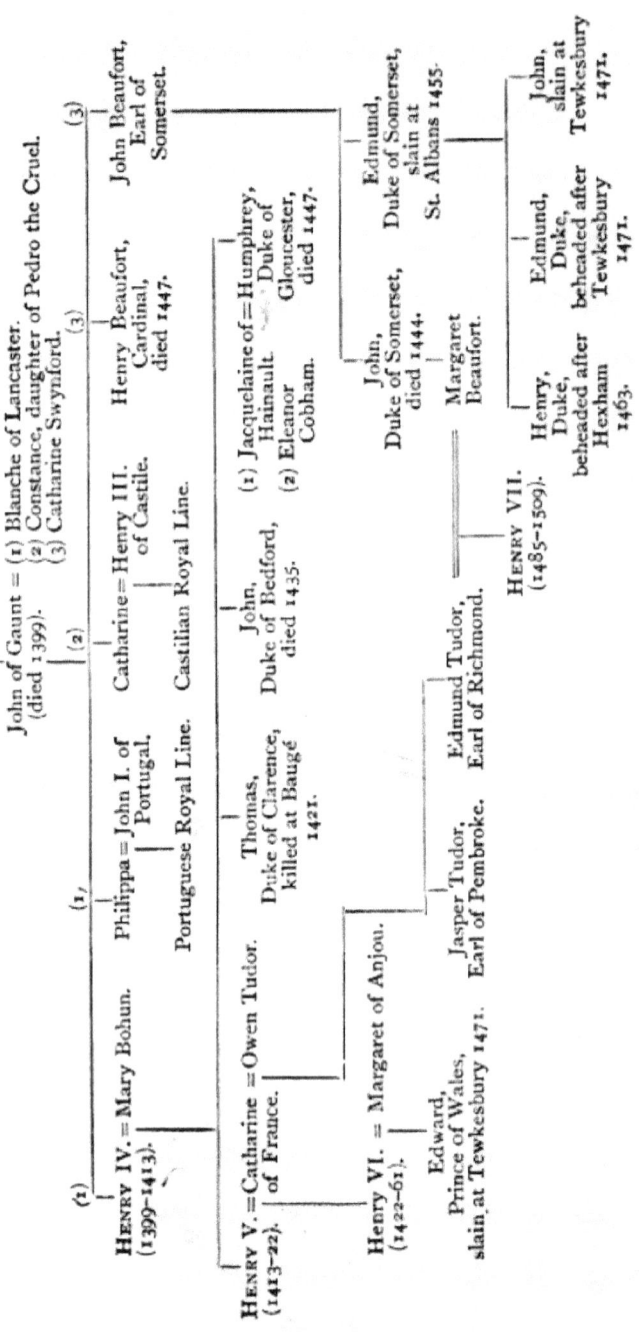

ALSO FROM LEONAUR
AVAILABLE IN SOFTCOVER OR HARDCOVER WITH DUST JACKET

OFFICERS & GENTLEMEN *by Peter Hawker & William Graham*—Two Accounts of British Officers During the Peninsula War: Officer of Light Dragoons by Peter Hawker & Campaign in Portugal and Spain by William Graham.

THE WALCHEREN EXPEDITION *by Anonymous*—The Experiences of a British Officer of the 81st Regt. During the Campaign in the Low Countries of 1809.

LADIES OF WATERLOO *by Charlotte A. Eaton, Magdalene de Lancey & Juana Smith*—The Experiences of Three Women During the Campaign of 1815: Waterloo Days by Charlotte A. Eaton, A Week at Waterloo by Magdalene de Lancey & Juana's Story by Juana Smith.

JOURNAL OF AN OFFICER IN THE KING'S GERMAN LEGION *by John Frederick Hering*—Recollections of Campaigning During the Napoleonic Wars.

JOURNAL OF AN ARMY SURGEON IN THE PENINSULAR WAR *by Charles Boutflower*—The Recollections of a British Army Medical Man on Campaign During the Napoleonic Wars.

ON CAMPAIGN WITH MOORE AND WELLINGTON *by Anthony Hamilton*—The Experiences of a Soldier of the 43rd Regiment During the Peninsular War.

THE ROAD TO AUSTERLITZ *by R. G. Burton*—Napoleon's Campaign of 1805.

SOLDIERS OF NAPOLEON *by A. J. Doisy De Villargennes & Arthur Chuquet*—The Experiences of the Men of the French First Empire: Under the Eagles by A. J. Doisy De Villargennes & Voices of 1812 by Arthur Chuquet.

INVASION OF FRANCE, 1814 *by F. W. O. Maycock*—The Final Battles of the Napoleonic First Empire.

LEIPZIG—A CONFLICT OF TITANS *by Frederic Shoberl*—A Personal Experience of the 'Battle of the Nations' During the Napoleonic Wars, October 14th-19th, 1813.

SLASHERS *by Charles Cadell*—The Campaigns of the 28th Regiment of Foot During the Napoleonic Wars by a Serving Officer.

BATTLE IMPERIAL *by Charles William Vane*—The Campaigns in Germany & France for the Defeat of Napoleon 1813-1814.

SWIFT & BOLD *by Gibbes Rigaud*—The 60th Rifles During the Peninsula War.

AVAILABLE ONLINE AT **www.leonaur.com**
AND FROM ALL GOOD BOOK STORES

ALSO FROM LEONAUR
AVAILABLE IN SOFTCOVER OR HARDCOVER WITH DUST JACKET

AN APACHE CAMPAIGN IN THE SIERRA MADRE by John G. Bourke—An Account of the Expedition in Pursuit of the Chiricahua Apaches in Arizona, 1883.

BILLY DIXON & ADOBE WALLS by Billy Dixon and Edward Campbell Little—Scout, Plainsman & Buffalo Hunter, *Life and Adventures of "Billy" Dixon* by Billy Dixon and *The Battle of Adobe Walls* by Edward Campbell Little (*Pearson's Magazine*).

WITH THE CALIFORNIA COLUMN by George H. Petis—Against Confederates and Hostile Indians During the American Civil War on the South Western Frontier, *The California Column, Frontier Service During the Rebellion* and *Kit Carson's Fight With the Comanche and Kiowa Indians*.

THRILLING DAYS IN ARMY LIFE by George Alexander Forsyth—Experiences of the Beecher's Island Battle 1868, the Apache Campaign of 1882, and the American Civil War.

INDIAN FIGHTS AND FIGHTERS by Cyrus Townsend Brady—Indian Fights and Fighters of the American Western Frontier of the 19th Century.

THE NEZ PERCÉ CAMPAIGN, 1877 by G. O. Shields & Edmond Stephen Meany—Two Accounts of Chief Joseph and the Defeat of the Nez Percé, *The Battle of Big Hole* by G. O. Shields and *Chief Joseph, the Nez Percé* by Edmond Stephen Meany.

CAPTAIN JEFF OF THE TEXAS RANGERS by W. J. Maltby—Fighting Comanche & Kiowa Indians on the South Western Frontier 1863-1874.

SHERIDAN'S TROOPERS ON THE BORDERS by De Benneville Randolph Keim—The Winter Campaign of the U. S. Army Against the Indian Tribes of the Southern Plains, 1868-9.

GERONIMO by Geronimo—The Life of the Famous Apache Warrior in His Own Words.

WILD LIFE IN THE FAR WEST by James Hobbs—The Adventures of a Hunter, Trapper, Guide, Prospector and Soldier.

THE OLD SANTA FE TRAIL by Henry Inman—The Story of a Great Highway.

LIFE IN THE FAR WEST by George F. Ruxton—The Experiences of a British Officer in America and Mexico During the 1840's.

ADVENTURES IN MEXICO AND THE ROCKY MOUNTAINS by George F. Ruxton—Experiences of Mexico and the South West During the 1840's.

AVAILABLE ONLINE AT **www.leonaur.com**
AND FROM ALL GOOD BOOK STORES

www.ingramcontent.com/pod-product-compliance
Lightning Source LLC
Chambersburg PA
CBHW031616160426
43196CB00006B/151